Advance praise for **Going Inward**

"In this important and scrupulously edited book, Alicia Fedelina Chávez and Susan Diana Longerbeam, along with their contributors—drawn from multiple disciplines—argue passionately and thoughtfully for the centrality of putting a strengths-based approach into our teaching in today's multicultural and multi-ethnic classrooms. The path they advocate is one that eschews performance, skillful lecturing, and disembodied teaching but rather honors the teacher bringing into the learning context her/his whole self—culture, identity, ideals, and assumptions—and encouraging the students to do the same. Introspection is critical to this approach for it can help the teacher or students 'discover the depth of culture, its beauty and origin, and the roots of [one's] previously unearthed strengths, failings, and biases.' This persuasive anthology will be of interest to those involved in education at all levels, especially in higher education; it is an essential book for those involved in working with student teachers. Embracing the message of *Going Inward* could well transform teaching."

—Andrew Garrod, Professor Emeritus of Education, Dartmouth College; Co-editor of *Growing Up Muslim: Muslim College Students in America Tell Their Life Stories*; *First Person, First Peoples: Native American College Graduates Tell Their Life Stories*; *Balancing Two Worlds: Asian American College Students Tell Their Life Stories*; *Mi Voz, Mi Vida: Latino College Students Tell Their Life Stories*; *Mixed: Multiracial College Students Tell Their Life Stories*; *Souls Looking Back: Life Stories of Growing up Black*; and *Crossing Customs: International Students Write on U.S. College Life and Culture*

"*Going Inward* should be essential reading for anyone genuinely interested in the humane aspects of teaching in the university classroom. Regardless of field of study or instruction, this collection provides the theoretical and rhetorical framework for a discussion of a new, introspective pedagogy. Encouraging instructors to turn inward, to consider the individual lived experiences and cultural backgrounds from which they spring, to inform how they teach and how they are perceived by those they teach, the essays in this collection provide examples of how to embrace and explore, rather than avoid and deny, the individual lived lives of university professors and the students they stand before. This collection is a call for a new kind of teaching, one that is informed by introspection and that encourages instructors and students alike to embrace the individual, complex, yet informing and essential, cultural, historical, and personal backgrounds from which they come. This collection is not only important for individual college or university instructors, it should also be the beginning of a conversation that can encourage a more introspective approach to higher education administration."

—Carlos Dews, Professor, John Cabot University, Rome, Italy; Editor, with Carolyn Leste Law, of *Out in the South* and *This Fine Place So Far from Home: Voices of Academics from the Working Class*

"The focus of this valuable anthology is exciting and long overdue. These compelling and courageous autobiographical stories offer useful insights and understandings, inviting readers into a state of self-reflection while also strengthening their ability to teach effectively across cultural lines. Highly recommended."

—Ann Todd Jealous, Co-author/Co-editor of *Combined Destinies: Whites Sharing Grief About Racism*

"The writers of these personal accounts tug at the intricate threads of their cultural backgrounds, gently pulling them through into the light of their own educational practices to see what can be found there. And what they find is that in coming to know the presence of their cultural roots in their teaching, they see themselves and students through a new lens. Across the stated themes in the essays that trace interaction between cultural routes and college teaching—place, tension, power, difference, and values—are three unstated themes about the qualities it takes to pursue such self-study in the service of students: unflinching honesty, persistent critical inquiry, and open-hearted vulnerability. Collectively the writers of these essays make one of the roots of the word courage visible—heart.

The essayists make the collection's stated and unstated themes visible, and demonstrate that their work is born of their deep conviction that as college teachers, college learners deserve nothing less. The authors share agreement that cultural introspection is perpetually unfinished business, and with this collection, they invite readers to begin."

—Linda K. Shadiow, Author of *What Our Stories Teach Us: A Guide to Critical Reflection for College Faculty*

"One can't help but go inward while reading these deeply moving essays by faculty reflecting on their diverse cultures and the powerful influences on teaching and learning. Woven throughout the book is the foundational belief shared by Chávez and Longerbeam that, 'Reflective writing changes the writer.' I quickly discovered that reading reflective writing changes the reader. Cultural introspection offers a pathway for educators to be more authentic, compassionate, and effective in their work with students who are in the process of discovering themselves. Much appreciation to the talented faculty for sharing their stories. I am changed."

—Jody Donovan, Assistant Vice President for Student Affairs/Dean of Students and Assistant Professor, School of Education, Colorado State University

"*Going Inward* requires deep-reflexivity, introspection, and most importantly, courage. The candid renditions presented in this book show us that we are pedagogues and simultaneously, we are learners. We continue to acquire new knowledge from *lo vivido*, the lived experience, from a deep understanding of who we are and where we come from. The compilation of these rich, culturally-diverse voices demonstrate that by tracing back our roots and telling our cultural-personal stories, our autobiographies, we are indeed gaining a deeper understanding of why we teach and hence how we teach. Whether in the college classroom or in the K–12 context, this anthology is bound to move the reader to be critically self-reflexive and tell our own *testimonio*, our own story—therefore, [to] grow and enhance our praxis."

—Judith Flores Carmona, New Mexico State University; Author of *Crafting Critical Stories: Toward Pedagogies and Methodologies of Collaboration, Inclusion, and Voice*

"*Going Inward* is a journey of discovery and enlightenment not only for those whose cultural stories [are] being shared, but also for all those inspired to tell their own cultural story simply by reading this transformative book.

Going Inward is a gift to today's diverse and complex world of higher education. This collection of deeply personal and introspective stories provides a powerful demonstration of how our cultural autobiography continually shapes our ways of 'being' a college teacher.

Going Inward teaches us the power of introspection and exploration of our cultural story and the strengths that lie within us all as teachers and learners. This rich collection of personal and insightful cultural autobiographies from 21 courageous college teachers sparks hope and inspiration to be more culturally responsive in our college teaching."

—Sue Hines, Director, Center for Excellence in Learning and Teaching and Associate Professor, Ed.D. in Leadership Program, St Mary's University of Minnesota

Going Inward

Questions about the Purpose(s) of Colleges & Universities

Norman K. Denzin and Shirley R. Steinberg
General Editors

Vol. 25

The Higher Ed series is part of the Peter Lang Education list.
Every volume is peer reviewed and meets
the highest quality standards for content and production.

PETER LANG
New York • Bern • Frankfurt • Berlin
Brussels • Vienna • Oxford • Warsaw

Going Inward

The Role of Cultural Introspection in College Teaching

Edited by Susan Diana Longerbeam
and Alicia Fedelina Chávez

PETER LANG
New York • Bern • Frankfurt • Berlin
Brussels • Vienna • Oxford • Warsaw

Library of Congress Cataloging-in-Publication Data

Names: Longerbeam, Susan Diana, editor. | Chávez, Alicia Fedelina, editor.
Title: Going inward: the role of cultural introspection in college teaching
/ edited by Susan Diana Longerbeam, Alicia Fedelina Chávez.
Description: New York: Peter Lang, 2016.
Series: Higher ed: questions about the purpose(s)
of colleges and universities, vol. 25 | ISSN 1523-9551
Includes bibliographical references.
Identifiers: LCCN 2016005930 | ISBN 978-1-4331-3104-2 (hardcover: alk. paper)
ISBN 978-1-4331-3103-5 (paperback: alk. paper) | ISBN 978-1-4539-1849-4 (e-book)
Subjects: LCSH: College teaching—Social aspects—United States.
Culturally relevant pedagogy—United States. | Introspection.
Classification: LCC LB2331 .G65 2016 | DDC 378.1/25—dc23
LC record available at https://lccn.loc.gov/2016005930

Bibliographic information published by **Die Deutsche Nationalbibliothek.**
Die Deutsche Nationalbibliothek lists this publication in the "Deutsche Nationalbibliografie"; detailed bibliographic data are available on the Internet at http://dnb.d-nb.de/.

The paper in this book meets the guidelines for permanence and durability of the Committee on Production Guidelines for Book Longevity of the Council of Library Resources.

29 Broadway, 18th floor, New York, NY 10006
www.peterlang.com

Printed in the United States of America

Table of Contents

Preface

From the beginning of our work with two cohorts of faculty at the University of New Mexico and Northern Arizona University, we cultivated a strengths-based approach to teaching across cultures—encouraging faculty to reflect on strengths from their own cultures and to also identify, notice, acknowledge, and engage strengths from their students' cultures in service of learning, in all academic subject areas. Faculty rose to this challenge, moving beyond laments they may have had about students to look candidly at their own assumptions and practices and to grow and develop in their teaching.

Engagement in culture and teaching autobiographies especially meant looking deeply inward and contemplating origins, meaning, and manifestations of cultural values and paradigms and relating these to their teaching. Cultural introspection facilitated many revelations among these cohorts of faculty, enabling strengths-based transformations and innovations to teach more effectively across the diversity of students in their courses.

In this work, we honor Indigenous cultures when we capitalize meaningful words such as Mother, Elder, and Indigenous. We also do not italicize words that do not appear in English, to center the importance of language that has no English translation yet evokes deep elements of the human experience.

OUR REFLECTIONS

Susan Diana Longerbeam

I am deeply moved and humbled by the insights of the faculty in this volume—by their compassion, keen intellect, and spirit of discovery. Every time I reread these essays, I discover greater depth, more nuance in culture, and deeper experiences of contradiction and intersectionality. I am especially moved by the ways the faculty in this book were generative in transforming their experiences of early learning and formal education, both positive and negative, to their work now with college students. They have applied the best of their learning and passed it on while learning from the worst, transforming the worst experiences by becoming better teachers and mentors for the next generation. This, to me, is the meaning of generative generosity.

Reflection does not come as easily to me now as life has become busier, and working with Alicia on this project for the past five years has been a gift of both rediscovery and discovery. At a time when I could have lost some of my connection to students after more than a decade of college teaching, I have rediscovered the importance of contemplation on my approach with and effect on students and their learning. I have learned through this work that the rediscovery begins with me, in my own culture of origin. Through going inward, I continually discover the depth of culture, its beauty and strength, and the roots of my previously unearthed strengths, failings, and biases. I have renewed my love for understanding culture, continued to uncover my own normative yet invisible cultural influences (what I call "peeling the artichoke" in my essay), and best of all recommitted to my love of students.

Alicia Fedelina Chávez

It was natural for me when I moved into professional roles to make time regularly to reflect. As noted in my essay in this book, I was raised in a family where reflection was encouraged, expected, and seen as necessary to life and to being a good person. I believe reflection is necessary to growth, to learning, and to professional development. When I became a professor and began to teach, it was second nature to weave reflection into my teaching practices and into student learning processes. It was also a given that reflection would be a foundational aspect of work with faculty on teaching across cultures.

I was also raised in a family where culture is discussed regularly and often deeply. It became essential for me when I began to attend and later work professionally in universities outside New Mexico to become highly introspective around teaching and learning. When I realized others were facing similar realities, it was natural for me to extend this to my scholarship and work with faculty. Collaboration with Susan Diana Longerbeam has been a joy and a blessing as we learn from each other across our cultures.

SPECIAL THANKS AND DEDICATIONS

We dedicate this volume to the faculty who contributed to this book. They worked with us over several years, chose to share their hearts and minds, dug deeply and courageously into their lives—ultimately for the benefit of others—and opened themselves to vulnerability with generosity of spirit. Thank you for choosing to work with us and for publishing your work as part of this book.

We also dedicate this work to Susan's son, Leo. Susan learned she was becoming a mother on the way to Albuquerque for our first meeting for this culture and teaching project to begin our work together. This book is a milestone for our work and for Leo, who just turned five. Leo was our inspiration throughout our work on teaching across cultural strengths, faculty introspection, and developing a culture of belief in students.

—Susan Diana Longerbeam and Alicia Fedelina Chávez

PART ONE

Overview

CHAPTER ONE

From Cultural Story to Teaching Insight

SUSAN DIANA LONGERBEAM & ALICIA FEDELINA CHÁVEZ

We each have a story to tell and a purpose in life to help positively impact our communities.
—Robin Minthorn

The culture and teaching autobiographies in this book emerged out of a faculty development program on culture and college teaching at two universities in the Southwest, Northern Arizona University and the University of New Mexico. Several years ago, we identified a shared sense of urgency about college success among underserved students, particularly for resident populations in Arizona and New Mexico, our home states. Teaching effectiveness across cultures is critical in a time of rapidly diversifying higher education environments. The faculty who chose to join us in exploring teaching across cultural strengths worked with us over several years, and most who began with us also chose to publish their culture and teaching autobiographies. Faculty wrote these essays within the larger context of the faculty development project on culture in college teaching, detailed extensively in our earlier work, *Teaching Across Cultural Strengths* (Chávez & Longerbeam, 2016).

Over several years, we have explored strengths-based and culturally resonant teaching to benefit student learning. We wrote of the need to draw on strengths from our cultural origins as faculty, in combination with the cultural strengths of students, and thereby balance our teaching to increase the possibility that all will succeed in college learning (Chávez & Longerbeam, 2016). We shared the journey we embarked upon with more than 30 faculty members at two institutions, exploring ways to transform our teaching practices by adopting a balance of cultural strengths to enhance student learning over time. The book offers faculty essays of cultural introspection applying in part the model, Cultural Frameworks in College Teaching and Learning (Chávez & Longerbeam, 2016) and from these essays many examples, narratives, and strategies to assist faculty in balancing pedagogical techniques and interactions with students across cultural epistemologies. This text also offers a variety of cultural introspection techniques.

Thus, this collection of faculty culture and teaching autobiographies is an outcome of several years' work on cultural introspection with the goal of improving teaching. The faculty are diverse by rank, discipline, and culture—and their perspectives and insights contributed to rich conversations on culture and college teaching. Throughout our work together, we shared and discussed our emerging culture and teaching autobiographies with one another. The faculty with whom we worked gave us the gift of their deep insights and enlivened teaching for all who participated in the culture and learning cohort. Toward the end of our faculty development project, Peter Lang made a commitment to publish these cultural introspections on college teaching, in honor of the faculty authors and through the recognition that no similar work on faculty cultural introspection about college teaching was yet available.

We hope you also are enlivened by reading these faculty culture and teaching autobiographies and find ways to purposefully go inward to learn from your own cultural ways of being as well as those of students you teach. We believe going inward can be transformational for teaching, because we discovered that when faculty reflected deeply on our early cultural influences on learning, we gained insight into our teaching practices, and we drew from the cultural strengths that students bring with them into college. Most profoundly, we discovered together a renewed focus on and compassion for students. These faculty authors are master teachers, and observing their teaching, discussing teaching, and writing about teaching throughout our work together has been an honor.

Returning to a focus on what enlivens us is important as many of us are strained by rapid changes in higher education. In particular, financial strain now emboldens a business approach to higher education, which often challenges higher education's core mission of teaching and learning. We believe counterbalances to the business model are needed in higher education now more than ever, as rapid changes in funding models result in a continual focus on business efficiencies. These trends exist at the expense of deep examination of our internal lives and of the processes that support learning, especially learning for those from increasingly diverse cultures. Instead of focusing on developing learning complexities, higher education institutions look for efficiencies and approaches with students and curricula that will work in uniform, efficient ways. These efficiencies often run counter to what actually facilitates complex learning in general and even more so across cultures and individuals. The business model permeating higher education is counter to what is needed to reach students in their worlds, worlds that are often different from those of faculty.

One of the ways to counterbalance these market forces in education is to return to a contemplative, introspective approach in our teaching and in student learning. We are referring to introspection as a way of going inward to understand ourselves better, followed by extending ourselves outward toward a deeper understanding of students. More specifically, we urge faculty to focus on cultural introspection; this book serves as a guide and inspiration.

THE IMPORTANCE OF FACULTY AND OUR CULTURES OF ORIGIN

College students must rely on faculty as their best mentors in academic learning. We have great opportunities to enhance our mentoring by extending ourselves toward a deeper understanding of our own teaching as well as student learning. Inside the curriculum and classroom exists a context in which we can create a bubble of presence and time with students—we have the "cocoon" to be with them—a sacred space of learning and developing and growing; we are entrusted with a sacred responsibility. We would be well served by learning from other faculty about our journeys in culture and college teaching. Yet, few examples of faculty introspective autobiographies on culture, teaching, and learning exist in the literature. There are, however, examples of college student autobiographies—students who have reflected on their cultures and the cultural connections to their learning.

Andrew Garrod and colleagues (Garrod & Kilkenny, 2007; Garrod, Kilkenny, & Gomez, 2007; Garrod & Larimore, 1997; Garrod, Ward, Robinson, & Kilkenny, 1999) have edited and published many books of autobiographical essays written by college students of varying racial, ethnic, and religious identities. Here we aim to do the same with faculty essays, with the expressed aim of exploring cultural origins on learning to shed insight into one's teaching.

We were honored and privileged to work with faculty who expressed a specific interest in examining their own cultures of origin, with the goal to better understand how their cultures influence their ways of teaching, thereby becoming more open to examining new ways of teaching that would better meet students' natural ways of learning. The faculty cohorts at two institutions involved faculty in writing their culture and teaching autobiographies (as well as interviews, teaching observations, and book discussions). These resulting 21 faculty essays make up the heart of this book. We hope you enjoy reading and reflecting on these essays in the same way we have over the past few years.

CULTURAL INTROSPECTION

Introspection simply means to look inside oneself. When we introspect culturally, we are looking at the ways in which our culture—including our behaviors, values, beliefs, and norms—influences who we are, how we think and behave in the world, and how we affect other people. Cultural introspection is the building block of cultural understanding. By examining our cultural influences, we begin to uncover our assumptions about education, learning, teaching, and students. These discoveries are often exciting and come in the form of "aha" moments. We found this particularly the case for those from European American cultures, for whom culture is often unexamined due to its normativity. One author in this book described his insight about students' level of investment in learning:

> As I write this document, however, I realize that some students who I may identify as "not caring" may instead be coming from a different cultural place and I may not be able to recognize when they care versus when they do not care. This lesson, among others that I'm sure I will find on this path of learning about different cultures, is one that I hope to explore in the years to come. (Gary Weissmann)

THE ONGOING ROLE OF INTROSPECTION IN DEVELOPING CULTURAL INSIGHT

The process of personal reflective writing has a transformative effect on the writer (Garrod, Kilkenny, & Gomez, 2007). The faculty writers in our culture and teaching group reflected on the ways in which writing the culture and teaching autobiography opened up insights into and connections between their early cultural learning experiences and their current teaching practices.

> These connections were not obvious to me until I started to write this (culture and teaching autobiography). (Laura Sujo-Montes)

By making connections between their own cultural influences and the ways they learn, faculty gained insight into the ways students may have also experienced cultural influences in the ways they learn. Indeed, a great benefit to these introspective stories, second only to the benefit to students, is in the way they contribute to a sense of ourselves in the academic collective, because reflection not only encourages personal connection and insight, it also develops our sense of who we are in community (Dewey, 1933/1998).

> This reflection has helped me to interrogate many values and behaviors that otherwise would have gone unexamined in relation to my work as an educator. (K. Maria D. Lane)

In their work on the importance of journaling as a reflection tool, Stevens and Cooper (2009) capture the necessity of writing one's insights in order not to lose them. They describe reflection as a conversation with oneself—to make meaning of our lives and to continue learning to address the tensions in one's life, between oneself and the world. "Every journey toward transformation begins with reflection on those things for which one cares deeply, and the relationships that exist in one's inner and outer worlds" (Cajete, 1994, pp. 189–190). Reflective writing changes the writer.

Shadiow (2013) reflects that stories she writes about her teaching stay with her. She notes that growth comes out of reflection on our stories, which change shape and meaning over time as we change. Our understanding of our stories changes as we change. And our stories stay with us for a reason, continually molding our teaching. Shadiow (2013) encourages us to return to stories, delving deeper into these same stories over and over again.

> I wrote the first draft of this essay nearly three years ago as an assistant professor. As I put together my application packet for tenure last year I realized how much the Culture of Teaching and Learning group had influenced my conscious growth as an educator (and lifelong student). The group articulated the deep, personal inquiry and desire to continually learn alongside my students. I have recently been awarded tenure, which I see as an indication that I must be doing something right. But more importantly I view this essay as a living document that will be added to and changed with time. (Katya Crawford)

VULNERABILITY AS A PATH TO UNDERSTANDING

Faculty found that the process of articulating their cultural values deepened their understanding of the risk of assuming other people shared their values, and the value of opening oneself to examining their assumptions. Through writing in a personal manner for an academic audience, they began to recognize their own vulnerability, and by extension that of students.

> "When you feel vulnerable yourself you don't recognize when you make other people feel vulnerable," wrote Kersti Tyson.

Most writing on stories in a collegiate environment is centered on assignments asking ***students*** to become vulnerable by writing their stories. Yet in *Crafting Critical Stories* (Flores Carmona & Luschen, 2014) a teacher reflects on writing her own story about identity and how the process of writing her story as a teacher opened up new knowledge about the ways her shame showed up in the classroom. Writing reflection gave her new insight about how to break up her silence on shame in the learning process, in the hopes of helping students who similarly experience shame in relation to learning. Flores Carmona and Luschen (2014) encourage faculty to critically reflect to find our own vulnerabilities—they urge us to "reflect calmly on knowledge that comes from within" (p. xx).

By opening ourselves to the vulnerability inherent in cultural reflection, we become more congruent with the vulnerable work we are asking of students. We must as teachers bring our whole selves to our work if we expect the same of our students (Tisdell, 2003). We are beholden to students when we ask for their reflection; we return their effort when we also engage in the effort required of going inward.

REFLECTION ENHANCES COMPASSION FOR STUDENTS

Telling stories is one way we make meaning of our teaching. And a great benefit of our stories is their effect on students and their learning.

> We are, as teachers, our cultured selves. Much of who we are manifests in our teaching and it is up to us to purposefully reflect, observe, and transform when necessary. I am continually discovering underlying lessons and experiences of my cultures and family through introspection and through the catalyst of working with a diversity of students as people, learners, and professionals. This is a sacred responsibility and humbling reality of teaching. Through teaching we ripple out through generations. (Alicia Fedelina Chávez)

Through our reflection on these essays (Chapters 3–23), we discovered that faculty intuitively and intellectually began to realize ways in which they extend compassion to students, and at times expressed a heightened intent to do so. For example, Laura Sujo-Montes reflects that she often gives students second chances. Through writing reflection, she realized that she could easily have been where her students are, struggling through academic requirements. Laura's culture and her Catholic faith guide her in her work with students. The writing process illuminated the connections between her cultural experiences, her faith, and her teaching approach. Laura's experience echoes the discoveries of Elizabeth Tisdell (2003), who studies spiritually and culture in higher education. Tisdell (2003) discovered that faculty who reflected on spirituality also tended to be most open to exploring their cultures of origin.

Reflection opens a vast array of opportunities to comprehend students—an important avenue for faculty who desire to better understand students. We discovered a similar urge to comprehend in the desire of physicians to understand their patients. Just as we attempt to understand our students better, Oliver Sacks wanted to understand his patients better (Gawande, 2015), and the processes of understanding are similar. His route to that understanding was also through reflection. Gawande wrote a tribute to Sacks in his epitaph. Gawande claimed Sacks used his gift in introspection to see his patients beyond their category of "patient" and into the whole person—just as we do when we extend our understanding beyond "student" to their whole being. Oliver Sacks discovered that the disease could not be understood without the whole picture, so he decided to look deeper into his own self, and into the selves of his patients. Sacks wanted to have deep compassion for himself in order to have deep compassion for his patients (Gawande, 2015), just as the faculty in this volume went inward, heightening self-understanding, thereby opening recognition of opportunities to extend compassion and understanding to students. Faculty authors recalled how they shared of themselves or centered themselves, making meaning of their own story, then extending that meaning to make a connection with students.

> I tap a student's potential by ... sharing my educational background and childhood stories as a way to potentially connect with students and help motivate them to see the possibilities ahead of them. (Judith A. Montoya)

> [Writing autobiography] is a way to make sure if I find value in who I am; I should make sure I find value in each student's background and life experience whether or not they are of my same cultural background. We each have a story to tell and a purpose in life to help positively impact our communities. It is my role to give those tools to my students to see them fulfill their potential and higher education goals. (Robin Minthorn)

The process of both storytelling and teaching extends a connection from those telling a story or sharing knowledge, to those receiving the story or knowledge. A faculty author shared his practice of brief reflection before beginning each class, as one way to heighten the connection between the teller and the receiver.

> When I am in front of students, as I am setting up for class and powering up the computer, I do an exercise I came to develop over the years. I casually look at the class, smile at them, and in my inner voice I repeat a few times: "Forgive me, I am sorry, I love you, thank you." I ask them for forgiveness for my shortcomings as a teacher, human being, and the role-model role I am being thrust into by standing in front of them. I am asking for their compassion toward me. Also, I apologize. By expressing my love for them, I am shifting the center of my being away from my mind, towards my heart. I have seen many people do good things, while being without love, being tense, unhappy, and in their minds. I don't want to be that person. Finally, I thank them for being there. I think the precursor for this exercise was watching Padre Pablo praying to give a good mass at the beginning of each service. Regardless, the exercise grounds me, makes me be present, allows me to acknowledge my students' presence, and makes me smile. (Matías Fontenla)

THE ROLE OF REFLECTION IN CHALLENGING ASSUMPTIONS

Reflection allows us to examine ourselves and become more open, because through reflection, we become able to see and examine our assumptions (Dewey, 1933/1998). Our learning becomes transformational when we open up the ability to question assumptions underneath our teaching practices, such as the following faculty author powerfully illustrates.

> Because of my high value on education and learning, I do hold this high expectation with students. My mantra has been: "If a student cares about their work, I'll bend over backwards to help them learn. If they don't care to work on learning, I don't have to care. They don't need a college degree to be successful in life." (Gary Weissmann)

When we examine our beliefs and assumptions, our teaching practices open up to change and development—because we are thinking anew about student learning. Asking ourselves to confront what we think we know is a fundamental way to develop critical thinking (Cajete, 1994). However, becoming aware of assumptions is difficult and we resist—moving beyond this resistance to reflect on one's own cultural influences on teaching requires courage (Brookfield, 1995).

STORY: AN ANCIENT TRADITION

Writing reflection is linked to the past in the ancient human cultural tradition of storytelling. Making meaning and making sense of our lives are as old as story itself. Though storytelling traditions are unique in each culture, reflective contemplation expressed through story is at the core of Indigenous learning. "Story is a way to root a perspective that unfolds through the special use of language" (Cajete, 1994, p. 30). Story is essential to learning and requires a deep journey into ourselves to unearth learning. Cajete claims, "Every journey toward transformation begins with reflection" (p. 189).

Storytelling is the oldest human form of teaching and human learning. We communicate our lives to make meaning of them, beyond ourselves (Vygotsky, 1978). We are made better by broad stories—of being human. Through stories told and retold, we may discover complexity and nuance; the harm of story without complexity is judgment. Chimamanda Adichie in "Danger of a Single Story" (2009) said the problem with simplistic stories is they flatten the human experience. To make a real connection to others, we must understand them in their entire complexity. These opening words in Adichie's famous TED talk evoke story's importance: "I am a storyteller."

Stories gives us a signpost, a place to remember lessons (Coles, 1989). Stories give an arc, a moral, a struggle, heightening our experience of ourselves. They reach beyond our minds to our hearts and spirits. This whole-person resonance is the reason stories last longer than theories (Coles, 1989). Sometimes stories stay with us in ways that dry theory cannot, and they change us because they live within us and keep us going, keep us surviving (Coles, 1989). Though we sometimes may not remember words, we likely remember images. A student of Coles claims, "stories become my images and sounds, part of me … you do this with a story—oh, like it says in the bible, 'the word becomes flesh'" (as cited in Coles, 1989, p. 128). Stories told of our own lives are particularly powerful for creating a life of meaning. "The whole point of stories is not 'solutions' or 'resolutions' but a broadening and even a heightening of our struggles—with new protagonists and antagonists introduced, with new sources of concern or apprehension or hope" (Coles, 1989, p. 129).

THE USE OF STORY IN TEACHING ACROSS CULTURES

Faculty in this volume shared many teaching stories through their culture and teaching autobiographies. Many became aware of how their teaching evolved from their cultures, and the ways in which their teaching was culturally distinct. Alicia became aware that she teaches differently from most other faculty early in her teaching career, when several Jewish women students approached her after class her first day to share that her teaching stories reminded them of their grandmothers' stories. Alicia reflected on teaching using story in her essay:

> I taught that first class session in ways natural to me, facilitating students sharing narratives of their lives and educational leadership experiences in relation to subject matter, relating my own experiences and family stories to explain concepts, having students discuss and apply theory to practice, and weaving in visual means including drawing, charting, writing, and then sharing. (Alicia Fedelina Chávez)

Some faculty used story to help students make the connection from the classroom to their future professional lives. A faculty member in our cohort uses story to illuminate the importance of our work as teachers and deepen narratives to make connections to our profession.

> I present the watchmaking industry to my class regularly, emphasizing the act of "telling time" (telling the story of the work we do) instead of "telling time" (the function of a watch). After this discussion, one student shared a powerful revelation: he said "I have to tell my mind to connect with the material, because that's what gives me an education and not just schooling." I consider that a high point in the year. This student, who had struggled with a lot of the material, and felt like the ideas were themselves "not easy to 'get'" later shared with me that he never felt like a "good student." After asking why, he noted with a profound but reserved sadness, "because I'm always in the boxes that are viewed as costs and as liabilities." (MJR Montoya)

Alicia uses story to inspire students' professional practice.

> I facilitate connections in many ways by designing meaningful assignments and class activities for them to choose and then delve into issues that matter to them in education and society. I include my own leadership stories as well as others' to inspire transformative professional practice by facilitating connection through narrative. I design many activities to integrate connections between their minds, hearts, bodies, and spirits. (Alicia Fedelina Chávez)

Story fulfills the role of engaging students so that their learning connects with them and, just as importantly, stays with them.

> The only way to enhance understanding is to tell the story of it or no one will understand. (Alicia Fedelina Chávez)

Adopting the role of storyteller is essential in Indigenous learning. Wilson (2008) begins his book *Research Is Ceremony* by telling the story of his family, his childhood, and his tribes. He says our work in teaching requires relational accountability—research as ceremony means bridging distance between ideas and people and asserts you cannot "take an idea out of its relational context" (p. 8). He framed his academic book as a letter to his sons, which helped Wilson to remember that whenever he felt his writing was becoming too abstract, he needed to tell a story. One story illustrates the idea of ontology, the nature of being. He shares a story retold by a six-year-old, who heard a story from his classroom teacher. In the teacher's story, a cat talks. The child questions whether the teacher is telling the truth (*I* think the cat does not talk!), challenging the entire ontology of the class. Wilson told this story illustrating ontology to evoke the personal voice, the relational element to explain an abstract philosophical concept.

A faculty author in this book told a story about his father instilling the value for education.

> When my brothers and I were younger, our father bought us a horse. It was a two-year-old red roan. He led the horse up to us and said, "He is yours now so take good care of him because he will take you far." I remember how happy and proud we were at the same time. I also remember how he would scold us for not taking care of the horse. He would say, "If you want something good in life, you have to take care of it, nurture it, and take responsibility for it." He said, "It is just like your education." ... I believe that my philosophy of education in the form of a horse helped me to make sense of who I am and where I wanted to be in life. More importantly, this cultural knowledge served as a strong foundation for me to build upon my own dreams, goals, and aspirations of pursuing an education that I desired and was good for me. Education is my horse in achieving and seeking a long harmonious life with good positive relationships with everything and everyone around me. (Vincent Werito, 2010, p. 1)

Reflective of the quote above, Laura Rendón (2009) sought faculty who taught from a perspective of contextual relationships and wholeness. She interviewed faculty who taught using intellect, emotion, and awareness. She was inspired to find the stories of other faculty like herself, who wanted to understand students more deeply. Rendón imagined a "pedagogical dreamfield"—a new way to understand teaching and learning based on the heart as well as the mind.

> In listening we can experience a deep presence and recognize how at a very basic, even spiritual, level sharing the stories of our humanity opens us to a deeper connection with others and ultimately with ourselves. (p. 51)

THE DIFFICULTY OF WRITING AUTOBIOGRAPHY IN AN ACADEMIC CONTEXT

Many of the faculty authors in this work wrote about how hard it was to reflect on their childhoods, cultures, and on early messages about and experiences with learning. They expressed the difficulty of engaging in "nonacademic" writing and the power of revisiting the emotions of their formative years. Yet, the experience of writing the culture and teaching autobiography offered rewards as well as challenges. One of the faculty authors reflects that in the writing, the process of remembering how she discovered she was different was painful, and she did not want to think about it. But she also felt the gift in remembering she did get through those childhood experiences, and she asserted,

> "I do know who I am; I am happy with who I am; I came from this culture" (Judith A. Montoya)

Some faculty authors expressed concerns at engaging in self-centeredness through autobiography. We reassured faculty that reflecting and going inward would serve their teaching and thus would heighten students' learning. The goal of going inward was not primarily to serve the self, but to serve students. We were reminded that as faculty we receive many messages about being too self-focused. But reflection is a different sort of self-focus—reflection for the benefit of our teaching. Reflecting is one way to shift the burden back to us as faculty, to find the ways our own learning experiences influence how we teach. Reflecting on our cultures is a hopeful antidote to continual laments about what is wrong with our students. Instead, we turn our focus back on ourselves to understand new ways of teaching that will reach students in their culturally natural ways of learning.

Another challenge in writing these autobiographies was driven by the stigma against writing from a personal voice in an academic environment. In the acclaimed book of working class faculty autobiographies, *This Fine Place So Far From Home*, the editors noted similar challenges to our own when engaging in personally reflective writing:

> To introduce one's childhood into a piece of writing intended for an academic audience feels inappropriate, "soft," or decidedly unprofessional to many of us trained in objective disciplines or academic conventions. Many of the contributors to this book, not just in this section, mentioned that they had never written in this style before and that the experience was both scary and exhilarating. (Dews & Law, 2010, p. 5)

We honor faculty voices in this volume; therefore, we did not screen them. We preserved their original voices, language, and words, words that often have no translation adequate to their meaning. Sometimes we extended the bounds of editorial style to retain voice. We made similar commitments as did Dews and Law (2010), who reflected on the experience of working-class faculty authors who had to think, feel, and write differently to succeed in the class-based environment of higher education; their writing styles reflected their class status and readers often judge those as less smart. The same judgments hold for those whose cultures originate in other than the Northern European middle class. We honor these faculty voices and their cultures of origin by encouraging each to write in their own styles and vernacular. Honoring voice communicates meaning best.

CULTURAL STRENGTHS AND STRENGTHS-BASED TEACHING

We avow the importance of faculty cultural introspection and cultural voice to enhance college teaching. Because reflection builds understanding and compassion, cultural introspection is consistent with viewing and working with students from a strengths-based perspective. When we understand culture and the influence of cultures of origin on learning, we are more apt to expand our narrow learning expectations to become inclusive of many ways of learning. For instance, we may look for evidence of student learning that extends beyond unidimensional assessments; we may seek to reach students through their own cultural ways of learning; and we may begin to build upon their cultural strengths. A cultural strengths-based approach to teaching and learning is consistent with positive strengths-based approaches to learning (Chávez & Longerbeam, 2016).

BOOK OUTLINE

In Chapter 2, "Place, Tension, Service, Difference, and Strength: How Culture Influences Teaching," we explore the culture and teaching autobiography themes, providing meaning and structure to the stories as a whole, through offering sample quotes from each autobiography. Chapters 3–23 include the culture and teaching autobiographies. In Chapter 24, "Developing a Culturally Introspective Practice," we offer concrete and pragmatic ideas for the reader's reflective practice, including basic guidelines for writing a culture and teaching autobiography. Chapter 25, "Reflecting into the Future," concludes with thoughts on the role of reflection in future faculty practice.

REFERENCES

Adichie, C. (2009, July). *The danger of a single story.* [Video file]. Retrieved from https://www.ted.com/talks/chimamanda_adichie_the_danger_of_a_single_story?language=en

Brookfield, S. (1995). *Becoming a critically reflective teacher.* San Francisco, CA: Jossey-Bass.

Cajete, G. (1994). *Look to the mountain: An ecology of indigenous education.* Rio Rancho, NM: Kivaki Press.

Chávez, A. F., & Longerbeam, S. D. (2016). *Teaching across cultural strengths: A guide to balancing integrated and individuated cultural frameworks in college teaching*. Sterling, VA: Stylus.

Coles, R. (1989). *The call of stories: Teaching and the moral imagination*. Boston, MA: Houghton Mifflin.

Dews, C. L., & Law, C. L. (Eds.). (2010). *This fine place so far from home: Voices of academics from the working class*. Philadelphia, PA: Temple University Press.

Dewey, J. (1933/1998). *How we think: A restatement of the relation of reflective thinking to the educative process*. Boston, MA: Houghton Mifflin.

Flores Carmona, J., & Luschen, K. V. (2014). *Crafting critical stories: Toward pedagogies and methodologies of collaboration, inclusion, and voice*. New York, NY: Peter Lang.

Garrod, A., & Kilkenny, R. (Eds.). (2007). *Balancing two worlds: Asian American college students tell their life stories*. Ithaca, NY: Cornell University Press.

Garrod, A., Kilkenny, R., & Gomez, C. (Eds.). (2007). Mi voz, mi vida*: Latino college students tell their life stories*. Ithaca, NY: Cornell University Press.

Garrod, A., & Larimore, C. (Eds.). (1997). *First person, first peoples: Native American college graduates tell their life stories*. Ithaca, NY: Cornell University Press.

Garrod, A., Ward, J. V., Robinson, T. L., & Kilkenny, R. (Eds.). (1999). *Souls looking back: Life stories of growing up Black*. New York, NY: Routledge.

Gawande, A. (2015, September 14). Oliver Sacks. *The New Yorker.*

Rendón, L. I. (2009). *Sentipensante pedagogy: Education for wholeness, social justice and liberation*. Sterling, VA: Stylus.

Shadiow, L. K. (2013). *What our stories teach us: A guide to critical reflection for college faculty*. San Francisco, CA: Jossey-Bass.

Stevens, D. D., & Cooper, J. E. (2009). *Journal keeping: How to use reflective writing for effective learning, teaching, professional insight, and positive change*. Sterling, VA: Stylus.

Tisdell, E. J. (2003). *Exploring spirituality and culture in adult and higher education*. San Francisco, CA: Jossey-Bass.

Werito, V. (2010). *The racialization of Diné (youth) in education* (Order No. 3440190). Available from ProQuest Dissertations & Theses Global. (857216561). Retrieved from http://search.proquest.com.libproxy.nau.edu/docview/857216561?accountid=12706

Wilson, S. (2008). *Research is ceremony: Indigenous research methods*. Winnipeg, Manitoba, Canada: Fernwood.

Vygotsky, L. S. (1978). *Mind in society*. Cambridge, MA: Harvard University Press.

CHAPTER TWO

Place, Tension, Service, Difference, AND Strength

How Culture Influences Teaching

SUSAN DIANA LONGERBEAM & ALICIA FEDELINA CHÁVEZ

As part of our yearlong faculty development project, participants wrote a culture and teaching autobiography. Due to the nature of culture as a complex mix of values, underlying assumptions, beliefs, and behaviors, deep work through cultural introspection is helpful to developing greater consciousness and understanding. This is even more helpful when cultural introspection goes beyond the personal to include analysis of how our cultural worldviews and ways of being manifest in our teaching practice. Further, when we begin to compare and contrast our cultural norms with those of our students, we are able to illuminate both ways we are similar and ways we are different. This assists us to gain deeper understandings and to further recraft our teaching practices with a greater balance across cultural mores. When we begin to incorporate and balance cultural strengths in addition to our own, we are on our way to balancing college teaching across cultural strengths.

WORKING TOGETHER ON CULTURE AND TEACHING AUTOBIOGRAPHIES

Through our work on these culture and teaching autobiographies, we stayed focused on supporting one another through the challenges of writing about our cultures of origin. We encouraged faculty participants to engage in this introspective process with a spirit of exploration and to consider the strengths originating in their cultures. We often reiterated our belief that all cultures have important strengths to contribute to teaching, learning, and to the world. This going inward process led faculty to a deeper, more enriched sense of self-understanding as well as to greater insights about roles their own cultural mores play in their teaching practices and interpretations of students.

As we noted in Chapter 1, autobiographical or more personal writing is not an easy thing for many faculty, especially when conducted as part of academic life. A focus on culture can also be difficult, especially in a society with people of many cultures, some who are ultra-aware of their cultural mores and some for whom culture is a largely unconscious aspect of life. Even those who are highly aware of their cultural epistemologies found challenge in considering their role specifically in their teaching practices. Another challenge in writing about culture is the risk of essentializing ourselves and others. Faculty resisted being reductionist about their origins, writing evocatively about the tensions and contradictions of culture (one of the themes). Yet despite the risk of essentializing, our culture and teaching-learning work was rooted in the belief that culture is best explored and discussed, rather than left unacknowledged.

Each faculty author in this book expressed and identified with culture in unique ways. Though all spoke of ethnic backgrounds, those backgrounds varied widely in their presence in the essays. Some focused primarily on regional influences, while others focused on religious backgrounds or significant life experiences in adulthood. Making sense of culture is a complex endeavor for every individual.

During the process of writing these essays, faculty often spoke with elders and researched ancestors; these discoveries were both fascinating and exciting. At times, uncovering these histories led to the greatest insights about the influence of culture on teaching. Learning about ancestral and familial cultural influences was helpful to our understanding of our own ways of learning and led not only to insight but also to compassion for ourselves and ultimately for students. As authors of these essays, we recognize that we understand students more deeply when we honor our cultural selves more deeply.

CULTURE AND TEACHING AUTOBIOGRAPHY THEMES

Each of the culture and teaching autobiographies was organized into one of five themes. Though each essay could be located in most of the themes, as all were complex and rich in depth and nuance, the essays were distributed according to a primary theme. Despite the risk of simplifying these complex writings, organizing the autobiographies by theme captures the core ideas across all of the essays, adding meaning and structure to the whole. We did not capture all of their complexity under each theme, and much more complexity exists in the essays themselves in the following chapters. We hope you are as enriched by reading these essays as we were by working with and reading the profound work of these faculty authors as we developed this book.

The essays are quoted in the order in which the authors appear in the book.

THE STRENGTH OF PLACE AND ITS INFLUENCE ON TEACHING

Some faculty authors reflected on their strong sense of connection to place. Faculty authors in this section made sense of their own cultural mores notably through meaning making about place. The influence of a region, and a connection to the land, embodied their culture and emboldened and influenced their teaching.

One faculty author reflected on the nonconfrontational nature of people in her home region of the U.S. northeast and the ways her regional culture influences her teaching.

> Embracing the northeastern nature of my ancestors, I am slow to anger and reluctant to confront. A low level of in-class talking or activity is comfortable to me, and I don't generally require a silent classroom. I recognize that not all situations meet all learners' needs. Many of the assignments or assessments in my classes feature elements of choice. I am comfortable having students choose questions to answer on a test or assignments to incorporate into a portfolio. I view choices as another way to demonstrate strengths. It is also one way to avoid confronting an assignment that might not be appropriate for a particular learner. (Melissa Birkett Greene)

Others made a connection between the religious values of a home region and their teaching in response to those values. One teacher resisted the dualism of her conservative religious hometown and chose instead to encourage the pluralism of her students' cultures and identities.

> The normative discourse of my culture avowed that there was a wrong way and a right way. ... By place I mean who we are and what we value, which is linked to where we come from but not determined by it. This understanding provides the substance for why I developed Places of Belonging as an assignment for my students. Through this assignment students are encouraged and allowed to share the essence of who they are. ... Through sharing the presentations, the assignment is an invitation to relate to a pluralistic way of knowing. (Jean Ann Foley)

Some wrote about working on the land and in the garden, evoking a deep connection to place.

> I realized in my early adult years that our family's garden was really a metaphor for life. Plowing the soil, planting the seeds, irrigating, weeding, harvesting, canning, all of these things prepared me for life. All of these things required motivation, curiosity, patience, attention to

> detail, perseverance, cooperation, forgiveness, problem solving, and a multitude of other skills and talents. … Growing things is essential. I maintain growing ideas and growing food are equally important. I try to guide [students] to view new information through many different lenses in order to develop an inclusive outlook. (Judith A. Montoya)

Faculty authors shared the joy of nature, its lessons in rest and balance, and in nature's ability to renew their connections to students and to their teaching.

> I recharge by going into nature and feel myself fade a bit if I don't have opportunities to go into nature on a regular basis. When things get to be especially difficult, I find a spot to sit in nature. In every city or town I've lived in, I find natural places close to home to recharge and find peace of mind, and in my teaching I try to find similar places for students to experience science in the outdoors. I often pause to look at the stars, clouds, moon, trees, and the world around me, and I encourage my students to do the same. (Gary Weissmann)

> Eventually no matter which place name is used or what story is true, each community values the diverse perspectives of its people as long as it is significant and meaningful for those who tell the story of the place. In much the same way, I encourage my undergraduate and graduate students, to be open and willing to listen to new perspectives and make new meaning from diverse perspectives. (Vincent Werito)

> My small family, the land, the village and its dwellers had, and continue to have, a profound influence on the way I understand and see the world. This view is embedded with values that influence my chosen field of study and the way I teach. (Katya Crawford)

THE TENSIONS AND CONTRADICTIONS OF CULTURE AND ITS INFLUENCE ON TEACHING

Faculty authors wrote about the inherent contradictions in and between their cultures of origin; while culture was influential, it did not always define their being. Many struggled with the contradictions between their origin and their current approach to teaching. They experienced contradictions as the tension of opposites. One wrote about lessons from her Swedish mother, followed by her approach with students later in her career.

> People can be rational if they try. Choices lead to clear and recognizable outcomes and rational people choose the wisest alternatives. Emotion should not enter into decisions. … I no longer believe this as completely as I once did and now understand that students have divided hearts, because I have a divided heart. (Leslie Oakes)

Another faculty author wrote of the contradictions within culture, within himself, and within the world.

> When I talk about culture I try to be as brave as my students. I talk about the Mora valley and I talk about my work with coltan mining, and in the spaces in between, the students help me

> through the contradictions I brought to the class with me. When they realize we are pilgrims of a common exile, I recognize not the teacher that I am, but the one I am becoming. This provides the best comfort I believe I can share as a teacher and public servant. …
>
> While cultural models and dimensions of culture are valuable, they are only good starts. From their very beginning, they seduce our minds into the comfort of categories, and as I work with students, these dimensions become very difficult to express in a dynamic way. In fact, I intentionally struggle with these concepts in front of them to ensure that this discourse is recognized as a meaningful problem that we all struggle with. This is why "thinking in front of my students" is ultimately an act of sorting out my own contradictions and discomfort with polished information—so they may see the value in making critical thinking an active part of their own learning process. I find the alternative to be dangerous. (MJR Montoya)

One faculty author wrote evocatively about the tension between judgment and curiosity. She found that resolving these contradictions fostered her inquiry for creativity and her compassion for students.

> When I make quick judgments about my students, instead of being curious to know who they are and how they've come to know what they know, I limit our ability to create learning and I increase the power differential between me and my students. …
>
> I continue to call on myself, my students, and my colleagues to begin with and to fiercely hold on to inquiry, to nurture our ability to be passionately curious about one another, and to listen to one another, especially when faced with our differences. In my own life, it is a call to invoke the deep curiosity about the world that I had as a child. …
>
> In my teaching, if I can be passionately curious about my students' lives, understandings, and stances, I can build more bridges to help them think and hear beyond themselves. … My mom taught me this powerful life lesson. Her demand for acceptance of something that I thought intolerable showed me the limits of judgment and helped me to rebirth my curiosity. (Kersti Tyson)

Another faculty author wrote about the contradictions between her early messages about individualism, in dynamic tension with her later adoption of community.

> I try not to retreat into the vast White distance, but instead overcome my early cultural influences and maintain deeper connections with students through drawing on a later cultural influence—that of community. (Susan Diana Longerbeam)

IN SERVICE TO STUDENTS: DEVELOPING NEW WAYS TO TEACH

> It doesn't occur to me to lament students' lack of engagement because it is my responsibility to engage their wonder, inspire their curiosity, and help them situate learning in their lives.
>
> —Alicia Fedelina Chávez

Faculty authors wrote about myriad avenues to teach and serve students, through recognizing many ways of learning, and through acknowledgment that not all students learn best in the ways that faculty themselves learn best. These master teachers developed pedagogies over time to reach students in creative ways.

> I use a variety of reflective and discursive techniques to involve every student whether in large or small classes knowing that we will all develop greater understanding through a collective of insights, interpretations, perspectives, and wisdom.
>
> I intersperse silent reflection to gather thoughts and process ideas, with animated discussion among partners, trios, small groups, and the whole class. I push and tease and encourage, thank and commend and laugh, not letting students remain disengaged. Like my own best family teachers, I am more than a bit intrusive, teasing students to "dig deeper" when they are clearly sharing a less than complex interpretation; asking a late student if they are OK, tracking down absent students to see what they need, and approaching students who seem in distress to offer a listening ear or a referral for assistance to campus resources. I talk with recalcitrant students to let them know in no uncertain terms that they are needed in the world, I know they can do better, and expect them to do so; something one of my former students describes as my "come to Dr. Chávez talk." (Alicia Fedelina Chávez)

Some faculty authors describe working toward the ultimate goal of helping students to become better humans. They spoke and wrote freely of allowing a place for passion and love in their professional lives, and were motivated by the desire to give something back to students, as they had been given by their teachers.

> Developing as human beings underlies everything in my teaching design and facilitation. This means that I constantly push and cajole, inspire and challenge students to see and understand our connection to all that surrounds us. I make constant connections to larger lessons in life and ask students to identify connections to current and future professional responsibilities. I do this hoping they will ripple through generations and I through them. This is how I was taught, how I see my responsibility and connectedness through teaching. (Alicia Fedelina Chávez)
>
> After all is said and done, though, what I care about most is motivating them to be the best human beings they can be. And to live a good life filled with passion, and love. …
>
> How do I assess whether my goals for this nontraditional class are met? My ultimate goal is impossible to measure in a quantitative manner. My ultimate goal is to help them develop into better, more caring and educated human beings, and for the class to have a positive effect for the entire rest of their lives. And further, that they use those experiences and knowledge to positively impact the lives of others. Perhaps a survey asking them about it 60 years from now would work. (Matías Fontenla)

Many of the faculty authors in this volume wrote about the importance of focusing on active rather than passive learning. One faculty member wants to help students learn about poverty through doing the active work of poverty amelioration. He ultimately wants for his students to have a more sophisticated story on the causes of poverty.

> Since our goal was for students to "live and learn" economic development, they were expected to keep a journal to foster the development of their own thoughts, to express their feelings, and to take notes. Rarely did we lecture, more often we would just moderate lively discussions. We did not give out answers, but we would pose questions. Then we would lean back and observe how they figured things out on their own, based on what they did that day. It was a wonderful, fulfilling experience seeing them "get it" on their own, their eyes sparkling with excitement. Students learn on their own, teachers are just facilitators.
>
> Only after having a hands-on, personal experience, talking to people whose situation did not fit neatly in a box, thinking about it themselves, that we could refute those simple misconceptions in the classroom, and build a more sophisticated story on the causes of poverty. Our discussions in class, their journal entries, and their final papers showed to me that most of them got it. (Matías Fontenla)

Ultimately, faculty in our cohort made a key shift from focusing on their teaching to focusing on student learning. They became interested in cultivating a passion for student learning, and what followed that shift was a focus on communicating with students to discover the means to facilitate their best learning, rather than a focus on accomplishing tasks. Through working with students who learn differently than he, the following faculty member identified that students were the ones who had transformed *him*.

> I realized that my people-centered passion as a teacher was better served by further shifting my attention from being a better teacher to helping my students become better learners. … I tell students that I admire their dedication to degree attainment while working and raising children and negotiate deadlines with students to respect competing commitments to family, jobs, and communities. Negotiating the learning process with students is a transformative change from the values I maintained when I was a student—an emphasis on the practical value of getting things done, which is likely another mark of my western European heritage. (Gary Smith)

FROM OPPRESSION FOR DIFFERENCE TO EMPOWERING THROUGH TEACHING

Some faculty authors wrote about continually negotiating their identities in contradistinction to dominant culture and confronting outsider status while recognizing the fluidity of identity and fighting back against simplistic notions of culture and identity. As a result of these experiences, they committed to recognizing the importance of empowering students, their cultural intersections, and their individuality.

> I awakened to the world around me to find cruelty, hatred, and animosity displayed outside my home. … I believe those early experiences taught me to value the individual distinctions of everyone, to recognize that divisions are often products of broader social and political forces, and celebrate those that stand in opposition to injustice of the dominant norm, which is what I try to impart to my students. …
>
> Individuals are always immersed in distinct and varied social groups. While the groups may display hard demarcations, the individuals within them do not as they live across social boundaries. Everyone holds multiple, rather fluid identities simultaneously. …
>
> I believe it to be vital for students to reflect on the particulars of their own conditions to identify the relations of authority and power that shape their world. For instance, in many of my courses I require students to collect and reflect on the presence of issues raised in the class and how they appear in the world around them and shape their perceptions. In a course on modern history, one such assignment starts with a long scavenger hunt for local items from Latin America, which, as students discover, are often hidden in plain sight in the community. The assignment ends by asking students to reflect on how these items reflect the economic and social position of Latinos in their community, who are also often hiding in plain sight. (R. A. Kashanipour)
>
> It was a hard lesson to learn, but ultimately I understood that being Other united me with more people who shared dual heritages in settings which were often hostile, intolerant, and unforgiving. The experience of growing up Black and Latino reminded me that being multicultural is not a luxury. …
>
> Growing up understanding my dual heritages has caused me to value the strength of different ways of thinking and feeling in a White-dominant, racially stratified society. These are the ways of thinking and feeling that students can bring to the classroom—that people embody different means of comprehending the world, and that their personal histories exceed simplistic stories or ways of learning. (Ricardo Guthrie)

These faculty further connected students' lives to the lives of others, to further understanding of the depth of varying life experiences. They continually challenge students to examine the human variation and depth of culture.

> In the classroom, I provide exercises for students to evaluate modes of expressing themselves, and how their knowledge compares with others. … Collectively, students evaluate film elements, and then discuss agreements and different ways of explaining particular scenes or the film overall. The groups report back to the larger class, share their perceptual analyses, and then the class as a whole compares and contrasts how the elements work together. In this way, a student who had direct experience working with Navajo communities could share her perspective on the images and ideas reflective of her culture—compared to others who had little or no interaction with Indigenous people before. Others, who were asked if they could identify with certain characters of different races and ethnicities, could see how similar or different their lives really were. (Ricardo Guthrie)
>
> A larger question is how do I connect with students who have similar and different cultural frames and values. … I do this by talking about borders. Whether they know it or not,

> students are constantly crossing borders; and crossing borders is not easy. Nothing about borders is easy. (T. Mark Montoya)

We were continually awestruck with the ways in which these master faculty transformed their own experiences into transformative, deep learning for their students.

> So, how do I reach those students who have put me in a box? I reach them with humor, with active learning, with sharing my teaching thoughts aloud, and with continual support for them as learners. Due to these box constrictions, I emphasize the need to "unlearn." Learning can actually be easy, but unlearning is hard. This is where and how I reach students culturally. I encourage them to share their stories. We become partners in teaching and learning. I am as much the teacher as I am the learner. The best pedagogical tool I have is when students allow me ways to adapt and adjust my own ways of teaching. When I teach without a box, students learn without a box; and hence cross borders in their learning and in their lives. They do this by drawing on their strengths, which come from the very hardships they have endured. (T. Mark Montoya)

Faculty authors wrote of disempowering and oppressive experiences in their own educational journeys. They wrote about committing now to overturning this pattern by empowering students through their teaching practice.

> My past experiences have provided me with a foundation for how I interact with students and how I teach in the classroom setting. I believe that we all have meaningful offerings and we should all be encouraged to use our knowledge not only to teach others but to learn from others as well. I consider it my responsibility as a facilitator of learning to bring out the pre-knowledge that all students bring with them to the classroom. … But this success did not come without many failures and starts and stops. I had to learn to be engaged in a place where I felt very uncomfortable. I have always been passive in teaching spaces. Often, I did not ask for help and I have never felt completely safe in the classroom. …
>
> As far as my culture is concerned I feel there have been few times in my scholastic experiences that my culture was upheld in the classroom; most times my culture was viewed as something exotic, something to be studied and scrutinized. I want my students to be able to express their opinions in my class, to contribute the knowledge they bring to the class, I want my classes to be open exchanges between me and my students. (Carissa Tsosie)

THE STRENGTH OF CULTURAL VALUES AND THEIR INFLUENCE ON TEACHING

Several faculty authors reflected on the influence of their (normative) culture of origin as substantial, its substantiality discovered through the process of writing and reflection. At times, dominant cultures, because they were presumed normative, were revealed through the power of insight; discovering culture was most powerful when it was most invisible.

> Yet in almost a decade of training on how to recognize and respond to the cultural identities that students bring to the classroom, I never considered what cultural identities I myself bring to the classroom. (K. Maria D. Lane)

> I have always operated on a misconception, that culture is something that defines others, not me. (Robert Neustadt)

As faculty gained further insight into cultural influences, they made connections to their teaching practice.

> If I additionally share with students my own thoughts about how culture influences my teaching, I believe we might make collective progress toward harnessing our cultural strengths and minimizing our cultural limitations in the classroom. (K. Maria D. Lane)

> If there are fibers of my cultural heritage that manifest themselves in my identity as a professor, I believe these reveal themselves in my provocative teaching style and activism. (Robert Neustadt)

This faculty author further illuminates the discovery of a great uncle:

> To my surprise and delight I discovered that Mordechai Kaplan, born in Lithuania in 1881, described by some as the "greatest American Jewish thinker," invoked a kind of Judaism that aligns ironically well with many of my own iconoclastic beliefs. (Robert Neustadt)

One faculty author wrote about the connection of her culture to her core value of developing relationships in community.

> This value of relationships is helpful as a teacher in that students can see from the beginning how important community is to me and how I am connected to my tribal and Indigenous culture. As well, this helps students to feel a part of the group and to be open to sharing their experiences and perspectives with respect to the learning and discussion. … It is important for me to acknowledge the different experiences and cultural backgrounds of the students and to value those as an important part of the community. (Robin Minthorn)

Another faculty author wrote about how extending compassion to students arises from her faith.

> In a way, being a religious person makes it easier for me to try to step into my students' shoes. … I usually tend to believe what the students write. Sometimes their stories present such a hard life that I wish I could do something right away to help them. (Laura Sujo-Montes)

This faculty author asked herself thoughtful, reflective questions about her work with students, questioning the congruity between her faith and teaching.

> Did I hold high expectations for her the same way I do for my students and for me? Did I show Christian charity toward her? How much of my actions were guided by my culture or by my religion? Can they even be separated?

> I try to constantly question myself: Am I being just and fair with my students? Should I believe the excuse they give me when they do not turn in work on time? What would happen if I were in their situation? Would I want an instructor who is compassionate and understanding? My religious beliefs also make me question my ability to embrace everybody. Since "all of us are creatures of God," then I must love every one, which, of course, I do not do. Also, "love each other as I love you" guides me to try to be an accepting and caring person to everybody … but I still have a long way to go to be able to get there.
>
> God acts through every person regardless of the person and, as some may say, in mysterious ways. I am careful to have this guiding belief present in my mind when my students ask for an extension to turn in the assignment because "life happened." After all, who am I to judge if they are being truthful to me? According to my faith, they will be judged after they die. (Laura Sujo-Montes)

WE ARE OUR CULTURED SELVES

These faculty authors enlivened the conversation about the importance of faculty culture in college teaching. While we expected their stories to be profound, the following essays in this book exceeded our expectations in their profundity and deep insight. In each theme—The Strength of Place; The Tensions and Contradictions of Culture and Its Influence on Teaching; In Service to Students: Developing New Ways to Teach; From Oppression for Difference to Empowering Through Teaching; and The Strength of Cultural Values and Their Influence on Teaching—we were given more depth and insight into the influence of early culture and family life, how those early lives influenced authors' natural ways of learning, and how those ways of learning now manifest in how faculty teach. We are grateful for the authors' depth of insight, honesty, and courage.

PART TWO

Faculty Culture AND Teaching Autobiographies

The Strength of Place and Its Influence on Teaching

In this section, faculty authors eloquently draw on their strong sense of connection to place to make meaning of who they are and how this influences their teaching practice.

CULTURAL LEGACIES ARE POWERFUL FORCES.
THEY HAVE DEEP ROOTS AND LONG LIVES.
THEY PERSIST, GENERATION AFTER GENERATION
- MALCOLM GLADWELL

CHAPTER THREE

NXSW

Cultural Legacies in Education

MELISSA BIRKETT GREENE

Neuroscience and Behavior
Northern Arizona University

> Cultural legacies are powerful forces. They have deep roots and long lives. They persist, generation after generation, virtually intact, even as the economic and social and demographic conditions that spawned them have vanished, and they play such a role in directing attitudes and behavior that we cannot make sense of our world without them.
>
> —GLADWELL, 2008, (p. 175)

One day, after lunch, next to the lockers in the hallway outside of Mrs. Simon's fifth-grade classroom, Michelle Lawrence kicked me. Hard. I wasn't sure why she did it, but I did what I thought was best in front the group of eleven-year-olds; I laughed and went out to recess. Six months later, Michelle and I shared a desk in Mrs. Anderson's sixth-grade English class, our heads bent together on essays and vocabulary definitions. Twenty years later, we are casual Facebook friends.

In his bestselling book, *Outliers*, Malcolm Gladwell describes the research of two social psychologists on a phenomenon dubbed the "culture of honor." The psychologists (Cohen and Nesbitt) studied reactions of male college students to a common experience—being insulted. The researchers found two different patterns of reactions. When confronted with someone blocking their path and uttering a single word ("asshole"), the participants tended to either laugh off the situation or get angry. Very angry. The researchers found that one unique characteristic predicted which participants would display which reaction: whether their families were from the northern or southern United States.

Gladwell (2008) goes on to explain how the southeast was settled by immigrants of Scotch-Irish descent. (Later research in this area extended this general finding to the western United States, including Arizona.) This remote part of the country remained partitioned into clan territories for generations, and people largely continued to lead herder lifestyles as they had in their cultures of origin. As Gladwell describes, the livelihood of a herding culture is under constant threat of theft. Herders must keep constant vigilance and aggressively thwart challenges to their family's stock or flock. Thus, a "culture of honor" surrounds the cultural legacies of herding clans and influences succeeding generations. Gladwell writes: "The 'culture of honor' hypothesis says that it matters where you're from, not just in terms of where you grew up or where your parents grew up, but in terms of where your great-grandparents and great-great-grandparents grew up and even where your great-great-great grandparents grew up. That is a strange and powerful fact" (Gladwell, 2008, p. 170).

In contrast, the northeast United States was settled largely by immigrants from Western Europe, many with farming rather than herding legacies. Small farms and townships (rather than isolated family territories) are the norm there. Cultural legacies of the people of the northeast trace their origins back to small communities of farmers and later included the rise of industry and a turn toward cooperative factory and mill work that required communal collaboration and discouraged a "culture of honor."

Can you guess where the angry college students were from? Can you guess where I am from?

Though currently living and working in Arizona, I am at least a fourth-generation upstate New Yorker. My cultural legacy traces its way back through my maternal and paternal great-grandparents to immigrants from the Netherlands, England, and Italy. Evidence for a deeply entrenched identity associated with a specific cultural legacy comes from my father, the amateur genealogist. Along one branch of the family tree, his cache of information reflects many of our family members' English names—Johns, Williams, and Josephs for the men and Anns and Janes for the women. Both my sister and I have middle names that were first used by relatives more than a century before we were born.

My ancestors were connected to the land and lifestyle of the rural, agricultural area that I too grew up in. Many of them were directly involved in agriculture or factory work, dependent on the collective work of a community to be successful. The local public schools I attended and the stages I walked across during graduation ceremonies were the same places my siblings, parents, cousins, great aunts and uncles, and even grandparents had been before me. The places and traditions that we all shared, extending to even our common educational experiences, provided familiarity, stability, and predictability that felt safe, comfortable, and valued.

My family is generally trusting but independent, and usually calm and reserved. We have no financial legacy, family property, or herds to protect, or buildings bearing our name. We typically avoid conflict at all costs. The heated discussions I've witnessed among family members are rare, and I've never witnessed an actual argument or confrontation. We personify Gladwell's description of northeasterners: calm, cooperative, and able to shrug off insult.

I recently learned that my parents had loaned money to family friends who were in danger of losing their house years earlier. The (former) family friends took the money and never repaid it, surely angering my parents and violating their trust. I would never have known. My parents simply stopped socializing with them, shrugged off the insult, and moved on.

While our family might not exemplify the culture of honor described by Gladwell and others, our relationships with each other are still important, extending beyond our shared geographic cultural legacy. As an adult, my education and eventual career took me to other parts of the country to study and work. Leaving New York has not always meant leaving my family, however. Although most of our family remained rooted in New York, twice my sister and I struck together to pursue opportunities in other places (first in Massachusetts, and later in Arizona). For her, these forays were temporary. With her eventual graduate degree in hand, she returned to upstate New York to raise her own family. Having her support before that, however, proved crucial to both of our educational and career successes. Not only did we pool resources that enabled us to pursue our goals, but together we compared observations of the different ways our new friends, students, and coworkers confronted situations and each other, and how they differed from the ways that we responded.

In my first semester as a faculty member, a male student did not agree with my lesson planning for the day. While I could only speculate about what his cultural legacy might have been, he felt comfortable enough to spontaneously walk to the front of the class, take the dry-erase marker from my hand mid-lesson, and write his own (uninvited) version for the class to see. For better or worse, just as I had in Mrs. Simon's class years before, in spite of feeling insulted by the situation, I defaulted to my cultural legacy, laughed it off, reclaimed my marker, and moved on. After the incident, several colleagues shared that they might have handled the situation differently.

My cultural, geographic, and familial legacies continue to influence my teaching today, nearly 10 years after the marker incident. Embracing the northeastern nature of my ancestors, I am slow to anger and reluctant to confront. A low level of in-class talking or activity is comfortable to me, and I do not generally require a silent classroom. I recognize that not all situations meet all learners' needs. Many of the assignments or assessments in my classes feature elements of choice. I am comfortable having students choose questions to answer on a test or assignments to incorporate into a portfolio. I view choices as another way to demonstrate strengths. It is also one way to avoid confronting an assignment that might not be appropriate for a particular learner.

For example, my reluctance to confront is manifest in the way that I ask questions of students in class. Although I work hard to learn all of the names of the students in my classes, I almost never call on students individually and publically in class. I found that type of confrontation painfully uncomfortable as a student. I don't ask it of the students I work with now. The stress of that kind of personal challenge was difficult for me as a younger learner. I was far more comfortable demonstrating my knowledge or engaging in learning in less confrontational situations. This doesn't mean that I don't hold students accountable for their learning; rather, it means that I approach it in a different way. In my classes today, you could reasonably expect to witness questions posed to an entire class (with a long wait time—being rushed is a form of confrontation too) or posed for small-group discussion or presented with time for each individual to write an answer privately.

The geographic legacies and "culture of honor" are an important aspect of recognizing how I might similarly or differently respond to situations faced in educational environments with students. For example, while I might be more comfortable looking past an awkward moment or interaction, a student (or colleague) with a different cultural legacy might feel more comfortable talking through a situation as a class or speaking directly with another person after a misunderstanding. It is helpful to recognize that our responses differ, depending, in part, on an individual's expectations and cultural legacies.

My cultural legacy influences my work and career in ways not only bound by my geographic heritage. I draw on additional aspects of my personal experiences to relate to students. I think of the role of my family, and particularly the relationship with my sister, that helped facilitate meeting my educational and career goals, and of the role geographic places can have on important decisions. Recently, a former student returned to campus to visit after graduating. He was visiting his sister (also a student at our school) and shared with me that he had returned to his hometown and had found his passion for teaching as an English teacher in his former high school. His hometown is located on the Mexican border, his students are different from those at our university, and his cultural legacy is very different from my own. At first he seemed hesitant to share his happy news. I suspected that he might have worried about what I thought of his decision to return home. But his decision resonated with me, and given the opportunity, I might make the same decision to return to work among the people I most closely shared a cultural legacy with too. Familial and cultural legacies are woven in our decisions, even when they come from different origins. They are a powerful influence.

Though Gladwell did not include it in his review of Nisbett and Cohen's work, their later research confirmed what I suspected when moving to Arizona; the Southwest, too, has a culture of honor. A culture of honor seems to play into more controversial aspects of education. Brown, Osterman, and Barnes (2009) investigated the role of culture of honor in school violence. They found that high school students in culture of honor states were significantly more likely to report bringing a weapon to school than students in non–culture of honor states. Further, they reported that three times as many school shootings occurred in culture of honor states. In reflecting on these data, the authors suggested that "school violence might be partially a product of long-term or recent experiences of social marginalization, humiliation, rejection, or bullying … all of which represent honor threats with special significance to people (particularly males) living in culture-of-honor states" (Brown et al., p. 1404).

Last week, four male students were shot by another male student on our campus, one fatally. Over 60% of the students on our campus reside in-state, suggesting that the majority of our students have some level of contact with a culture of honor. How does this knowledge influence my interactions with students?

It means understanding that students will vary in their perspectives toward violence. It means a realistic assessment of the likelihood of violent situations arising. It means that I might expect to encounter students affected by violence in my classes. It means that my experience with my own cultural legacy may be different from that of the students I work with. I continue to try to reflect on how my personal experiences and cultural legacies frame the way I view education and how I interact with students.

Although not always comfortable, an exploration of aspects of my own cultural legacy, sometimes spanning generations, bestows a stronger sense of identity on my work as a teacher in higher education, particularly in the context of a culture that is in many ways different from my own. It highlights some of the strengths and weaknesses inherent in my approach and provides additional room for reflection not only on my development as an educator, but in what I recognize and respond to in the learners I work with. I draw on my understanding that individuals are influenced by sometimes tacit cultural legacies and an appreciation of the many factors that students must balance in their decisions to pursue higher education and careers, for example, the difficult decisions to leave families and hometowns and the influence they can have in our education and careers. It also means bringing my own approach to the situations that arise when interacting with others, and sometimes reexamining whether my cultural legacy serves me well in my decisions as an educator.

REFERENCES

Brown, R. P., Osterman, L. L., & Barnes, C. D. (2009). School violence and the culture of honor. *Psychological Science, 20*(11), 1400–1405.

Gladwell, M. (2008). *Outliers: The story of success.* Boston, MA: Little, Brown and Company.

CHAPTER FOUR

A Discovery Process

Identifying My Multicultural Roots

JUDITH A. MONTOYA

Geography, Planning & Recreation
Northern Arizona University

CULTURAL IDENTITY THROUGH THE LENS OF FAMILY AND CHILDHOOD

When I began thinking about my cultural identity, I quickly realized that I have had some notion of my cultural identity since I was very young. I was raised in what I now know to be called a very rich "multicultural" environment. Growing up in Tularosa, New Mexico, in a multigenerational family home of authentic adobe whose original room was built by my great-great-grandparents provided me with a solid foundation of love, family, and community. My cultural identity is molded by this place that is my home. The progression of how my cultural identity has evolved to the present encompasses a rich mix of culture, family traditions, experiences, and place, which I will try to convey in the following narratives.

MY HOME AND FAMILY

The Tularosa basin is located at the foot of the Sacramento Mountains, with the Mescalero Apache Indian Reservation up the mountain to the east and the White Sands National Monument to the west. It is an oasis of giant pecan and cottonwood trees as a result of the original acequias (irrigation ditches) that line the streets of the village. The original part of town was laid out in 49 blocks, and each home included an acequia and water rights that still exist today. There are an abundance of fruit trees and gardens in every back yard. Tularosa gets its name from the red willows that grew along the banks of the Rio Tularosa, or "Tulie Creek" as we call it. It originates in the high mountains where the Mescalero Apache Reservation is located. The Village was established in 1863 and later, after the battle at Round Mountain between the settlers and the Mescaleros, more people began to settle in the area.

My cultural identity cannot be described without first introducing my family. I was lucky enough to grow up with great-grandparents, parents, an uncle, two cousins (boys), two brothers, and three sisters all living under the same roof. My Dad's name was Demetrio Montoya, and he was a major influence in my life. While he never completed a college education, he placed value on getting an education. He was an active member of our community and held leadership roles with the local school board, Optimist Club, City Council, and was the mayor of our town for 12 years. My Mother, Patricia Dorame Montoya, also did not complete a college degree but always worked outside the home in a professional setting. Both of my parents were employed by the nearby air force base, which exposed them to a diversity of ideas, perspectives, and people from all over the world. Their experiences and resulting perspectives were passed on to us at an early age. Both were incredible role models in my life, and they always supported me in my goals.

My great-grandparents were Frank and Blasa Dorame. We moved in with them when I was four years old, and shortly after that, my aunt passed away, so my Uncle (Mom's brother) moved in with his two sons. My extended family consisted of numerous Aunts, Uncles, and cousins. Older cousins were referred to as "Aunt" and "Uncle," so for many years as a child, I thought that all older cousins automatically became Aunts and Uncles! My great-grandparents raised my Mom from birth along with her brother because her Mother died from complications at childbirth. At that time my great-grandparents were working for the BIA on the Mescalero Apache Indian Reservation. My Mother attended school on the reservation until she was 16 years old when my grandparents retired and moved to Tularosa. My Grandpa was Yaqui and my Grandma was half Black and half Hispanic (probably Mexican). My great-grandparents played a significant role in the development of my cultural identity. I first discovered I was *not* an Apache when I was about six years old.

WHAT? I AM NOT AN APACHE?

Some of my earliest memories of being with my great-grandparents are of times spent visiting friends in Mescalero and Three Rivers, which were both on the reservation. My grandparents were Godparents to what seemed like hundreds, and everyone seemed to know them and regarded them as elders with much love and respect. One recurring visit was to Three Rivers to visit Bertha Tortilla (daughter of Shanta Boy). During the summer she lived there in a wikkiup, which was a type of shelter made with walls and roof of pine boughs or other tree limbs and dirt floors. The inside was dark and cool with a pleasant smell of pine pitch and smoke. I remember there being intermittent rays of sunlight breaking through between the leaves and branches of the walls and roof. In the middle of the room was a wood fire with large pots, usually filled with beans and red chili, one filled with hot lard for making fry bread, and another cast iron flat plate for cooking tortillas. I remember Bertha as being elderly, but not as old as my grandparents. Her hair never seemed to be combed and she was missing most of her teeth. She conversed with my grandparents in both Spanish and Apache, but I never heard her speak English. Despite her appearance, there was something endearing about her, and even though I was usually hiding behind my grandma and holding her hand, I was very curious about her. I wondered why she lived there alone, why she didn't comb her hair, and what happened to her teeth! I always looked forward to our visits with Bertha Tortilla. She always greeted me with a soft smile, and I remember thinking that she must be someone's grandma too. On one particular visit I remember the conversation being centered on the upcoming July 4 Feast, which was the time of the annual puberty right ceremony for the young Apache maidens. Someone in the Shanta clan would be participating, and the talk was of food preparation and setting up of teepees in Mescalero at the feast grounds.

After returning to Tularosa later that day we were sitting outside under the big walnut tree in the back yard, and I asked my Grandma when I would be able to celebrate *my* feast. Her answer was not what I expected. She said "Mija, you can't have a feast, you're not an Apache." "I'm not! Then what am I?" She replied, "you are a Yaqui Indian, your grandpa is Yaqui, not Apache." My next question was, "What is a Yaqui Indian?" I was six years old.

WAIT ... MY GRANDMA IS A NEGRO?

As a child I attended St. Francis de Paula Catholic School from grades 1 through 6. There was no kindergarten, so I began school with first grade. Over the years there were many families from the surrounding towns who sent their children to our little school. Some children came down from Mescalero, which was 15 miles up the mountain to the east; others came from Alamogordo, which was 12 miles to the south; and others were from La Luz, which was six miles away between Tularosa and Alamogordo. Because my grandparents knew so many people, many of these kids would walk home with us from school, which was only three blocks away. We would have a snack and then play outdoors until their parents picked them up after work. When I was in fourth grade, an Anglo girl named Carla

Tidwell from La Luz began attending our school, and Grandma knew her parents, who were ranch owners. One day after school we were sitting on the bench under the walnut tree having a snack when Carla turned to me and said, "I like your Grandma, I didn't know she was a Negro woman!" Before I would have a chance to respond, her Dad came driving up the driveway, and off she dashed to greet him. I was 10 years old.

Later in my life I would learn from other non-family members that my great-great-grandfather, Andres Crawford, was a Black Buffalo Soldier. It was never discussed in the presence of my grandparents.

WHAT IS A MESIKIN?

After completing sixth grade in my Catholic school, everyone went on to enroll in the junior high school (where the "Publics" attended). Coming from the Catholic school, we all grew up thinking that we were "Catholics" and they were "Publics." I didn't have any hesitation with my transfer to the public school. After all, I knew plenty of "Publics," and they were no different from me. My grandparents and parents had plenty of Public friends who visited our home. In the summers I played softball, rode the Recreation bus to Alamogordo for bowling, swimming, and skating, and I had been a Girl Scout Brownie, which had meetings in the basement of a non-Catholic church. I was excited! This was the first year in the public schools that girls were allowed to wear "pants," and it was the first year I was not required to wear a uniform! One of my first new friendships was with a girl named "Giffy," which was her nickname. Apparently her little brother could not pronounce Vicky. Junior high was a time for girl birthday parties, slumber parties, and screaming parties in general. Giffy and her older sister had lots of girl parties at their house out on a farm/ranch, and I happened to get invited to one. This was a slumber party, and I remember the image of girls rushing toward me and the sound of screaming as my Mom dropped me off at her house. As other girls were arriving, we remained in the front yard turning cartwheels and flips with intermittent screaming, doing what girls do, and having fun! Suddenly, with great urgency, Giffy yelled, "Quick, everyone inside and into my room!" "What's wrong?" someone asked. "My Daddy is coming down the road and he doesn't like Mesikins!" she answered. As I was running down the hall to her room, I remember thinking to myself, "What's a Mesikin?" I was 12 years old.

DISCOVERY OF YSLETA PUEBLO ROOTS

After my Dad passed away four years ago, we learned from an Aunt that we had Ysleta Pueblo ancestry. In fact, my Grandma Margaret Montoya (Dad's Mother) was half Ysleta. I was familiar with the Isleta Pueblo (spelled with an "I") along the Rio Grande just south of Albuquerque, New Mexico, but I learned that the Tigua of Ysleta del Sur Pueblo were also Pueblo Indians related to the northern Pueblo people. They are the southern-most of the Rio Grande Indian Pueblos that extend northward to Taos Pueblo (above Santa Fe), New Mexico, and are located in Texas along the Rio Grande just over the border of New Mexico, about 100 miles from Tularosa where I grew up. "The Ysleta Mission, founded by the Tigua Indians in 1682, is the oldest parish in the State of Texas" (Houser, 2006, ¶3). These Pueblo people remained loyal to the missionaries and broke away from the northern Isleta group during the Pueblo Revolt of 1680 to head south with the Padres. "In Spanish 'del Sur' means 'of the south' to contrast it with the mother pueblo of Isleta of the north, that is located just south of modern-day Albuquerque, New Mexico. The old Spanish spelling with 'Y' has been retained for Ysleta del Sur Pueblo in El Paso, Texas" (Houser, 2006, ¶3). While we were aware we had relatives in that area, this recently discovered identity took my family by surprise. Even now, in my 50s, I have a new cultural identity to explore!

NEW MEXICO IS THE STATE BETWEEN TEXAS AND ARIZONA

After completing my undergraduate degree at Western New Mexico University in Silver City and working for two years, I then completed my graduate degree at the University of New Mexico in Albuquerque. I got married, and while my husband was ABD he accepted a position at Springfield College, Massachusetts. I was excited to be moving to New England, a new place of culture and people and adventure. I was promptly hired by the diocese as a physical education teacher in one of the K–8 schools in an "Irish" neighborhood. I quickly learned that each neighborhood school was identified by a certain ethnicity. There was the Italian school, the Puerto Rican school, the German school, etc., and they didn't mix much. I found this interesting, but mostly I found it odd. The faculty at the school was a combination of lay teachers and nuns, all "Irish" as they proudly described themselves in their introductions to me. Since I was obviously not Irish, the other teachers assumed that I was Puerto Rican, probably because I was brown and they were the only familiar point of reference. One of the nuns complimented me on my English and how I had no accent! One morning Sr. Margaret, the principal, was out in the parking lot while I was parking. Naturally, being from New Mexico, I drove a truck. Not only did I drive a truck, but it had a camper shell and kayak and canoe racks rigged on top. As I approached Sr. Margaret I could see that she had the most befuddled look on her face. "Good morning, Sr. Margaret," I said. She quickly blurted out a barrage of questions. "What is *that*? Is it a van? What is it for? Is it difficult to drive?" All the while she was looking at my four-wheel-drive Toyota pickup. "It's a truck," I answered. "We do a lot of backcountry backpacking, camping and kayaking and canoeing. It gets us where we need to go and hauls all of our gear," I proudly answered. After an inspection of sorts she ended with, "I guess you come from a pretty wild place, but you won't be needing that thing here." The next week when classes started, I made my introduction to my first-period class, which happened to be eighth graders. I started with my name and said that I was from New Mexico. One of the girls raised her hand and said, "My parents love that place! They go there every year to spend time on the beach and they always come back with a great suntan like yours." After the introduction my first lesson for the class that day was a geography lesson, not physical education. "*New* Mexico is the state between Texas and Arizona."

These stories of some of my life's experiences are elements of my cultural identity that I have linked together to demonstrate the progression of how my cultural identity evolved throughout my life. They are the antecedents to my values, which I will review next.

WHAT ARE MY VALUES?

The things that I value most in my life are centered on family, traditions, food, place, and nature. Most of my childhood was spent playing outdoors with siblings and helping in our family's garden. I realized in my early adult years that our family's garden was really a metaphor for life. Plowing the soil, planting the seeds, irrigating, weeding, harvesting, canning, all of these things prepared me for life. All of these things required motivation, curiosity, patience, attention to detail, perseverance, cooperation, forgiveness, problem solving, and a multitude of other skills and talents. As a child and continuing into my adult life, I have never felt alone because of these values. I've been able to make a "home" in most places I have lived and keep centered as long as I could carry on my family traditions and re-create some of those processes. Growing up I felt that there was always someone there to hold my hand, literally and figuratively. My solid foundation centered on family culture and traditions is what has enabled me to venture out away from "home" and enabled me to "hold my own hand" when necessary. How do these values translate to what guides me? I will try to illustrate this in the following section.

BELIEFS AND ASSUMPTIONS THAT GUIDE ME

My values are what have set the stage for my beliefs to develop and guide me along the way. They direct me in assuming the following:

- Everyone is important and capable in their own way. I strive to view all of my students in this way by purposefully looking beyond a face sitting in the classroom. I have learned that providing the students with an online space to introduce themselves to the class in written form solicits more information voluntarily and provides a much broader sharing process for understanding who they are.
- Children are treasures and should be nurtured. I strive to view all of my students in this way as well. As a child, I gained great confidence from feeling treasured and nurtured by adults in my life, which enabled me to explore and experience success.
- Food and family together always make things in life better. I strive to incorporate a sense of community in the classroom. I do this by reminding my students at the onset of each class that we will all be working together equally toward a common goal.
- Home is a place of comfort. I strive to take them back to that place in class discussions. I encourage them to use life experiences to make sense of new ideas and put things in perspective.
- Growing things is essential. I maintain growing ideas and growing food are equally important. I try to guide them to view new information through many different lenses to develop an inclusive outlook.
- Being outdoors and maintaining physical fitness is imperative. I strive to live this lifestyle and be a role model for my family and my students by actively participating in a healthy lifestyle in our community where we all live together.

IMPACTS OF VALUES ON MY TEACHING

I have come to believe that tapping a student's potential and motivating the student to reach it are two of the greatest challenges for an educator, especially when teaching students who do not come with the cultural capital of the mainstream culture. I often do this by sharing my educational background and childhood stories as a way to potentially connect with students and help motivate them to see the possibilities ahead of them. I was one of those students and always managed to find a teacher somewhere along the way who took that perspective. As a result, my educational goals revolve around treating students as individuals, recognizing their educational and cultural backgrounds, and creating opportunities for them to actively participate in their own learning process. I believe this approach emphasizes a positive relationship between the teacher and student. This relationship requires an inviting learning environment that is based on open and frequent communication, fairness, trust, and mutual respect. Providing and prompting an opportunity for one-on-one communication with me often works with students who are unlikely to speak up in class otherwise. Over the years I have found that this is how I learned best and these are all familiar components of communication that I grew up with in my culture, and I try to carry that on in my teaching.

As a teacher, I have always tried to motivate the students to raise their educational expectations, and I act as a resource and facilitator to help them achieve those expectations. I learned and practiced this teaching strategy from being a Mother of two daughters and helping them to grow and thrive in this way. I believe in a teaching approach that combines class, community involvement, experiential learning, and the use of current technology in a culturally safe environment. I think this approach will prepare the students to be confident and successful in the real world. As a learner, I was most successful and responded best to teachers who conveyed that to me. All of my courses include assignments that place students in the community as volunteers to further enhance their learning process of diverse communities and inclusive practices. Other assignments include "doing" what they are learning such as conducting an accessibility compliance survey on a facility or surveying their community for culturally influenced events and activities. With each new semester I strive to view each class with enthusiasm and convey my commitment to their learning process.

Currently my teaching approach is based on the fact that our college population now reflects the increasing ethnic, racial, and cultural diversity of our society. After teaching in higher education for 28 years, I have come to the conclusion that the term *typical student* is no longer applicable. I believe curricula in higher education need to adjust to these demographic facts to handle the changing face of our student body. I strive to take a leading role in this process to ensure that each of my students is getting her or his needs met and reaching their full potential. Because of my cultural background, I have never been in the category of "typical student," and therefore I will never be in the category of "typical Teacher" either. I am very proud of my cultural identity and how it has translated to my teaching philosophy and values. My hope is that students will see themselves in me and know that all things in life are possible!

I am Judith Dorame Montoya Campbell from *New* Mexico, I am Mestisa, I am:

- a daughter,
- a granddaughter,
- a sister,
- a cousin,
- an aunt,
- a wife,
- a mother,

- a student,
- a teacher,
- a friend,
- very grateful, and
- very proud to be who I have become!

REFERENCES

Cave, D. (2011). *God's warrior: Father Albert Braun, OFM 1889–1983—Last of the frontier priests.* Santa Fe, NM: Sunstone Press.

Houser, N. P. (2006). History of Ysleta del Sur Pueblo. Retrieved from http://www.ysletadelsur-pueblo.org/tigua_trails.sstg?id=16&sub1=29

CHAPTER FIVE

One Way Interrupted BY Two-Eyed Vision

JEAN ANN FOLEY

Teaching and Learning
Northern Arizona University

My cultural heritage comes from France, Scotland, and England. My cultural roots are embedded in a small town in eastern Oklahoma. It is these roots in Oklahoma that I describe and relate to my teaching. I am not dismissing the idea that my ancestry influences my values and choices; however, it is through a persistent, clinging fog of a discursive white American privilege that I search for clarity and purpose as a teacher. Students are from diverse walks of life, and to successfully be their teacher, I need to recognize my privilege to embrace their cultural and social contexts. It is within a frame of resistance to oppression and love for understanding that I write about my culture and its effects on my teaching.

I first use the broad brushes of religion and gender roles rooted in Oklahoma to render a sketch of my culture as it related to informing my values through adolescence and young adulthood. The messages I received from school, church, and family about how to be female tethered me to a myopic view of culture. Next, I discuss influences that began to broaden and disrupt my understandings. Finally, I draw from my current teaching position at Northern Arizona University in the College of Education as a way to connect my past with the present and explicate my teaching practice. I share a student example and my own presentation from an assignment called Places of Belonging to demonstrate the influence of my cultural roots on my teaching practices.

ONE WAY

Religion played a central role in shaping my cultural values. My parents were cofounders of a Southern Baptist church in my small town; they were Sunday School teachers and choir singers; my dad was a deacon. They were sincere in their beliefs. As central to most Christian traditions, they believed that there is one correct or acceptable way to salvation. They were not zealots in their faith but saw the church as a place to develop moral character and to build healthy ties with like-minded people to strengthen our society.

Gender roles were clearly assigned in my culture. Before I "got my period" in seventh grade, I believed with all my heart I could be and do anything I chose. Even with three brothers to compete with, I could hold my own with climbing trees, catching frogs, back-talk, and fixing my bike. However, in sixth grade, when those in my class who were privileged enough chose their instruments for the elementary school band, I was stopped cold. A girl was not allowed to play the drums in 1964. After defaulting to the flute, going through puberty, and experiencing a coronation of the Girls' Auxiliary (GA) in my church, I began to see there was a big difference between what was expected for boys and what was permitted for girls.

I need to write a bit more about the GA, because it was through this organization that I learned a great deal about my position and identity as a female in my culture. Girls' Auxiliary was a missionary organization founded in 1914 by the Southern Baptist Convention. It was an offshoot of the Women's Missionary Union for young girls and teenagers in grades 1–12.

When I was a member of GA beginning at age 11, there were four levels of accomplishment: Maiden, Lady in Waiting, Princess, and Queen. The focus for the organization was memorizing Bible verses, reading and reporting on books about missionaries, and sewing. I never could figure out what the sewing was about. The primary theme, as I understood it, was to remain pure and prepare to go to third world countries to share Baptist doctrine or, as others might say, "preach the Gospel." This was confusing to me because women were not supposed to be preachers, but to support men who had been called into service. The motto was "Arise, shine, for thy light has come." The song was "We've a Story to Tell to the Nation."

When I turned 12 years old, I had met all of the requirements for moving up from the level of Maiden to Lady in Waiting. Becoming a Lady in Waiting was a big step. There was a coronation for this occasion that could be described as a marriage ceremony with no groom. All girls participating in the ritual wore a white dress and a green felt octagonal badge pinned on the left side of her dress. We filed through the aisles of the church holding candles and singing "We've a Story to Tell." Parents and other relatives sat in the pews with happy but reverent expressions. When we arrived at the altar, the white felt star was pinned to our green patch, which indicated we were now Ladies in Waiting. It was something to see: 15 white girls, all in white, and carrying white candles. The Queen with a scepter, at the center of the altar, helped with pinning on the stars. I liked the attention prior to the coronation. I got a new white dress, some panty hose, and black shoes with an ever-so-tiny heel. I liked the singing and carrying the lit candle. But, overall, I felt empty and alone. I found I could not relate to becoming a "Lady in Waiting."

My reflection on my experience as a GA provides insight for how I imagine some of my students feel when immersed in a dominant culture that does not mirror their deeply seated values and understandings. When there is little space in a classroom for dialogue that might disrupt the status quo, I believe that all students are deprived of understanding the impacts of social and political power of dominant belief systems. When only one truth is presented, a singular view of personhood contains, constrains, and oppresses everyone.

TWO-EYED VISION

As I entered the University of Oklahoma, the dominant discourse of my culture was reinforced through my sorority, the Baptist Student Union, and most of my courses. However, my culture began to expand through reading Henrik Ibsen, William Shakespeare, and Arthur Miller, to name a few. Being self-centered at the time, I was sure that *A Doll's House* had been written about me, and I was pretty sure Willy Loman was patterned after my dad's search for the American Dream. King Lear absolutely broke my heart. Although these authors were part of the literary canon of dead white guys, their fiction exposed a raw realism that was not a welcome visitor in my culture. They pierced a passion in me that provoked a critical questioning that was troubling and yet a breath of life. It was as if I had been asleep and the prince's kiss had awakened me. But the prince was literature, and the kiss was with eyes wide open.

On the surface, I blended in with my culture, but underneath I was questioning perceptions of power, gender roles, race inequities, socioeconomic privilege, and religious certainty. I began to doubt my culture's claim that everyone was the same and had the same opportunities. However, I could not locate a safe space for discussing or even posing the questions that were dogging me. I use Places of Belonging as an assignment in my courses to introduce safe spaces for validating diverse identities.

There was an incident one Christmas break when I returned home from school for the holidays that marked a critical moment of insight that shapes my teaching today. When I arrived home, following the two and half hour drive from Norman, Oklahoma, the family home looked and smelled wonderful. The comfort of everything being the same, the house lights, the Christmas tree, the aroma of the roasting turkey was heaven. I went to my bedroom at the end of the hall, unpacked my clothes and books, and went into the kitchen to visit with my mom. Everything went as expected until my mom came across a book that I had brought home to read over the break. She was extremely disturbed by the title, *Truth Is Two-Eyed* (Robinson, 1979).

How could a mere title generate so much anxiety? I don't think she would have been as upset if she had found a baggie of marijuana in my book bag. Finding this book was an assault to her. They had sent me off to college, where they had graduated, where my two older brothers were attending, and where I was learning to become a teacher in the arts, music, dance, or some such acceptable thing, and here I was reading a book that wasn't even part of the curriculum. She was quite serious when she said that there is only one truth (not two as the book title suggests), that I should not own this book, and I certainly should not read it.

The book was about understanding Christianity by expanding one's vision by studying Eastern religions. Robinson (1979) explained, "Readiness to look at reality through both eyes at once brings the promise of extra dimensionality and depth, but presents the labor of a fresh learning and focusing process" (p. 17). This quote captured my desire to see my culture and other cultures with more depth. When I was growing up and forming values, I could only see the surface of my culture. I was oblivious to the complexities, the oppression, and the singular dimension of my cloudy vision. I had no intention of exploring two-eyed vision with my family, but the new possibilities for understanding felt like a cockleburr in my hair that remained embedded no matter how I tried to disentangle it.

Vision is neat and tidy with blinders on. The normative discourse of my culture avowed that there was a wrong way and a right way. Power was a commodity to be leveraged at all times. Sides needed to be taken, and there were rewards for standing fast. Communication was about convincing the "other" that they were wrong. From this perspective, there is only one "correct" way.

After reading Robinson and being exposed to diversity beyond eastern Oklahoma, I realized there were multiple ways of living and understanding. Each was rich with purpose and passion. All had substance to contribute to the understanding of being human and searching for liberation and empowerment. Robinson explained that dialogue was a process for meeting across differences.

TWO-EYED TEACHING

The notion of one way always seemed a bit hateful to me as well as bland. Although I felt isolated and oppressed by my culture, I also experienced a great sense of belonging. However, for me, to belong meant to abandon my personal identity. When I chose theater as my major (with a teaching certificate), I found a new culture that required two-eyed vision and encouraged sensitivity of touch, smell, and taste. It is a culture of exploration and creativity that feeds my teaching pedagogy.

In opposition to a one-way perspective, I believe that learning should tap into our streams of experience that move beyond the singular self to include circumstantial and dynamic factors composed of historical and cultural context. Information that is related to our place is embedded in our lives. By place I mean who we are and what we value, which is linked to where we come from but not determined by it. This understanding provides the substance for why I developed Places of Belonging as an assignment for my students. Through this assignment, students are encouraged and allowed to share the essence of who they are.

At the core of my teaching is a desire to intrude on the dominant culture by encouraging relationship and dialogue to advocate for liberation and human dignity. Ayers (2009) summarizes my philosophy of education: "Education is where we ask how we might engage, enlarge, and change our lives, and it is, then, where we confront our dreams and fight our notions of the good life, where we try to comprehend, apprehend, or possibly even change the world" (p. 77).

As my students prepare to become teachers, I want them to know themselves so that they might be fully present in the classroom and be more accepting of their students. Through sharing the presentations, the assignment is an invitation to relate to a pluralistic way of knowing. The classroom becomes a collective of realities. These realities we share are not externally constructed but originate from within and emanate outward.

In each of my teacher preparation courses, I devote the first five minutes of class to an assignment I call Places of Belonging. It is an occasion to honor what makes each of us unique and similar at the same time. Each member of the learning community (which includes me as well as the students) is provided the time, space, and challenge to reacquaint and reunite with the contextual experiences of our lives that remind us of who we are.

I believe this assignment is related to my GA coronation, but with a twist. Now, the story we are telling is our own, and the language we use is unique. The assignment is to provide an interpersonal and intrapersonal link for each student and the class as we struggle "to affirm diverse knowledges" (Dei, 2002, p. 122).

The assignment is an effort to begin the process to reunite ourselves with our culture, our reality, and our passion and then enter into a relational bond by sharing this individual knowing with the classroom community. I believe validation of our innate culture can invigorate our agency to liberate ourselves and society. Noddings (2002) explained, "The self is a relation. It is constructed in encounters with other selves and objects and events in the world" (p. 116).

In my descriptions below, I offer my interpretation of one student example and share my Place of Belonging.

Eugenia. Eugenia is a Navajo student in a predominately Anglo class. She typically wears contemporary clothing with her long black hair pulled back, low and held with a rubber band. Today, Eugenia's hair is loose with a shine that reflects the deep hue of the feathers that are tucked behind her ear and curve to the base of her neck. Her long skirt, pleated white blouse, and brown suede moccasins communicate simplicity, beauty, and strength.

Eugenia delicately places feathers, photographs, and books on a table in front of the classroom while Native American flute music fills the environment with a faint drum keeping a solid heartbeat. She stands at the front of the classroom. She waits for focus, silence, and respect.

As the hush falls and the attention is locked, she begins to read in a strong and reverent voice her original poetry about growing up on the Navajo reservation. She talks about the land and how it might appear barren to an outsider, but to her and her family this land represents their roots.

> From the midst of the brazen land
> Comes a withering smile,
> Her smile that accepts
> This hostile, barren land.
>
> —Eugenia Sloan, "My Grandmother's Land"

Eugenia smiles gingerly as she collects her things and returns to her seat while the students pause from the reading and then heartily applaud. I sense a connection between her grandmother's accepting smile and the classroom landscape.

Jean Ann. I sit on a table in front of the classroom, cross-legged, dressed in a black leotard and jeans. This is not my professional attire. I share with my students my aspirations from high school to be a music and dance teacher. I then explain that one summer afternoon before my senior year, a car ran a stop sign and smashed into the car I was driving. My car was totaled, my passenger was a bit bruised, and I was unconscious. It took the rest of the summer through the month of September for me to heal.

This incident shifted my intentions for future employment, but it did not shake my passion for dance and music. I tell them that rhythm and beat puts me at ease and calls me into my body. It is an organic part of me that frees my spirit, heightens my awareness, and engages my heart.

I explain to them that rhythm and movement are integral parts of my teaching. Playing music at the beginning of class as students stroll into the room is more for me than for them. Hearing the music helps connect my head to my heart. It is a sort of preparation for the teaching and learning dance.

I ask the students to please stand up and spread out throughout the room. As they shuffle about, I turn on my CD player, crank up the sound, and say, "Let's dance!" Cymbals begin to crash, a guitar sets the beat, and Kenny Loggins sings out, "I've got this feeling this town's just holding me down. I'll hit the ceiling or else I'll tear up this town. Now gotta cut loose! Footloose!"

I lead them in free-form versions of the Jerk, Swim, Grapevine, and Twist while they add some of their own moves that we all try to follow. When the song ends, I catch my breath, wipe the sweat off my brow, and thank them for the dance.

The presentations stand alone as an offering to the community of learners as passage for knowing one another as we prepare to learn about relational teaching. There is little or no discussion following these pieces. There are a few questions to the presenter, a verbal thank you, and usually applause as acknowledgment and validation. The presentations describe connective tissue that colors a context for who we are and where we come from.

Eugenia demonstrated a connection with the layers of home place, her beginnings, and her ancestors. I invited my students into a personal space that represented freedom and a commitment to physical engagement that defied conventional professorial behavior. These Places of Belonging presentations called forward samples of authentic existence and provided an opportunity to publicly acknowledge our beginnings as we relate our personal place to our present continuation of being.

As I have described, religion and assigned gender roles of my eastern Oklahoma culture served to narrow my view of possibilities. Through a fierce desire for liberation, I sought a culture that was not dominated by a unilateral discourse of one way being the only way. Because of my experiences and in spite of them, I approach my teaching through a commitment to "two-eyed" pedagogy.

REFERENCES

Ayers, W. (2009). Untitled article. *Journal of Curriculum and Pedagogy, 6*(1), 75–78.

Dei, G. J. S. (2002). Spiritual knowing and transformative learning. In E. V. O'Sullivan, A. M. Morell, & M. A. O'Conner (Eds.), *Expanding the boundaries of transformative learning* (pp. 121–133). New York: Palgrave.

Dewey, J. (1934). *Art as experience.* New York, NY: Perigree Books.

Noddings, N. (2002). *Starting at home: Caring and social policy.* Oakland: University of California Press.

Robinson, J. (1979). *Truth is two-eyed.* Philadelphia, PA: Westminster Press.

Sloan, E. (2002). "My Grandmother's Land." Poem presented in class, Northern Arizona University, Flagstaff, AZ, 18 June.

CHAPTER SIX

Tapping into the Roots of My Approaches to Geoscience

GARY WEISSMANN

Earth & Planetary Sciences
University of New Mexico

I was born and raised in Denver, Colorado, in a home with one older sister and three younger brothers. My extended family mostly lived in the Washington, DC, area, so I only saw my grandparents, aunts, uncles, and cousins when they visited Denver or we visited them (this happened regularly, however). Many cultural identities influenced my upbringing and the person who I am today. Growing up in Colorado, I was immersed in the natural setting of the Colorado Rockies, and I still center myself by going into nature, preferring either high above tree line or in badlands country. I have a strong identity with others from the Rocky Mountain West. My childhood home was a moderately traditional Jewish household, and I was raised in the Conservative tradition of Judaism. I consider myself to be a spiritual Jew and participate in ceremonies and holidays, though I do not follow all of the strict traditions. My faith, however, has taught me to be aware of social issues, and I could be labeled as a "liberal" because of my interest in social equity and justice. Being raised in America, I took words about freedom and justice to heart, and I believe that the freedom of speech and religion as well as opportunities for education are critical for self-determination. So, if I had to name my cultural background, I would call it "Jewish American Liberal from the Rocky Mountain West."

My father was born in Germany, moving in 1936 when his father and mother realized that their son couldn't get an education because he was Jewish. My father is an only child. My mother was born in New Jersey but moved briefly to California and then to Washington, DC, where she spent most of her formative years. She is one of four children in her family. Her father was born in New Jersey and has Russian ancestry in his background, and her mother was born in Hungary but moved when she was 16 to the United States (an interesting story in and of itself). My grandmother was the "glue" for my extended family, and because of this I know and am close to many of my cousins. I was fortunate to have known all of my grandparents and one great-grandmother.

Many of the values that I've developed thus far in my life can be traced either to my parents (and their parents) or to my wife. The themes of education, equity, fairness, and cooperation with others resonate with each of them, and I can only imagine that many of my ancestors carried these same values.

In this autobiography, I will outline some of the ethical values that I view as most significant in my teaching and approach to work. These include my beliefs that

1. education is of primary importance, and that an educated population is necessary for human advancement and development and for our society's success;
2. equity and fair treatment of others are critical and necessary;
3. peace can be found in natural settings, and thus wilderness plays an important role in my being; and
4. assimilation of other cultures into the "American" culture will make an individual successful (this is from my upbringing, but not a value I hold anymore).

I know that these few points can't capture the whole of my ethical and cultural background, as many aspects of my approaches to life are much more varied than this simplified assessment can capture, and many may not be clear to me and are probably subtle. Additionally, words alone can't truly capture the values that formed me (at least for this scientist who is not trained in this manner!). As such, this is an imperfect representation of my cultural life and values I carry.

VALUE 1: EDUCATION IS CRITICAL AND IMPORTANT FOR SUCCESS IN LIFE

Throughout my life, an emphasis has always been placed on education. From an early age, my parents would talk about the significance of getting a good education, equating this to success in life. I can hear my father saying that he goes to his job every day and that it is my job (and that of my siblings) to go to school and do well. Excellence was also critical and expected, though occasional failings were still accepted. We were also taught that academic subjects, such as reading, language arts, math, and science, were more important than art, music, and physical education (not something I hold as a belief anymore).

This value of education is rooted in my Jewish tradition. We learn lessons about the Talmudic scholars, arguing and discussing points in a collaborative learning approach. We also learn that there are several potentially correct answers to difficult questions, and each can have equal footing in society. Just as in the science that I try to do, multiple hypotheses in life are important.

Underlying this value are several assumptions:

- Education, though not necessary for success in life, can make life easier.
- I would go directly to college after graduating from high school (though in hindsight I think waiting one or two years through doing service may have helped me better appreciate my college education).
- Learning and thinking are some of the most important things one can do in life.
- Individuated learning is most valued.

MANIFESTATION IN MY TEACHING AND LIFE

My career, and my approach to life, reflects that I followed these "rules" for education. Though I agree that education is critically important for success of a society and that it allows for an easier life in many ways, relatively recently I realized it need not be done along the rules outlined for my life.

In my current teaching, I work to emphasize my personal enthusiasm for learning. Even when I'm teaching the Blue Planet class, with its large population of students who don't like science, I work to create an environment where students recognize the value of the broad education that they're receiving. One of my stated goals for the class is that students will be able to read popular science literature and news upon leaving the class. I believe that an educated population is needed to face the challenges of global warming that are approaching, and this class offers the students some background to help them understand these challenges.

One of my favorite things to do in a class is to discuss the census statistics about educational level in America. Approximately 26% of Americans over age 25 have a bachelor's degree or better. This educational level must come with a responsibility, and I try to bring that to every class I teach. We are a privileged class to have the opportunity of higher education, and we should recognize the responsibility that comes with this privilege.

Along with these efforts to relay my ethic that education is critical, I also carry some assumptions that influence how I might interact with students. I see that gaining an education is a responsibility and that this is the student's job (or one of their jobs) and that the student should take it seriously.

VALUE 2: EQUITY AND FAIR TREATMENT OF OTHERS ARE CRITICAL AND NECESSARY

All people have the right to be treated fairly and equitably, no matter their personal status in society. This value was often a point of discussion in my family, and was often a point of discussion during my religious upbringing. Several lines in both biblical teaching as well as scholarly writings discuss welcoming "the stranger in your land" and treating people fairly in business and other settings.

This ethic permeates through all of life. As children, we were taught that all people have a productive place in society. My father is a retired physician; however, he lived this ethic by treating the cleaning staff in his office with respect as well as his other employees. He taught us that nothing in the office could work without all parts—his expertise in medicine, the nurse's assistance and her expertise, the billing and clerical staff, and the cleaning staff. Loss of one part equates to loss of the business. He and my mother taught us that society works the same way. An important component to this is general respect for our fellow humans.

In the 1970s, I bought into the idea of belonging to a "colorblind" society, where all people would be treated the same and opportunities would be offered equally no matter a person's cultural background or the color of one's skin. An assumption behind the ideal of a colorblind society, however, is that the dominant culture would dictate how people should act and approach life. I don't believe in a colorblind society anymore. Rather, I believe that we should revel in the richness of difference, and learn from each other a broad way of approaching life. I strive to accept others at face value, leaving space to learn who that person is as an individual without judgment of biases and stereotypes that our society teaches us.

Underlying this value are several assumptions:

- People are mostly the same, with similar emotional issues, feelings, and desires. Not all people act these feelings out in the same way, but they all deserve some level of understanding, and initially, all people deserve respect.
- All people should be treated fairly unless they do something to lose that trust.
- Opportunities in life should not be based on socioeconomic status, and society is responsible for working toward offering equitable opportunities for all.
- Ultimately, the world could achieve a state where opportunity can exist for all people to succeed to the best of their ability if mutual respect for each other could be achieved.

MANIFESTATION IN MY TEACHING AND IN LIFE

I believe this value plays an important part in my teaching. I strive to approach all students with equal respect and work to make my classroom accessible for all students. Additionally, I expect the students to treat each other with the respect they each deserve. This ethic has been realized in my classroom in several ways.

In geosciences, we teach that the Earth is 4.6 billion years old. Many of my colleagues will roll their eyes when students have a belief system that says Earth was created in six days and is not close to 4.6 billion years old. I strive to build the environment where we explore what science teaches, how science explores the world, and that it is based on observations and supporting evidence for interpretations of these observations. Faith is based on one's learned beliefs and does not need to be supported in the same way science does. The distinction is one where I strive for mutual respect, not confrontation. I respect a student's right to have their faith but still firmly teach what science tells us about the Earth. They don't have to believe the observations from science, however. I have been thanked by several students for this approach.

Another way this ethic could be observed in my classroom is from work I did with visually impaired students. Geoscience is a visual field, and graphics, photographs, and other visual aids are commonly used to teach the subject. When several visually impaired students signed up for my Blue Planet class, this approach wouldn't work. I was able to hire a teaching assistant; we translated lecture PowerPoint slides into a format they could read; we provided tactile objects for accessing visual information, and we arranged to have the information set into formats these students could access. I believe it to be my responsibility to do this, mostly because of my strong belief in equity. As a result, my first visually impaired student told me that this was the first time she was able to earn a B in a science class.

VALUE 3: NATURAL SETTINGS, OUTDOORS, AND WILDERNESS ARE IMPORTANT

Growing up in Colorado, I was fortunate to have opportunities to explore nature. Often, my family would drive to the mountains to "explore" different areas. For family vacations, we would travel to national parks to "check on our properties," as my father would commonly say, regarding public lands as "ours" in the broadest sense. I learned backpacking skills and was encouraged by my parents to enjoy the backcountry.

Through these experiences, I learned the value of wilderness. When I need to be "recharged," I find myself going to the wilderness.

Underlying this value are several assumptions:

- Most people can find solace through nature (though now I think that this is not necessarily true).

- Observations of nature are important for human understanding of our place in the world. We should all be aware of seasonal patterns, phases of the moon, and other natural phenomena that we can observe daily.
- Nature and wilderness have intangible value beyond any economic value that may be placed on the land.

MANIFESTATION IN MY TEACHING AND LIFE

I recharge by going into nature and feel myself fade a bit if I don't have opportunities to go into nature on a regular basis. When things get to be especially difficult, I find a spot to sit in nature. In every city or town I've lived in, I find natural places close to home to recharge and find peace of mind, and in my teaching I try to find similar places for students to experience science in the outdoors. I often pause to look at the stars, clouds, moon, trees, and the world around me, and I encourage my students to do the same.

I teach environmental sciences classes, and in doing so I am able to share my love of nature with students. My lectures and class projects are filled with images of nature, not only because I am covering this material but also because of the aesthetic beauty of it all. I also have the opportunity to take students outdoors for study. These experiences allow me to share my enthusiasm for this beauty with students who may not have had opportunities to travel into nature.

VALUE 4: ASSIMILATION INTO THE DOMINANT CULTURE IS NEEDED FOR SUCCESS IN THAT CULTURE

When my father's family arrived in the United States, they did everything possible to fit in. They learned English and worked to avoiding speaking in German. They would watch movies to learn what it "meant" to be American. They dressed as "Americans" and they did whatever they could to be American. They assimilated in many ways.

This assimilation led to success for my family. My grandfather's five-and-dime store made his family financially secure, allowing him (and my grandmother) to travel widely and retire comfortably. My father successfully completed medical school and became a family practice doctor. He considers assimilation as important for this success. For quite some time, I believed this to be true, as well. It took years to recognize the flaws in this concept of assimilation.

Underlying this value are several assumptions:

- English is necessary for success in American society.
- Assimilating into society allows you to integrate and participate in the success offered by this society.

MANIFESTATION IN MY TEACHING AND LIFE

I don't know when I stopped believing this "value." Part of it may be my sadness at seeing the Yiddish language disappearing because it didn't fit with the need to assimilate. This language, though not in my heritage since it is mostly an Eastern European language, is so full of life and represents the beauty of my culture in a way that English cannot.

I see this in other languages and other cultures. Such richness exists in many aspects of different cultures, most having things that are beautiful and full as well as aspects that are not so desirable. I see joy and richness in my life by experiencing (or often observing) other cultures. It doesn't diminish my own beliefs and values, but exploring how other people successfully navigate life enriches my own experience in life. Today, I enjoy opportunities to experience other cultures, though I am often uncomfortable doing so.

I don't know how this value manifests itself into my teaching. There was a time when I may have expected students to just fit into the university culture, and that learning and education are "the way out" of … of what I'm not sure, but probably out of their culture and into the mainstream American culture. Now, I believe that education and learning are important to make contributions to society as a whole, but I don't believe that it has to come at the expense of assimilation and integration into the mainstream culture. I can only imagine that this ethic comes out somehow in my teaching, but I am not sure how.

WORKING WITH OTHERS AND MY ABILITY TO WORK AND TEACH IN A DIVERSE SOCIETY

How my cultural background affects my teaching is still partially unclear to me. I know it must because we are all reflections of our experiences and environments, but beyond the specifics already described, I'm not sure.

The ethic of equity causes me to work to allow all students access to materials in a way that best suits them; thus, I tend to be more open to different styles of learning and observing students working in different ways. I strive to teach toward different styles in an active way that retains the context of material. I don't believe this is true for most of my colleagues. I believe they were, for the most part, successful in school because they learn through lectures or were motivated self-learners, and therefore they expect students to learn in this same manner.

Because of my high value on education and learning, I do hold this high expectation with students. My mantra has been the following:

> If students care about their work, I'll bend over backwards to help them learn. If they don't care to work on learning, I don't have to care. They don't need a college degree to be successful in life.

This attitude is one reason I teach at the college level rather than high school. As I write this document, however, I realize that some students who I may identify as "not caring" may instead be coming from a different cultural place, and I may not be able to recognize when they care versus when they do not care. This lesson, among others that I'm sure I will find on this path of learning about different cultures, is one that I hope to explore in the years to come.

SUMMARY

I approach the world with general comfort in my own culture, both holding dearly the more positive aspects of this culture and questioning the not-so-positive aspects of the culture. In this comfort, I am learning an openness to other cultures. I can be exposed to others from different cultures and not feel insecure in my approaches to life. Differences do not diminish my own approach.

As I continue exploring diverse cultures and how this relates to my teaching and work with others in academia, I hope to become more comfortable feeling uncomfortable with difference. I'm not sure that makes sense, but there is an uncomfortable feeling of being the outsider when one is placed into a different culture. As a tall white guy, I stand out as different when I walk through the grocery store in Chinle, Arizona. This must be how minorities feel when they walk through most of the country—this sense of discomfort of being the minority. In the future, I hope to learn from this discomfort.

This self-assessment has been a beautiful starting point to gaining additional comfort with who I am, opening the door to learning about others and relishing in differences. I firmly believe that *every* faculty member should be required to spend time writing a self-assessment, and every incoming first-year student should do the same. Through this exercise, we would gain an appreciation of where we are and who we are with on this ride. Maybe, through such an exercise, we would finally be able to approach a culture that values diversity, and appreciate and feel the value of diverse approaches to answering societal questions.

CHAPTER SEVEN

Education AS Our Horse

On the Path to Critical Consciousness

VINCENT WERITO

American Indian Education
University of New Mexico

Yá'át'ééh shee'ałtaaháásį́į́łgo	Greetings … to all who listen
Shik'éí	… My blood relatives
Shidine'é	… My people
Shi t'e'ázání	… My clan mothers
Bił kéíhaasht'į́į́nií	… People of my community
Shi de'áyaní	… All others.

Ta'neeszahnii nishłį. Naakáí Dine'é báshíshchíín. Kinłichiiníí dashichéí. Tódichiiníí dashinálí.[1]

I begin this essay by sharing how I was taught to properly introduce myself whenever I address an audience. This proper way of Diné introduction begins by establishing my relationship (k'é) with the supernatural cosmos as a child of the Holy People or as Ni'hookáá' Diyin Diné, Five Fingered Earth Surface Spiritual Beings. In acknowledging the Holy People in the four directions, I affirm the sacredness of our language by being mindful about what I say. Next, I greet clan relatives, clan mothers, and other Navajo people who may be related to me through clan affiliations (adoone'é) followed by recognizing other people in my community. This proper way of introduction entails proper cultural protocols about respect, kindness, and goodwill toward others, particularly in how we greet an audience and in how we approach our audience in a proper manner by "stepping" first with our right leg. In Navajo thought, the right side of our body is associated with the Beauty way teachings (hozhóójį na'nit'in). Through proper clan introductions, not only do I establish positive harmonious relationships with everyone around me but

I share the core aspects of my Diné spiritual, common, social, and physical image (Aronilth, 1994) that are expressed through k'é and adoon'é.

K'é embodies Diné core cultural values of sharing, reciprocity, community, and peace. K'é is the shared value of establishing and maintaining positive healthy relationships with others in the community. These relationships could be with close family, clan relatives, the natural cosmos (i.e., the earth, sun, moon, stars, and natural elements) and/or the natural environment (i.e., plants, animals, insects, and all other life). So for me, being Diné means that I am part of a larger community of four legged, winged, and other five fingered 'peoples.' Therefore, authentic, reciprocal, symbiotic, and sustainable relationships are the core of Diné values and beliefs as expressed and lived through the concepts of k'é and hozhǫ́ that inform our social behaviors, social organization, social responsibilities, and our sociocultural values and beliefs with language at the center.

I am from the Ta'neeszahnii matrilineage. I was also born for or into the Naakáí Dine'é matrilineage. My maternal grandfathers are from the Kinłichiiníí matrilineage My paternal grandfathers are from the Tódichiiníí matrilineage. To nonǫNavajos, these clan matrilineages may be unfamiliar but to other Diné (Navajo) people they establish our relationship with one another through k'é. These Navajo clan affiliations (or adoone'é) stem from the recreation of the Diné clans by Changing Woman (Asdzą́ą́ Nadlééhí). Each clan has a unique history, stories, and teachings (knowledge) that are manifested through natural behaviors, creative orientations, characteristics, skills, traits, and unique personalities of the Diné people today. These innate, critical cultural understandings and features along with the habits of the people are what contribute to Dine thought and knowledge in the past and present contexts. By internalizing this, we believe that we are not just Indians, Navajos, or racial stereotypes like the Redman. Instead, we are leaders, artists, healers, poets, philosophers, environmentalists, educators, and we are Diné—an embodiment of the natural and spiritual world that we live in.

As a child growing up in a Diné community and learning the Diné language first, I learned these important Diné values and beliefs like ké' and hozhó (Werito, 2014) that still resonate and come through my teaching, scholarship, and research today as an Indigenous scholar, researcher, and educator (professor) at the university where I teach. Growing up in a Diné home, I developed a Diné worldview that is very different from the Western forms of knowledge that are so overpowering in schools and institutions of higher learning. For example, in my childhood I often heard my mother and father encouraging us to express ourselves properly to our relatives to reinforce k'é or to be reverent during ceremony and behave in a proper manner or to listen carefully and with purpose to what is being said by elders in the spirit of hozhó. By learning these core values through Diné socio-cultural contexts of learning I internalized a pedagogy or way of teaching and learning that continues to inform my core values, beliefs, and understanding about teaching and learning as a dialectical and dynamic process for engaging others.

I am originally from a small rural Navajo (Diné) community called Na'neelzhiin by some families in the community but also called Ya'neelzhíín by others. Depending on which families you talk to you will hear how the place got its name. The place name Naneelzhíín translates to a Dark Horizontal Streak in the Distance referring to the use of game corrals that were used by Navajos hunters to trap deer in box canyons. The other name, Ya'neelzhíín translates to A Pile of Flat Rocks Stacked High referring to a geographical land marker that was placed atop a high mesa possibly by Navajo hunters or by Spanish conquistadors who traveled through the area looking for Navajo warriors. Thus, the Spanish name of this place is Torreon meaning tower. It was settled after the return of the Diné to their homelands from Bosque Redondo. After the signing of the Navajo Treaty of 1868 with the United States government, the Navajo were allowed to return to their homelands after being confined at Fort Sumner, New Mexico for four years (Denetdale, 2008). Eventually no matter which place name is used or what story is true, each community values the diverse perspectives of its people as long as it is significant and meaningful for those who tell the story of the place. In much the same way, I encourage my undergraduate and graduate students, to be open and willing to listen to new perspectives and make new meaning from diverse perspectives. Further, I want Indigenous youth and other students of color to become familiar with their histories, cultures, and oral traditions and to accept who they are, and not to imitate others. These fundamental Diné values that I have described continue to be a significant part of my epistemology, ontology, and axiology, and they have a significant influence on my cultural identity and cultural orientations as a Diné as well as informing my perspectives anew on teaching and learning.

> When my brothers and I were younger, our father bought us a horse. It was a two year old red roan. He led the horse up to us and said, "He is yours now so take good care of him because he will take you far." I remember how happy and proud we were at the same time. I also remember how he would scold us for not taking care of the horse. He would say, "If you want something good in life, you have to take care of it, nurture it, and take responsibility for it." He said, "It is just like your education." Although education has always been a big thing in my family even before this time, I did not understand what he meant by that statement at the time. (Werito, 2010, p. 1)

While Western historians like to point out that the horse was not indigenous to North America, in many Indigenous oral traditions, there are stories and songs about the origin of horses and their existence and purpose to humankind. For example, Diné oral traditions tell how the horse was sung back into existence at Sísnaateel and recreated out of white shell, turquoise, abalone, and black jet stone.

Accordingly, Navajo oral tradition relates how the night sky was created when two great beings, a white shell horse and a turquoise horse, raced across the night sky and left in their footprints the vast Milky Way to guide humans in determining their lives and fate in the future. Hence, for the Diné, the horse embodies spiritual and natural powers or life energies (bigáál) that are found in the physical natural world (sunlight, rainbows, lightning, and rain clouds) and cosmology (sun and stars) of the people. For the Diné this belief is symbolically represented in the spirit and on the body of the horse as seen in its hooves, ears, eyes, and torso. This idea of life energies is also found in East Indian and Asian philosophies as spirit and matter describing the dynamic and static natural forces of nature. More recently, quantum physics relates the study of quantum waves to a deeper understanding of life energies as subatomic matter or particles. Based on these different systems of knowledge, the horse guides, teaches, and informs and reconnects its rider to the natural balance of life and life forces. In Navajo, we say łį́į́' nihígáál at'é. That is, the horse is our transportation in life. Similarly, we say nanit'in dóó óhoo'aah nihigááł at'é. That is, the Diné philosophy of education is our transportation in the form of a spiritual horse (Aronilth, 1994).

As I continue to reflect back on my childhood experiences with schooling now, I believe that my first experiences with school involved experiencing alienation, marginalization, and racism. For example, when I first went to boarding school I remember the stress of learning English and the strict regimentation designed to assimilate me into White cultural norms and values. As I was encouraged to speak English and reprimanded for talking Navajo, I quickly realized that English is the language of the White man's school. Moreover, I began to understand that schooling or the White man's schools, *bilagáana yázhí bi'oltá'*, were different from my own teachings or education at home. It became glaringly apparent that my Diné cultural identity and language were always in conflict with what was expected of me in schools. So, I had to make many compromises in terms of what was expected of me and who I was. Despite all these challenges, I believe that my philosophy of education in the form of a horse helped me to make sense of who I am and where I wanted to be in life. More importantly, this cultural knowledge served as a strong foundation for me to build upon my own dreams, goals, and aspirations of pursuing an education that I desired and was good for me. Education is my horse in achieving and seeking a long harmonious life with good positive relationships with everything and everyone around me.

As my early experiences with schooling become an important focal point for critical reflection in my life, in my teaching, and in scholarship, it has become clear for me to see how a racial and ethnic identity was imposed on me within the U.S. school system. As these early experiences began to shape my thinking of who I am and my place in the educational system, I began to understand that my place in school and society was that of a racialized "Other" (Said, 1993). As I reflect back on experiences now, I believe that I was being assimilated to think that I needed to learn the White man's ways and language if I wanted to fit into their schools and to achieve success in their society at the expense of losing my own. Since I began teaching graduate-level courses in the field of education, I have been introduced to educational philosophies, theories, and studies that are critical of the status quo in education. Over time, I learned about the asymmetrical relations of power that operate in schools as well as the structural inequities that play out in society. For example, I understand how universities can continue to assimilate and marginalize Indigenous and other youth of color if university faculty do not change their practices. As a result, some students of color begin to believe that who they are and what they bring is not valued as much as Western knowledge in academia and, as a consequence, they internalize feelings of inferiority as racially stigmatized youth (Lopez, 2003). Inevitably, students and faculty of color learn unconsciously through White supremacist discourse that their languages and cultural knowledge are not held in high regard within academia.

In contrast, for many who become aware of the challenges they face, they become more aware and conscious about what they need to learn and what they feel is important to their overall schooling and academic experiences. Indigenous and critical perspectives are crucial for the younger generations to acquire and learn, especially in the contemporary contexts where critical issues such as language shift, cultural change or erosion, and homogenization are part of their realities and existence. For example, from high school on to the present, not only did I discover other ways to identify myself—such as Native American, American Indian, or Indigenous—I also begin to affirm my true Diné identity that was always there. This is idea is called t'áá hwó 'ajiit'éego in Navajo. Translated to English, it means, "it is up to you." It was up to me to "find face and heart" because what I needed and knew was already within me (Cajete, 1994). I just needed to bring it out by reconnecting my educational philosophy to the process of achieving hozhǫ́, thereby achieving critical consciousness in the process. I have strived to encourage my students to find their voice, speak or relearn their language and their cultural beliefs and values. Endogenous education (Cajete, 1994) is an Indigenous-centered pedagogy that can help anyone become (re-)centered in life and help them to reaffirm their identity within the processes of schooling.

To this day, I often wonder if our early Navajo (Diné) leaders such as Barboncito, Chief Manuelito, and Ganado Mucho who survived confinement at Bosque Redondo at the hands of the White man and lived to sign the Treaty of 1868 would have agreed to let their children be educated in the White man's schools if they knew that it would also be at the expense of losing their Diné identity, language, and culture. Although Western "education" was promised by the U.S. government to our early Navajo leaders in the Treaty of 1868 to make their lives better after being incarcerated for four years at Bosque Redondo, they have also become sites of struggle and contestation over the value of holding on to a Diné identity and the Diné language and cultural knowledge. Yet, given the circumstances at the time, even if they knew, the return to their homelands was a more pressing issue along with the survival of the people as a whole.

There were many Navajo who were also never captured and incarcerated during this time and remained resistant to the U.S. government. Consequently, as descendants of these resisters and those who survived the Long Walk, we can confidently embrace the knowledge that our ancestors retained Diné thought and identity, including their philosophy of education with honor, humility, integrity, and pride. Therefore, in pursuing a Diné education, we can speak confidently and on equal footing with the White man about our sovereign rights to land, water, life, and education because of the sacrifices that were made by our ancestors. We have retained what it means to be Diné in our mind, thoughts, our cultural values, and our philosophy of education. Diné sovereignty is not only premised on the Treaty of 1864, but it is alive in our words, our actions, and commitment to one another, and most importantly in our responsibility to our children in the future. Therefore, we must reclaim our own education just as our ancestors reclaimed the horse.

In the end, I return to how I embraced education as my transportation in the form of a horse. As I continue teaching in higher education, it is becoming more important for me to know and share with others that it is important to achieve a clear mind and a critical consciousness (Freire, 2000) while engaging in the process of schooling, because schooling and education are two different things. Over the past seven years of practicing Aikido, a form of Japanese martial arts, and meditating on these thoughts, I have come to understand that to seek balance or harmony in my life I must continue to reflect on myself and find new ways to always strive to achieve my full potential physically, mentally, and spiritually as a human being. By synthesizing my cultural traditions with newly discovered knowledge, I find that I must also continue to strive and not be lazy if I want to achieve hozhǫ́ by learning to balance my personal, social, and professional life as well as my relationships with the natural world or universe around me. I have learned through my own Dine philosophy of education, the principles of Aikido, and critical educational studies that learning and teaching entail a synthesis or blending of new and traditional forms of knowledge that are consistent with my core values and beliefs, much as my ancestors did in the past. More importantly, learning and teaching must be embedded in my immediate contexts (Gay, 2000; Cleary & Peacock, 1998), connect with my innate and natural ability to learn, and it must be a creative participation of seeking/finding inner strength (Cajete, 2000), beauty, peace, and allowing it to flow out and blend with the universe around me. I share these aspects of my cultural background to inspire the younger generations of Indigenous youth and others willing to listen to carry on the teachings of their ancestors and to reaffirm and find new meanings within these traditions that are steeped in critical knowledge and perspectives about conflict, change, and traditions. Finally, achieving hozhó as an aspect of Diné critical thought and theory is a way to rearticulate our identity, our sovereign rights to language and education, our knowledge of geography, place, and history that is wrought with colonization, warfare, slavery, but more importantly it is part of our survival, nation building, and language and cultural sustainability.

NOTE

1. This proper way of introduction was explained to me by Dr. Wilson Aronilth at Dine College in Tsaile, Arizona, in a course titled Navajo Philosophy, NIS 371.

REFERENCES

Aronilth, W. (1994). *Diné Bi Bee Óhoo'aah Bá Silá: An introduction to Navajo philosophy.* Center for Dine Studies. Tsaile, AZ: Navajo Community College Press.

Cajete, G. (2000). *Native science: Natural laws of interdependence.* Santa Fe, NM: Clear Light.

Cajete, G. (1994). *Look to the mountain: An ecology of Indigenous education.* Rio Rancho, NM: Kivaki.

Cleary, L. M., & Peacock, T. (1998). *Collected wisdom: American Indian education.* Boston, MA: Allyn & Bacon.

Denetdale, J. (2008). *The long walk: The forced Navajo exile.* New York, NY: Chelsea House.

Freire, P. (2000). *Pedagogy of the oppressed* (30th anniv. ed.). New York, NY: Continuum.

Gay, G. (2000). *Culturally responsive teaching: Theory, research, & practice.* New York, NY: Teachers College.

Lopez, N. (2003). *Hopeful girls, troubled boys: Race and gender disparity in urban education.* New York, NY: Routledge.

Said, E. (1993). *Culture and imperialism.* New York, NY: Alfred A. Knopf.

Werito, V. (2010). *The racialization of Diné (youth) in education* (Order No. 3440190). Available from ProQuest Dissertations & Theses Global. (857216561). Retrieved from http://search.proquest.com.libproxy.nau.edu/docview/857216561?accountid=12706

Werito, V. (2014). Understanding Hozho: A contemporary Diné interpretation of living according to the philosophy of Sá'ąh Naghái Bik'eh Hózhóón. In L. Lee (Ed.), *Diné perspectives: Revitalizing and reclaiming Navajo thought.* Critical Issues in Indigenous Studies Series. Tucson, AZ: University of Arizona Press.

CHAPTER EIGHT

Roots

A Personal Cartography of Values and Teaching

KATYA CRAWFORD

Landscape Architecture
University of New Mexico

In 1967, on the island of Crete, a 30-year-old American writer and a 34-year-old Australian journalist meet. The American is well educated, having gone to the University of Chicago, the Sorbonne in Paris, and finally Berkeley for a master's degree in English literature. He has published his first novel and sold the movie rights. Young and quite well-off, he buys a Mercedes. For him, this is less a status symbol than a love and appreciation for a beautifully made machine. His parents live in a suburb of San Diego. His father is a shop teacher and his mother an elementary teacher and painter. His grandparents and mother (she was three) migrated from Germany, and his father migrated from Canada, and before that Scotland. They believed in hard work, education, and the American Dream.

The Australian dropped out of school at 16 to start her early career as a journalist. She believed that education took place in the world, not necessarily in the classroom. At the age of 21 she moved to London and got a job with the J. Arthur Rank Organization. She interviewed the likes of Marlon Brando, Sophia Loren, Elizabeth Taylor, Frank Sinatra, and blossoming stars such as Michael Caine. She is warm, fearless, and outgoing. Her mother taught her to "live in the day, because tomorrow you could get run over by a bus." Her Australian family is Irish and Swiss Italian on the maternal side, and English on the paternal side. She hasn't seen her father since the age of 16. Her mother is powerful, eccentric, a world traveler, a painter, and a poet.

My mother and father, the Australian and American, are married within three months and have a son a year later in Dublin, Ireland. My mother has no interest in coming to America, but my father is anxious to show his son to his parents. After a year they take a ship to New York. All their belongings are packed into the Mercedes, which makes the journey with them across the ocean. They move to San Francisco, close to the family but not too close. It is not the life my mother had imagined—raising a son alongside political demonstrations and riots coupled with a sexual and drug revolution. They sell the Mercedes, buy a VW van, and follow new friends to Dixon, New Mexico. Dixon is a small Hispanic farming village of about 3,000 people nestled in a valley along the Rio Embudo. My mother instantly falls in love with the landscape ("like Greece without the ocean") and with a village that seems "un-American." With the last of the film money they buy three acres in El Bosque, with hills to the north and the river to the south. The land has a dozen apple trees, an acequia, and a field of sunflowers. This is where I was born.

My parents, along with a handful of other Anglo transplants, adopt the Spanish tradition of building their own home from adobe and living off the land. For many years our house is only two rooms—a kitchen and a bedroom with an outhouse. Like a family member, the house grows with time. Rooms slowly get added on, and the house takes on the L form typical of the region. My parents establish a rhythm of farming and building in the spring, summer, and fall, and writing in the winter.

When I describe my childhood to friends it sounds simple and idyllic, which is the life my parents were in search of. In many ways, it was. Our days were structured by the daily rituals of survival (collecting water, chopping wood, farming, cooking, building, etc.) and the order imposed by my father's German upbringing. We ate meals together at exactly the same time every day, took naps every afternoon, completed chores by dinner, listened to NPR while cleaning up, and we, the kids, were in bed by 7:00 p.m. with an hour to read. We were detached from the world of consumerism and found joy in friendships and the complex makeup of the land we inhabited. It was simple but not necessarily easy. We were poor, and my brother and I were acutely aware of being outsiders, even though this was the only home we knew. We were blond with fair skin and light eyes—our father had long hair and our mother a foreign accent. We ate strange food (tofu, goat's milk, whole wheat bread) and were godless children in a Catholic and Presbyterian village. We didn't have a TV and many of our clothes were handmade. Elementary school and junior high were a daily physical and mental battle as we struggled to become native to place. We both agree that it took roughly 17 years to earn our place in the Embudo Valley. Ironically, I left six months later.

My small family, the land, the village and its dwellers had, and continue to have, a profound influence on the way I understand and see the world. This view is embedded with values that influence my chosen field of study and the way I teach. Here are the values that I am aware of. I am sure there are others that are unconscious and may be revealed over time.

COMMUNITY AND INDIVIDUALISM: TWO PARTS TO A WHOLE

Both community and individuality are strong values within our family. Without the knowledge of the Hispanic elders and the building and harvesting parties, we would not have had a home or a livelihood. The other handful of Anglo transplants were also far removed from their extended families, so we relied on each other as families do. If someone was sick, meals were made; children were cared for, houses were cleaned, gardens were weeded. There was even an instance when the village raised $60,000 for a woman's hospital bills. Between the houses scattered along the river there was a constant exchange of children, food, tools, and knowledge.

In our family, individual expression is as important as the notion of community. My mother and father fully support the idea of finding one's calling, however long it takes and however it changes. There was never a pressure to succumb to the traditional American measure of success. Suspicious of monetary wealth, my parents urged us to find riches in diverse life experiences and to follow our hearts. Their philosophy, which I too hold, is that one's contribution to society will be more meaningful if joy and passion are involved.

These values, a life of joy, individual expression, and community engagement, directly influence my teaching. Students enter the Landscape Architecture Program for three years. I urge students to treat their cohort as a family—to support and challenge each other in the exchange of knowledge and ideas. I stress the notion that the success of the group is equally as important as the success of the individual. Peer reviews, group discussions, and student-led teaching sessions are built into the syllabus. Assignments are balanced between individual and group projects.

EDUCATION: AN ATTITUDE AND A PRIVILEGE

Within my family, higher education is seen as a privilege, and the resources and time are not to be wasted. We understand that great teachers can make a lifelong impression, but we also believe in the individual responsibility to challenge one's self and to take initiative in building an engaging and enriching experience. In other words, education is not a consumer good with a one-way relationship, but a rich exchange between students, teachers, the institution, and the world (family, community, city, country, etc.).

This value was reinforced by my own experience at The Evergreen State College, where students are largely responsible for articulating their own path of study. At Evergreen there were no exams, and in lieu of grades we conducted self and teacher evaluations. Teachers were true advisors and mentors, and I am still in touch with many of them today—23 years later. To have so much responsibility placed on my own learning experience helped me dig deep in finding and engaging my interests and place in the world. Despite having to use grades at UNM, this model of self-evaluation and personal responsibility works its way into my classes. Students are invited to help build assignments. If a student doesn't find value in a particular assignment, he or she may propose his or her own assignment and outline clear learning objectives.

LAND ETHICS

My family places incredible value on environmental issues, which we see as inseparable from all issues. Having grown up on an organic vegetable farm, we see the land as our home, our livelihood, our teacher, and our source of spiritual fulfillment. Climate change and environmental justice are at the forefront of our concerns, discussions, and work. We are also aware of the privilege associated with American environmentalism, and that whole global populations are struggling just to survive.

I have noticed that students coming into the Landscape Architecture Program hold similar values, regardless of ethnicity. In the most basic sense, the goal of landscape architecture is to design socially and environmentally sustainable places that are also beautiful. The most heated and richest discussions in class come from perspectives on what contributes to social sustainability (depending on cultural and physical context) and our cultural notions of beauty. As we design for people other than ourselves, it is critical to situate our biases and values and question our assumptions.

For example, my students are currently engaged in the design of a waterfront plaza in Detroit, Michigan. Before going on a class trip to Detroit, I had the students make a perception collage. Through imagery and text the students explored their perception of the city as outsiders. The collages revealed urban blight, violence, and racial tension mixed in with Motown music and the glory days of the automobile industry. It was a bleak picture, but after visiting the city the students challenged their preconceived ideas. We were blown away by the generosity of spirit, kindness, urban wilds, the profusion of grassroots organizations filling the city with art and agriculture, and the overwhelming evidence of beauty, hope, and optimism blooming among the ruins.

TRAVEL: LEARNING THROUGH LEAVING

As a studio, we could not have understood the site in Detroit from data sets alone. Going to the city, interacting with people, eating the food, shopping at the markets, smelling the fumes and wildflowers, touching the surfaces, and observing everything firsthand was invaluable in our quest to understand place.

Travel—the experience of new places and new cultures—is high on the list of my values. Outside of the United States, my father lived in France, Greece, Ireland, Colombia, Mexico, and Japan. My mother has lived in Australia, England, Italy, Greece, and Ireland. I have lived in Italy, Spain, and Australia. My brother has lived in England and France. We have all traveled extensively and will continue to as long as we are able. Travel presents itself clearly as a value because we have never been rich by American standards, yet we always find ways to make it happen. My parents funded many of their trips through grants, and my brother and I worked like mad, and instead of buying a reliable car or putting money toward a savings account or retirement, we travel. We all share a thirst to see, witness, and experience the greater world. Traveling helps us understand and challenge who we are, what we believe, and our place in the world. As transplants, travel offered all of us a chance to discover our roots in Italy, Ireland, Germany, and England. In short, my experiences from traveling and living in other countries have shaped who I am as much as the village I grew up in. To experience the tastes, sounds, art, rituals, and languages of other cultures contributes to a global understanding of place and can foster a humanitarian sensibility.

I bring the value of travel into my teaching. I have not only run a study abroad program in the Netherlands and taken students on trips within the United States, but I try to bring the values I associate with travel into the studio. The majority of our students are from out of state, and we also have students from India, Iran, China, the Czech Republic, Mexico, Nepal, Thailand, and Brazil. International students offer insight to diverse cultural ways of learning as well as seeing and designing landscape. International and out-of-state students give the rest of us fresh perspectives on Albuquerque, and we can give them insider knowledge. This exchange makes for a richer studio environment.

I have also observed an invaluable bonding that occurs between students (and professor!) in travel. The experiences of eating, walking, and planning together, along with the unexpected situations of any adventure, bring us all closer through shared experience. When travel is not part of a design studio, I make a concerted effort to provide opportunities for bonding that tend to come naturally with travel. For example, I'll have the students over to my house for a meal, invite them to an art opening, or set up a monthly happy hour gathering at a local establishment. I have also had them take walks in pairs, or in groups of three, and meet an hour later at a coffee shop to discuss a particular topic relevant to urban design or landscape architecture.

WORK ETHIC AND THE CONSTANT SEARCH FOR BALANCE

My family has a strong work ethic, which perhaps stems from American and German values. This is a value that I continually battle with. It is so ingrained in me to work relentlessly that I find myself feeling guilty if I take a day off. None of us (my immediate family) actually believes in this on an intellectual level, but we can't seem to help ourselves. Two major events happened in 2010 and 2011 that changed my perspective, yet I am finding myself reverting to old patterns.

In May of 2010 I was diagnosed with breast cancer and found out that I carry the BRCA gene. What this meant was that unless I took drastic measures, the likeliness of the cancer coming back was upwards of 85%. It also meant that women in my family, many I had never met, had been dying and surviving from breast cancer for decades, and possibly centuries. I also learned that this gene is associated with Jewish bloodlines, bringing about questions of secrecy and my German heritage. Because this gene passes through paternal lines, I had to reach out to distant family and urge them to get tested—not the best way to make a first impression (!), but privacy could cost lives.

But the real point of this story is that last summer and fall, while I was going through numerous operations, was one of the most difficult (physically) yet amazing times of my life. Suddenly what is really important to me became crystal clear, and for the first time in years I took days off with *no guilt.* I took long walks, made art, watched movies, went swimming, cooked meals with friends and family, slept well, and laughed a lot. I was spoiled rotten and treated like a queen by my friends, family, colleagues, and students. My life had a spiritual richness, joy, and balance, and it took cancer to give it to me.

The second event was collaboratively working on a garden competition in France and winning. A small team of us got to travel to the Loire Valley and build our design for the Chaumont International Garden Festival. We had 11,000 euros and 10 days to complete the project. In the United States we would have been working around the clock, but in France it was entirely different. Work started at 9 a.m. and ended at 5 p.m. We had a leisurely breakfast, wine with lunch, and spent several hours over multiple courses at dinner. There was no work allowed on weekends. We pantomimed and laughed through language barriers and forged lifelong friendships. It was one of the most joyous and valuable life experiences, and the project did in fact get completed in 10 days.

I have always demanded a tremendous amount from my students, and I hold myself to the same standard. Working all night before deadlines was par for the course. Coffee, sleepless nights, and diminishing health seem to be firmly embedded in design tradition. Ironic, as the designs we propose seek health, beauty, and sustainability. I have realized the often toxic nature of the design studio and have taken a new approach, stressing health, rest, and rejuvenation. I can't say it is totally successful but am working hard to develop a healthy and joyous learning environment. Some of the methods I've experimented with include humor, better organization on my part, respite and catch-up days, meal sharing, and mandatory breaks.

Joy, humor, and enthusiasm are infectious. At the beginning of each project I ask students to consider what it would take for them to "fall in love" with the task at hand and what sort of working environment would bring them joy. I urge them to take this question seriously. They may share their responses with me or keep them private. When I sense tension or frustration building, I have them go back to the question, and if there is something I can do to activate a block, to let me know.

I also worked with the dean and students to set up a park-like space on the third-floor terrace (it had been locked for two years). Students now use this space for breaks, to eat lunch, or have team meetings. Being able to easily pop outside, stretch, and watch Central Avenue below or the Sandia Mountains in the distance has been an excellent move in creating a positive learning environment. In addition to the terrace park, we converted an underused room (just adjacent to the terrace) to a community kitchen with a refrigerator, microwave, and kettle. Students now bring healthy food from home and have meals together on the terrace.

And finally, I never assign projects over fall break, allow reflection time and breaks between projects, and work with the other instructors in coordinating deadlines. Simple effort and organizational skills on the part of the instructor can greatly reduce unnecessary stress on our students.

REFLECTIONS ON THE CULTURE OF TEACHING AND LEARNING

I wrote the first draft of this essay nearly three years ago as an assistant professor. As I put together my application packet for tenure last year, I realized how much the Culture of Teaching and Learning group had influenced my conscious growth as an educator (and lifelong student). The group articulated the deep, personal inquiry and desire to continually learn alongside my students. I have recently been awarded tenure, which I see as an indication that I must be doing something right.

I view this essay as a living document that will be added to and changed with time. There are probably too many cultural values to even list, but the ones above are at the forefront of my consciousness and have the most influence in my teaching.

The Tensions and Contradictions of Culture and Its Influence on Teaching

In this section, faculty authors explore the inherent contradictions in and between their cultures of origin, often exploring the tension of opposites that influence their teaching.

CHAPTER NINE

A Mixed-Up History, A Divided Heart

LESLIE OAKES

Accounting
University of New Mexico

SCENARIO ONE

I am sitting on the floor with the new Sears and Roebuck catalog. My sister and I are picking out wedding dresses, furniture for our first homes, baby things (cribs, changing tables, diaper bags). All the models in the catalog are White and neatly dressed. They all appear happy. Nearby, my parents are reading the Sunday paper from cover to cover, complaining about the Vietnam War. I am eight years old. We live in Boise, Idaho.

This scenario captures much of my deepest identity or what Bourdieu (1980) would call the habitus, which is White, middle-class, heterosexual, and gendered. We speak English in our house and our community. We watch White people speak English on TV. Our teachers are White Americans of European descent. We have no close extended family and are expected to leave home when we go to college, never to return. We are expected to get an education and have careers, but not take them too seriously (my parents would like us to take careers seriously, but in Boise girls get married and have families). We are expected to vote and keep our yards clean.

We are taught that we are individuals responsible for our own lives and actions. We do not ask for help. We are on time. We work hard. Emotions are to be overcome. Complaining gets you nowhere.

COMPLICATIONS

Scenario Two

My sisters and I are sitting on the floor of the YWCA with a group of antiwar activists, including Pete Seeger and others. My parents, who do not believe in God, have joined the Unitarian Church, which meets in the Y, so that my sisters and I will meet other nonbelievers. On this night, we all sing antiwar songs and songs of the Civil Rights Movement. Then, all the Unitarians in Boise listen to speeches about supporting conscientious objectors. Later, there is a long debate about whether the church should become a sanctuary. It is 1967. I am wearing an OUT NOW button that my father bought me after we had a heated argument about the war. I have become the rebel child, although I still like to look through the Sears catalog.

My father, who voted for Goldwater in the last election hoping the United States would get out of Vietnam, has mixed feelings about the world. He was born to a poor family in the Ozarks, but his family became middle-class by bottling Coca-Cola. He fought in World War II and was patriotic in a jingoistic way. Later, however, my father went to Harvard on the GI Bill. Although he remained a registered Republican, he never voted Republican again. He will also became an outspoken supporter of civil rights in all its forms, although his family in Oklahoma continued to refer to a part of Tulsa as "N(word)town" decades later. My father hated Oklahoma. He wanted to get away from his family and that part of the country, but he had to fight against his own prejudices all his life. He was a conflicted person.

My mother, who was born to Swedish immigrants in northern Mexico, also went to Harvard. She could only sing in Spanish. She could only tell jokes in Spanish. She was often called to translate for the Mexican housekeepers who worked in our neighborhood. On the other hand, her parents were dour, puritan Swedes who did not express emotions, never admitted weakness, and were extremely solitary. When I asked her the meaning of life, she said there was no meaning. Humans were no better or worse than ants on an anthill. We were a solitary family, and we spent long hours in our separate rooms reading or working.

Although my mother was a registered Republican, she quit voting for Republicans in 1964—the same year she threw out all the books about fairytales. We could read anything from their extensive library (including *Das Capital*, *Mein Kampf*, Cervantes in Spanish, or *Macbeth* in Portuguese), but she didn't think it was good for girls to read about mythical princes riding to the rescue. Later, she worked in a Tijuana free clinic, crossing the border several times a week for the last 30 years of her life. She never accepted a salary. She lived all her life on the Mexico/U.S. border—either symbolically or in reality. She was a conflicted person.

So I am the conflicted child of conflicted people. Bourdieu argued that the habitus is so deeply imbedded in how we think, speak, walk, and even move that it is almost impossible to be aware of the foundational rules of our behavior. I agree.

ANALYSIS

Scenario Three

It is Tuesday morning. My students have a large assignment to turn in. I have encouraged them to work together and have set up workshops on the weekend and Monday night where they can meet and where I can help them complete the assignment. During the workshops, students of mixed ethnic background and different ages cluster around computers, eating lumpia and doughnuts. The room fills up. A few have brought their kids. A quiet student who seldom talks in class is helping another student who seldom speaks at all use Excel. I think, *Good. Now he'll have a friend.* The disabled vets have found each other and are working in the back corner. I am happy and stay longer than I planned and until all the questions are answered.

The next morning, I am about to start class. Most of the students have turned in their assignments. When the clock in the room clicks to 9:30, I pick up the assignments and put them away in a bag. Out of sight. Unreachable. Several students come dashing into the room late. Their assignments are not stapled. Three have not brought a folder as instructed. I am annoyed. I will not accept their smaller, weekly homework assignments late. "No way," a student protests when I refuse to take her assignment. "Yes way," the class responds. They already know the rules about late work, but they can drop almost half of these small assignments so the penalty is small. They cannot drop the larger assignment grade.

I am torn.

I do not like students being late. I find it personally insulting on some deep level. Work is work and play is play. Individuals are responsible for their own destiny and must follow the rules. Also, I know from experience that most of the students who are late will not have completed their assignments anyway. Most, but not all, and I really want the students to succeed. I want them to feel good about themselves. Our lives are not fair. Some of these students have family obligations, commute from other places, are struggling with PTSD and have other barriers to education that I never faced. "OK," I concede. "Just this one time." (Ironically, I turned in the final draft of this essay late, and I am ashamed about it.)

SOME OF THE OTHER VALUES THAT I STRUGGLE WITH

Underlying Assumption

Education is work, and work is serious, solitary, and silent, done in black ink on white paper. Learning is done sitting still in a quiet room. To overcome this assumption, I work to make my classes colorful, noisy at times, physically active, and fun. We draw accounting concepts. Sometimes we chant (students have to remember certain accounting rules). Sometimes we act things out; we pound on our desks whenever we talk about annuities due. We boo liabilities and cheer assets.

I pair up students in class. I call pairs up to the board to demonstrate solutions to problems. I encourage students to work together on everything except two in-class exams. I have those exams in part because of the pressure of colleagues who only have in-class individual exams and in part because I am conflicted.

Underlying Assumption

Success is an individual responsibility. Students in college should be responsible enough to complete the homework on their own and to study and prepare for class. If they fail, it is their own fault. To overcome this assumption, I set up lots of chances to practice with feedback that is not costly in terms of the final grade. I give in-class practice quizzes where I check their progress step by step. I use I-clickers. In my undergraduate class, I give low-point assignments that can be dropped but that encourage students to keep up. I do not limit the number of As and Bs arbitrarily or pit students against each other—or at least I try not to—but I still get annoyed when students seem to be whining about why they can't get something done or why they didn't do well. I am conflicted.

Underlying Assumption

Some people (people with formal education in recognized colleges) are smarter and better than others. My colleagues like to use the lobster metaphor. When you throw a bunch of lobsters into the pot, the biggest will claw their way to the top. Maybe the metaphor is about crabs. They like a really tough exam with an average around 60%. They are happy if only a few students do well.

I like the metaphor that says that to grow, lobsters have to shed their shell and during this time are terribly vulnerable. Students are the same way. I don't like competitions unless they are fun and no one really cares who wins. I don't insist on a curve. I give the majority of class points for exercises that can be done together. I want my assignments to be clear and I want students who understand the material to succeed. But still, I sometimes get annoyed with students who don't understand what I am teaching. I try not to show my annoyance, but I'm sure they hear it in my voice. Maybe somewhere in my subconscious I am still trying to overcome the feeling that as a women I don't really know what I am doing, that, after all, I am still a silly girl.

Finally, I was raised with an enlightenment mentality that believed in education, science, etc. In this model, people are born tabula rasa and soak up their culture and knowledge. People can be rational if they try. Choices lead to clear and recognizable outcomes and rational people choose the wisest alternatives. Emotion should not enter into decisions.

I no longer believe this as completely as I once did and now understand that students have divided hearts, because I have a divided heart. Maybe we have lived previous lives that influence our choices in this life and cannot be undone. Maybe notions of individuality are all phenomenological. Maybe we have spirits that are given to us by a higher being. Maybe Freud was correct that we have a shared consciousness. Surely the habitus that we inherit/learn is deeply embedded and irrational in the classical sense. Perhaps liberation emerges from the crack between that habitus and contradictions of the world. Perhaps creativity is also sparked by the same painful disjuncture that makes us uncomfortable in our own skin. I just don't know anymore, so I keep experimenting in my classroom, to the extent I can experiment when teaching accounting.

REFERENCE

Bourdieu, P. (1980). *The logic of practice*. Stanford, CA: Stanford University Press.

CHAPTER TEN

Keeping Contradictions as a Teaching Tool

Cultural Intelligence in Content and in Practice

MJR MONTOYA

International Management
University of New Mexico

The village of Mora is located approximately 45 miles on either side between Taos and Las Vegas, New Mexico. During the early 20th century, it was known as an important stop for the trade of hides and furs, and it was also a significant ranching and packing area. One can find many buildings that are reminiscent of late Victorian-styled Western boom towns. The old, vacant general store serves as a reminder of a time when commerce and business thrived in the region. I was reminded by my grandparents that when they grew up, they could remember a lot of traffic coming through Mora. The way they recount it, it was a fleeting glimpse of the possibilities and limits of American progress. For them, it was bookended by a life of poverty. While much was happening in Mora in the early 1920s, it was only happening for a few people, and the rest lived a much simpler life in the hills and the higher country. Most people raised sheep, or they were hard-working carpenters and masons, responsible for keeping the village from falling into the hard marshland that surrounded the river valley. My grandparents were one and the other. Francisco (Pancho) and Dolores (Lola) Martinez were both raised in families of carpenters and builders. Ambrocio (Bocho) and Celina (Cel) both came from ranchers and farmers in a town called Lucero, which was nestled high into the hills where the Canadian tributaries were the strongest. Both of them recounted to my parents and their brothers and sisters (16 total) that living in Mora was like watching the rest of the country wrestle with its own poverty. "We were always poor," my grandpa Pancho used to recount, so when the Great Depression hit, things were very much the same in Mora. It has always been a place where the engines of progress move at a tangent to everyday life. I hesitate to call Mora a much simpler part of the world. I choose to understand it as a different place, where concepts such as poverty and progress are not understood in the same way as in places where wealth is accounted for by the amount of money one has in a bank account, or by the level of conspicuous consumption one is able to afford. I am a child of a place that has occupied various worlds, meaning it is a place where people have adapted, changed, and grown accustomed to many different worldviews over many centuries, but that still maintains a particular cultural value system. Some people call this Mestizo, others Chicano, and others Hispanic/Native American/Latino. I have struggled with these categories, mostly in recent years, and often find that identity politics reach their height of ambiguous power when they are bureaucratized. I've often wondered what the implications are for people who enter "other" in a census sheet. Latinidad, or Latin American identity is a complicated construct. I like many other Northern New Mexican Chicanos have found the category of race (which for Hispanics is categorized as "white") problematic, and even though there is an ethnic category, Hispanics and Latin American identifiers are still very complex. Therefore, I, like many people I know, simply indicate "other" as either an ethnic or racial category, particularly because it also does not represent my Native American roots as well.

I now often refer to myself as Norteno, a cultural affiliation that lets me think more about place than people. It is the mountains of the Sangre de Cristos that give me much of who I am, and even though I've traveled to many places throughout the world, the peaks that line the mountain valley are mine in a personal and spiritual way. If you pass through Mora, you will invariably notice the roads that wind through complicated systems of hills and rock. Geologists swarm to this region because of the diversity within the geological system that leads into the Mora Valley. As a result of this, you can sometimes see the hills sparkle under the morning sun, and sometimes you can imagine a time when the water ran through these powerful curves. I feel ancient sometimes, because the place I occupy has seen so much. La Jicarita is a part of me, as is the Mora River and the way it smells like Hierba Buena on a day when the infrequent rain visits the sometimes harsh climate of the desert mountains. It is a place that served as the staging grounds for new relationships between the Pueblo, Ute, Comanche, and Spanish settlers, then later French traders and Lebanese immigrants. After the Pueblo revolt, this land was a land of many cross-pollinations, due in part to colonialism and partially to the forces of latent capital reaching once communal worlds. The power dynamics have shifted to and fro in this place, much like the infrequent rains and the hardened but merciful soil that farmers planted on. Sometimes farmers and ranchers from various communities got along, sometimes they had to get along, and sometimes they created rifts between one another. Mora is a land of contradictions and hard-fought solitude. It has both embraced progress and rejected it at similar times. I think of this place as home, and this place that I call home often represents the contradictions in my own being. If

I am to speak or write intelligently on the subject of culture from a personal perspective, one must first understand that I bear these contradictions as part of what culture is and what it achieves in social and political spaces.

Geert Hofstede (1997) often refers to culture as "the collective programming of the mind that distinguishes one group of people from another" (p. 5). I refer to this definition because it most closely relates to my introduction to the academy as a professional. As a member of the business school, I am in another culture (the culture of the business world) that views culture as a "soft skill" or as an ancillary part of larger economic models. *Programming* is a word I have wrestled with, because it seems too structural a word, devoid of the emotional sentiment that makes culture a vital component of identity. However, as my contradictions manifest, I like the word very much, because it gets one to think of the broad and dynamic nature of culture. Culture is as simple as one stopping on a busy street when they see a red octagon or silencing one's cell phone in a theater. It's as nuanced as eating your eggs poached with red chile on top because your family has a history of heart disease, and in an attempt to eat healthier while enjoying the tastes that make family gather, you join two relatively strange food practices together. It's as compassionate as learning to cut your cousin's food before everyone eats because he has early-onset MS and can't cut his meat like he used to. It's as cruel as insulting another person for not practicing the same faith or, worse yet, killing someone for looking, acting, and thinking differently. I have read the big books on culture from the 19th century, and the distinctions of class, race, gender, sexuality, and creed create a vocabulary that describes less than half of what I sense about culture. I have visited many parts of the world, and I sense the danger of rigid classifications, the part of Hofstede's definition that entails *distinguishing one group from another*. In the 21st century, boundaries are both soft and rigid, belying classifications while relying on them all at once.

I accept culture as a part of my teaching because it is the thing that I always wrestle with, and as a scholar, how can one effectively build a home around their ideas while inviting others to be a part of that home as well? My intellectual home has many family members who live in it, drawn from my professional and personal life. My first year teaching at UNM was a moment I considered a "homecoming," and in preparation for my first class, I prepared a section on "building cultural intelligence." To teach international management, scholars emphasize the institutional dissimilarities that pose challenges for businesses to cooperate effectively. But like the contradictions we all bear, the field of business contains many contradictions, particularly when dealing with culture. On the one hand, businesses tend to view institutional similarity as a value-added and tend to view diversity as a cost—what our textbook would refer to as *translation and transaction costs*. While much effort is placed on emphasizing these costs as sources of great potential, on the surface it views one's differences as a liability (commonly referred to in the field as "the liability of foreignness"). This requires that I get students to think critically about the contradictions that we bear as policymakers, as decision leaders, and as business managers. I ask my students to recognize the way they constantly bear their own contradictions in their identity. Sometimes I quote *Alice in Wonderland* and emphasize how she is never the right size and the spaces she explores never really fit. It is this Othering, this foreignness that is endemic to ourselves. While cultural models and dimensions of culture are valuable, they are only good starts. From their beginning, they seduce our minds into the comfort of categories, and as I work with students, these dimensions become difficult to express in a dynamic way. In fact, I intentionally struggle with these concepts in front of them to ensure that this discourse is recognized as a meaningful problem that we all struggle with. This is why "thinking in front of my students" is ultimately an act of sorting out my own contradictions and discomfort with polished information—so they may see the value in making critical thinking an active part of their own learning process. I find the alternative to be dangerous.

That is why teaching and learning about culture as a pedagogical practice is one of the greatest challenges we face in the academy. We must and should allow ourselves the ability to separate culture from ideology, to let culture have a place in our teaching that doesn't neatly categorize students or anything else in the classroom as X or Y. Being Latino, or rather Norteno, is an important part of my identity, but I quickly grow resentful of the essentializing potential that associating one aspect of culture does to a person. And it happens quickly. As the first native New Mexican Latino to win a Rhodes Scholarship from UNM, I was thrown into a world (Oxford) where class politics and social dynamics were completely foreign to me. The work ethic that I had learned from my family was no longer valued, at least not my need to be physically helpful to others. I was encouraged to separate myself from laborers and from staff in an attempt to reinforce the divide between the educated and the uneducated, which in England is still a profoundly class-related issue. I quickly became the exotic artisan, incapable of high-level scientific inquiry. My cohorts encouraged this romantic idea of me as the gypsy-like artist. Because I played guitar and wrote poetry, I was somehow incapable of being a serious thinker on the subject of politics and philosophy. It was here that I met a watchmaker in Oxford who became a personal friend, who taught me how to value the handmade efforts of workers, particularly those in the world of luxury and fine art markets, who are erased from their work by those with large sums of disposable income. I found these structures of class played heavily in my collective programming. Watchmaking for me symbolized yet again one of the many contradictions of culture, the kind that can easily erase human dignity and subjectivity from one's work, regardless of how much talent or skill is present in that work.

Today, I present the watchmaking industry to my class regularly, emphasizing the act of "telling time" (telling the story of the work we do) instead of "telling time" (the function of a watch). After this discussion, one student shared a powerful revelation: he said, "I have to tell my mind to connect with the material, because that's what gives me an education and not just schooling." I consider that a high point in the year. This student, who had struggled with a lot of the material, and felt like the ideas were themselves "not easy to 'get,'" later shared with me that he never felt like a "good student." After asking why, he noted with a profound but reserved sadness, "because I'm always in the boxes that are viewed as costs and as liabilities." For him, overcoming the liability of foreignness was about the contradictions present in intelligence itself, about the system of forces that were present for him in the classroom. He struggled in my class, and in a hopeful way, I'm glad he did, at least in the sense that through his struggle he was able to find a way forward. As a teacher, I cannot provide intelligence, but I can foster the spaces that make intelligence proceed from a mind willing to struggle.

These struggles followed me throughout my graduate school career. The amorphous concepts of culture and identity presented significant challenges, especially when I studied at NYU and Emory. Both institutions revealed the social disparity and cultural distances between rich and poor in the United States despite the democratic project the country so proudly believes in. At NYU, I often heard students lament their economic conditions, and they wrote about their poverty in their art and lamented their economic conditions in political science classes. And yet, I would find these same students spending thousands of dollars a month on designer clothing, which mostly came from trust funds or from "modest" family support. At Oxford, I sat in rooms with princes and trust-fund kids, sons and daughters of industry leaders and celebrities. All the while, I was called on to be Latino, and this for me became a tiring and crude exercise. I was the students I now work with, fighting to not be a liability to myself and my mind. I had to laugh when I thought of how often people were surprised that I listened to the Outlaw Country of Waylon Jennings, that I knew all the lyrics to contemporary rap and hip-hop, and that I played guitar much like my favorite Scandinavian death metal bands. I was expected to listen to Mexican polkas (which I dance to quite well), to make tortillas (which I do quite well), and speak in the language of my ancestors (which means I would speak a combination of Spanish/Latin/Aramaic/Basque/Dine/French/German/Hindi). Culture is so dynamic and so rich in its intersections that I can draw a line in the sand regarding who I am and how I wish to represent myself, but it would hardly represent who I am and who I am becoming.

In this increasingly technologically integrated world, teaching culture outside of personal experiences then becomes additionally challenging. Most of my students have difficulty separating the "I feel" and "I think" elements of their engagement with subject matter from the "this is" or "this can be" descriptions that are equally valid and valuable skills. The "collective programming" of self-reference serves as a reminder to me that culture is transcendent, and as a challenge for teachers, I must navigate not only the conventional ways that culture is understood, but I must also place those conventions in the context of newly derived social patterns. For example, I recently taught a class on conflict minerals, more specifically how the use of smartphones and other technological devices are connected to the proliferation of child soldiers in the Republic of the Congo. I explained how the mining of columbite-tantalum (or "coltan"), a rare earth mineral used in most laptops and cell phones, is one way our own consumption patterns have a strong impact on societies that are invisible to us on a daily basis. In a response paper to that presentation, one student wrote about how bad she felt about the situation, but then proceeded to spend the remainder of the exercise exploring how bad she felt. This is common, and I challenged her to help me understand how her legitimate feelings could be used to understand how to describe and address the problem itself. The next day, as papers were being discussed, she raised her hand and bravely shared her personal epiphany: "I realize that this phone lets me be me, but it also prevents others from being themselves." This was a small but powerful victory for her, and as class broke for the day, others gathered around her nodding and giving her support. The next series of papers I received from students demonstrated a significant reach beyond themselves and more into the lives and systems that produce these tragic forms of human exploitation. Bearing the contradictions of our own production and consumption produced the cultural intelligence we fought so hard to develop in class.

Thus, the contradictions inherent in culture serve as a pedagogical problem of the highest difficulty and, equally, of the noblest intent. We are asked to recognize cultural patterns in our students, provide access and greater sensitivity. Moreover, we are asked to help place those cultural patterns in the context of an ever-changing world, asking students to step inside and outside of themselves with sophistication and dedication. I must also let my collective experiences serve me. They must be a valuable addition to who I am in the classroom, and I try my best to lay bare the core of my being, so that students understand me not only as a complicated human being, but as a person with intellectual aims and goals for myself and for my students. When I talk about culture I try to be as brave as my students. I talk about the Mora valley and I talk about my work with coltan mining, and in the spaces in between, the students help me through the contradictions I brought to the class with me. When they realize we are pilgrims of a common exile, I recognize not the teacher that I am, but the one I am becoming. This provides the best comfort I believe I can share as a teacher and public servant.

REFERENCE

Hofstede, G. (1997). *Cultures and organizations.* New York, NY: McGraw-Hill.

CHAPTER ELEVEN

Relearning Inquiry, Unlearning Judgment

The Autobiography of a Curious Girl

KERSTI TYSON

Teacher Education
University of New Mexico

I was raised driving back and forth between Taos, New Mexico, and Albuquerque, New Mexico, a 2.5-hour drive. Quite literally, from the time I was four until the time I was about 30, if I was living in New Mexico, I made the drive just about every other weekend, either from Taos to Albuquerque or vice versa. This back-and-forth also meant that I attended many different schools—three elementary schools, four middle schools, and three high schools. I handled the transitions by keeping my nose in a book. Reading was my ultimate escape and comfort. On the one hand, my drives to Taos kept me connected to my grandmother—the matriarch of our family and someone who helped to raise me, especially when my parents' paths made living with them untenable. On the other hand, I lost my sense of belonging to any one place. There was a constant sense of disequilibrium in my life.

Eventually, in high school, my sister, brother, and I all ended up living in Taos with my grandmother, and we spent less time driving back and forth. My grandmother was a loving, forceful, and private lady. She taught me the power of unconditional love and the power of a look. When I first started teaching, she helped me to develop my own look. My grandmother's look was called a "double whammy" in my family. And we all feared it. It was a mix of disappointment and "straighten up right now," and we were all loathe to be on the receiving end.

My grandmother was a stubborn Norwegian, born to parents who immigrated to the United States from Valdres, Norway, as children. She was the youngest of eight, and by the time she was a teen she lost both parents and four of her sisters. I have often wondered how such tremendous loss at such a young age affected my Grandmother. She never talked about it with me, but we visited her families' graves on visits to her hometown in Minnesota.

Throughout my life, my grandmother gave us a home. I treasured driving up her driveway in the shadow of Taos Mountain—the home that was the one steady place in my life. I treasured spending days reading in the quiet of the thick adobe walls and sharing meals with my grandmother, relatives, and friends. My grandmother definitely liked to have things her way, and when we lived in her house, it was under her rules and guidance. Certainly we had disagreements, and sometimes we had to agree to disagree. Even if my grandmother was adamantly opposed to a choice we made, she was able to say, I love you and I disagree with this choice you are making. I wish today that I had asked her more about why she disagreed—and heeded her advice. She was usually right.

When my grandmother died, her children sold her house. My grandmother's home had been a haven for me, but when it was gone, it was gone; it was a haven when she was there. At the same time, I believe that my grandmother lives on inside of me—even a decade after her death, I still hear her voice, her laughter, and if I'm really paying attention I can catch her blue sparkling eyes wondering at me. I still try to avoid the double whammy, though.

Growing up, I was the curious one. I had a million questions about everything and always wanted to know "why." I can remember my Grandmother shaking her head and saying, "Kersti, you and your questions," with a twinkle in her eye. At times, I wondered if there really was a problem with asking too many questions, but I kept asking them, much to my Grandmother's chagrin. It was in her kitchen where I felt most able to ask the myriad questions on my mind. When I was with my Dad, there was not much room for my curiosity. My Dad is like a walking encyclopedia, and there was little room for anything except his monologues on whatever topic crossed his mind. My Mom had a wonderful sense of fun and great intellect, but this side of her was overshadowed by making ends meet as a single mother or, later, homemaking for her husband. Over the years, I realize that somewhere I stopped asking questions as I did when I was young. I started feeling self-conscious about it. I stopped being curious. I'm not sure why or how, but my curiosity waned and, in turn, I became more and more judgmental (mostly in my head). Primarily and most harshly, I judged myself, but I also developed a habit of judging and labeling others. Perhaps judgment was a more solid construct in a life that had much disequilibrium. Perhaps it was something I picked up from those around me; I can remember most of the adults in my life always having a quick opinion about so-and-so and such-and-such.

As I reflect on this shift I now see that as my curiosity waned, I became more guarded. Perhaps that was because as I became more and more judgmental in my own head, I assumed that others were judging me in the same way. Was my curiosity stamped out by judgment—my own and others'? Over time, I lost track of the curious girl I once was as I delved further and further into adulthood. It wasn't a sudden shift; rather, it was something that happened subtly over time. I don't think I'm alone. I think our dominant culture is more supportive of judgments than curiosity, and this cultural norm is especially strong in schooling and academia. For example, in education, our cultural norm is to grade students, and even schools, often using metrics that don't offer clear evidence or feedback for the assigned grade. Often, I find that the grade overshadows everything, the work it represents, the people involved, and even the learning. This overshadowing happened to me too. Slowly over time and without really noticing, I somehow stopped asking questions and instead moved to unquestioning judgment. Instead of approaching situations with curiosity and delight as I once did, I approached them with an idea of "right" or "wrong," "good" or "bad." Over time, this stance put distance between me and the world.

The first place this stance started to unravel was in my teaching. As a novice teacher, I quickly realized that my mathematics students were much more complex than the right or wrong answers they gave on a test or homework assignment. In fact, I've learned that if I judge my students and what they "know" too quickly, I miss knowing them, which in turn hinders my ability to teach in ways that are responsive to their needs and interests. As a teacher, I started to be curious again, ferociously curious about my students' lives and their knowing.

My aim now is to buck this norm, to revive my curiosity and curtail my judgments. This seems especially important in my life in academia—in my research and teaching. If I fall back into old habits and neglect to be curious about people, and instead find myself judging and categorizing people too quickly—certainly a habit we have in our current iteration of education—I find that judgment narrows my world, especially when it comes to judging myself. I make assumptions and create realities about myself and others that are narrow, often untrue, and certainly limiting. When I make quick judgments about my students, instead of being curious to know who they are and how they've come to know what they know, I limit our ability to create learning and I increase the power differential between me and my students. In my research, I find that judgment limits my ability to hear and seek understanding from colleagues and other researchers. It creates competition between my ideas and theirs, instead of seeking understanding to see if and how ideas and understandings can build, challenge, and strengthen what we know and understand about our common interests and passions. For example, if a student offers the "wrong answer" in a discussion, if I can be curious about her thinking and what led her to that answer, I have the opportunity—and so do her fellow students—to understand the problem in a deeper way. More often than not, I find that the best learning is born from trying to understand someone's thinking about a misconception because it helps to tease apart the assumptions we may have about a construct. It also helps me to understand another person's thinking process, to momentarily gain a window into a different way of seeing the world.

One of the reasons my siblings and I ended up living with my grandmother in high school was because we missed living in Taos. Another reason is because my mother and stepfather were alcoholics, and life with them was unpredictable and increasingly impossible. Growing up with a mother whose "life had become unmanageable due to alcohol" taught me perhaps one of the most valuable lessons and has greatly informed my values. My mother was an amazingly functional alcoholic. She couldn't remember a conversation from one day to the next, but she always had dinner on the table for the family, managed to work when necessary, managed a household for my stepfather, and more than anything she managed to always be there for her children. Whenever we really needed her, she always pulled through and had my back. My stepfather was also a functioning alcoholic—he would lecture/yell at us for hours and not remember but was fully functional at work.

For many years, from the time I was a teenager and could track what was going on, I spent a lot of time monitoring my mother's drinking and wishing my mother wasn't an alcoholic. I had a lot of judgment around it; perhaps it was my way of seeking something solid in a chaotic and unpredictable life. As a result, I spent a lot of years rejecting her. One fight we had, although it took years for it to settle, changed that. I remember leaving my Mom's house, once again crying and yelling because she was drinking again, and I told her I could never accept that she was an alcoholic. Her reply humbles me to this day. She said that her alcoholism was a part of who she was and was something to accept. I fought this acceptance for many years and then, with distance and time, I realized that alcoholic or not, she was my Mom and I loved her. In realizing and accepting this reality, I became clear that if she was drinking, I would take care of myself and not spend time with her, but that I still loved her. This realization changed our relationship. I was no longer fighting it and I no longer counted or tracked her drinking. If someone asked me if my Mom was drinking, before, I would have had a detailed answer and judgment about it. Now, I responded that if they wanted to know the answer, they would need to ask my Mom. This realization helped me to learn, at another level, what acceptance and unconditional love meant. It also helped me to lead my own life rather than tracking my Mom's drinking. Funny how when there is dysfunction, that is where we tend to focus instead of on what is functioning. My Mom stopped drinking the last years of her life. Admittedly, it was sometimes hard to tell, because alcohol had taken its toll on her health, but my doubts gave me an opportunity to test my newfound stance, and it proved to be a healthy stance—I loved my Mom, drinking or not—although I much preferred the not. This realization and acceptance of reality gave me my Mom back. It also helped me to crack open my curiosity. It opened up the opportunity for me to try to learn more about her experience from her perspective, rather than my—and others'—judgmental ideas about it. It is interesting to realize that it wasn't her lack of drinking that gave me my Mom back, but rather my lack of judgment about it that gave me my Mom back. I'm happy to say that in our last few years together I enjoyed my Mom more and more. She died, suddenly, a few years ago in April, and I'm heartbroken that it happened just as I finally found my way to be in relationship with my Mom. I feel like I squandered time and would do it much differently if I had to do it again. I'm thankful that we were at peace when she died.

My Mom taught me this powerful life lesson. Her demand for acceptance of something that I thought intolerable showed me the limits of judgment and helped me to rebirth my curiosity. I strive to implement this lesson in all parts of my life. When faced with behaviors or opinions that are different from my own, my first response is often a conditioned one, to judge and reject. But my Mom taught me that the more productive response is to accept and engage, even if it is something I disagree with, to take a curious stance. I'm far from practiced at doing this work. Often I find myself jumping to judgment, about myself and others. More often than not, I realize that my judgments are wrong because they are based on limited information and clouded perception. When I am able to take a step back and take a stance based in inquiry, I learn more about the situation and the people involved, and the solutions to problems are more creative and less daunting.

As I learn to navigate the new roles I've taken on in the last few years, of being a mother, wife, friend, professor, and colleague, I find that when I lapse into judgment about myself and others, inquiry and connection *stop*, whereas in the moments I can foster inquiry, especially in the face of adversity, creativity and connection are born. In my teaching, if I can be passionately curious about my students' lives, understandings, and stances, I can build more bridges to help them think and hear beyond themselves. In my research, if I can be passionately curious about my colleagues' ideas, I have stronger theoretical ground to stand on and rich understandings to draw from. Similarly, if I continue to keep inquiry open as I learn with the teachers and students who co-participate in my research, I am able to learn more deeply with them.

With my students I work to help them develop an inquiry stance—to help them practice being passionately curious about each other's and their future students' lives and understandings. This stance is a careful balancing act in education. On the one hand, as an educator, I have an idea about what I want my students to learn, and as the "teacher" my role is to judge my students on the basis of whether or not they are learning what it is I have to teach. On the other hand, if I become too attached to these judgments, I lose the ability to inquire into the insights and ideas my students have about the thing I'm trying to teach them. When judgment is pervasive, my own learning stops and my students' learning stops. When my work in education, as a teacher or learner, becomes about my students "getting it" instead of understanding what my students understand, I miss the opportunity to learn from and about my students' lives and thinking, and they lose out on the opportunity to bring their ideas and lives into the conversation. When my learning about my students is stagnant, my students' learning about the topic and one another is stagnant.

In our current culture of standards and assessment, I fear that the balance in society has tipped too far on the side of quick judgments about who our students are and even what they are capable of. In my work as a scholar and teacher, I work to find ways to nurture *our* human potential through curiosity and inquiry, especially in a world that is so divided along lines of difference. I do this by attending to how I am listening to my students' ideas and experiences. Judgment darkens and deepens the lines between our differences, whereas inquiry has the potential to blur the lines and help us accept and renegotiate the boundaries of difference. And as I continue to forge my way in this new realm as an academic, I continue to call on myself, my students, and my colleagues to begin with and to fiercely hold on to inquiry, to nurture our ability to be passionately curious about one another, and to listen to one another, especially when faced with our differences. In my own life, it is a call to invoke the deep curiosity about the world that I had as a child. Perhaps it is a call to all to tend to and nurture the curiosity we come into the world with.

CHAPTER TWELVE

Finding Community Within White Distance

SUSAN DIANA LONGERBEAM

Student Affairs & Higher Education
Northern Arizona University

I reach back into the cultural influences on me to understand my influence on students. What continues to drive me on the journey to better teaching is a search for the connection between who I am and how I educate. I want to understand not only my impact on students, but how I can expand my ability to reach students, many of whom experienced distinct cultural influences than did I.

My early cultural influences communicated a strong value of individualism. By individualism I mean a focus on independence and self-reliance. These cultural influences gave me strengths. They also led toward a feeling of separation from others.

I identify as a White Northern European American woman, and central to my ethnic identity is an internal experience of separation, what I call the vast White distance. I yearn for connection. Out of this yearning to create greater connection within myself and with others, I try not to retreat into the vast White distance but instead overcome my early cultural influences and maintain deeper connections with students through drawing on a later cultural influence—that of community. The vast White distance exists in a sense of hanging back; when I want to respond, sometimes I do not. I know a moment is powerful but experience a loss for words.

> I am observing a discussion between a Navajo and White student. The Navajo student responds to a comment of his peer with "I do not really think that way about the world." I realize this is a moment of potential deep learning, of sharing ontological differences. The White student seems to dismiss the comment. I want to jump in right then, but I hang back, not saying a word.

This teaching story represents a missed opportunity I regret—one that motivates me to close the distance. I regret not saying something, anything. I wish I had said to the White student: "This. Right now. This may be your deepest learning experience in graduate school. Listen very carefully." This is what I mean by the effect of White distance on my teaching.

PEELING THE ARTICHOKE

I have tried to overcome the separateness and distance of my youth through understanding my cultures of origin and through finding community. Searching for lost culture is like peeling an artichoke, a vegetable of my California childhood—the reward is the heart, the sweet nibbles of cultural knowledge. I am continually searching my cultural roots to get to the heart of how those roots manifest now in how I teach. The values I explore here of my origins are those of individualism; my later cultural influences, from young adulthood, are those of individualism soothed by, and now blended with, community.

Some of my most poignant and sharpest early school memories are related to feeling embarrassed by teachers and administrators. I believe these teachers were rooted in a competitive, individualistic culture. They encouraged me in my individual achievements, and I did well in their eyes, in response to their care. But also, an early memory: A kindergarten teacher referred to me derisively: "She thinks she is so cute." Another memory: seeking others at school, ordered to the principal's office (running around the classroom, talking too loudly, playing with friends), the deep shame of it. The visceral knowing I did not behave properly. Given that I remember those things first, I know I never want to create those memories for students. Consequently, I try to avoid shaming students. I do not deride them, I believe in their individual goodness and strength and beauty—and I extend unconditional positive regard (Rogers, 1961).

A SORT OF TIMELINE

This is a "sort of timeline" because linear, chronological timelines are rooted in my own Scandinavian, German, and English cultures. So I use the term *timeline*, but I aim for a less rigid understanding of linear time. Nevertheless, honestly I lead with my cultural influences, as I imagine many of us do. I lead with low context communication, and in low context cultures, we tend to derive meaning from interaction through verbal and written communication, tasks, rules, and time sequences. In contrast, high context cultures (most cultures besides White Northern European) tend to derive meaning from the broader context of nonverbal communication, situational knowledge, and relational, connectional cues—between people, things, and situations (Hall, 1976). My timeline begins with my early cultural influences of individualism, those that sometimes created distance. My response to the distance was to embrace community, my predominant influence since young adulthood.

My later cultural influences in community were the antidote to separation. I pursued community to alleviate individualism and pushed myself toward new cultural influences in college at UC Santa Cruz. I was influenced by professors who identified as socialist and feminist and lesbian. I majored in community studies and embraced the learning inherent in collaboration and in emotional work, a term we used in the "second wave" of mainstream predominantly White feminism. It was good, tough, whole-person learning. And I became new through education, through the discovery of community. Now I urge students to form community in cohorts, and to support their campus and local communities through service and care to those who are struggling.

UNDERSTANDING INDIVIDUALISM: THE ARTICHOKE IS GETTING SMALLER

My low context culture did not emphasize the context of our surroundings and our cultural influences. I was raised in Livermore, California, a place of working-class people, suddenly populated in the 1950s by scientist transplants from other places. My father was one of those transplants, a navy scholarship student from an Oklahoma farm, beginning a career with a young family as an electrical engineer at the Lawrence Livermore Laboratory, and continuing to the end of the Cold War (a career spanning from the late 1950s to the early 1990s). For me growing up, Livermore was a place of rootlessness, the nuclear family suburban town in a Native and Hispanic land. Most of us children of scientists were growing up in a low cultural context environment, born of uprooted parents. In that environment, it did not matter where we were from, because all was new and we believed we could make ourselves anew. The price for the newness was low culture and little contextual awareness of our identities.

In Livermore I learned to embrace individual striving. I was raised in the public school system, a public system supported by those scientist parents, with a strong emphasis on math and science courses. Because we had no history in the place we were living, the only memory I had of learning about our place was a superficial paper maché building exercise to depict the California Missions. As an educator, I seek to deepen cultural understanding. I want for students the truth I lacked, so they will know from whence they come. The process of understanding this historical context has been a long one and will continue throughout my life. Uncovering a dominant culture that was presumed the only relevant one is complex, but with help from mentors, with education, and with courage, I am getting to the heart of the artichoke, my cultures of origin. Now I want to offer students a pathway to wisdom, authenticity, and well-being.

A more recent awareness of my culture is a continual counting, parsing, and tracking of time, time broken into segments. Still now, I use time in 20- or 30-minute blocks: in writing, in meetings, in exercise and staring into space. As a child, it was 30-minute segments of homework, piano, and swim lessons. I am grateful for these cultural influences.

I ask myself how all this counting affects my connection with students. I hope I do not impose this counting on them too much. I try to put relationship first, and sometimes that means I show up late. I think I offend students who run on absolute time. I share with students I sometimes run seven minutes late, so if they are present within seven minutes, I do not consider them late. Those minutes are often for taking care of oneself or others—sometimes in simply traveling safely to class. I am always looking for the balance in various cultural notions of time. I end class "on time," telling the class members I respect their time. But acknowledging from where I come, and the ways I've been acculturated to time, helps me to remember the reasons those 20-minute writing segments work for me, and why they may or may not work for students.

I am determined to peel the artichoke to learn from where I come to better reach students. For instance, I lead with traditional research papers; they may also produce a video or another kind of art project. But these "nontraditional" forms of pedagogy are an add-on, the disabled entrance; my courses are not yet fully designed for the universe of learners. My focus on traditional pedagogy comes from my roots in European American educational and cultural environments. Though I do still tend to lead with theory, I am also using case studies, stories, and experiential learning to illustrate theory.

A VAST SPACE OF ROOTLESSNESS

I remember childhood experiences of the competitiveness rooted in individualism: In first grade, reading Dr. Seuss books, along with the thrill of learning to read (!) but also knowing that my friend Lisa was reading more than me, according to the numbers we had to submit to our first-grade teacher, she must have been speed reading, and perhaps she was inflating the numbers (she also beat me in tetherball)? I decided to be in second place. And later in 4-H, second place again, and then it seemed I would always be in second place. Why did this matter so much? The place that counted was first place. These are core memories, examples of the competitive, individualistic mind. I remember a constant feeling of not being good enough, of having to prove myself through competition. Now, I use mostly cooperative pedagogies so that students have many ways to demonstrate their unique learning.

SO DELIGHTFULLY EARNEST: IN SERVICE TO INDIVIDUALISM

Individualism manifests in how I focus on the best challenge and support of each individual, a truism of my profession. I also want students to challenge me, and I appreciate those who do. Embracing this challenge is part of how I use individualism to honor each person, especially those who challenge me to think differently than I do by cultural instinct. I seek to recognize students for who they are. I extend earnestness in seeking to meet each of their individual needs. *Earnestness* is a word that evokes my sense of my Northern European White culture. In my culture of origin, we are often so delightfully earnest. It is a kind of striving, a constant questioning, and a continual searching that comes out of our cultural experience of seeking connection.

Now, I think acknowledged White identity involves a kind of continual earnestness. For instance, I think back further: I remember the children of color in my schools, but it is a hazy, distant, lonely memory. Where were they in my childhood and how do they remember Livermore? What was their experience of the public schools? Due to my focus on individual achievement, and my assumed privilege, I am ashamed to say that I do not know.

Why did I have to run all over the world to find community? The assumption in that, the privilege in believing I could access the world. An undergraduate mentor, Rosa, taught me that White folks went all over the world because our spirit is lacking, and we are searching for wholeness in other people. That is why Helms (1990) calls it pseudo-independence; the irony of which is that we, while claiming our individualism, are actually in debt to many peoples and cultures. I felt this as a child. I felt it viscerally. I knew deep in my heart this was not my people's land. I could feel it when I played in the creek, the Arroyo Mocho behind my suburban track home. It is easier now to acknowledge this pain than to be sometimes in denial and sometimes unaware.

And only later I realize how different I have become, sometimes through the eyes of my family and friends. My worldview has changed. It has deeply changed, and I also still lead with who I am, which is still at the heart of the artichoke, individualistic. But now, also communal. I seek to demonstrate the power of both to students: by showing pride in my heritage, illuminating the strengths in European American cultures, and by adopting communal ways in teaching.

TEACHING: NOT AFRAID TO CALL IT LOVE

Loving students is not difficult, I think because the college years were so tough for me. I extend gentleness because I experience life as a difficult journey. Only their sometimes posturing I resist, when their hubris interferes with their learning. But most often, I remember how tough college was, and it is easy to extend compassion. Maybe because I see myself as quirky and individualistic, I am able to teach to each of their individual spirits. I believe that if we fail to reach even one student, we fail to uphold our inclusive values. I use individualism in service to inclusivity.

> In a class on counseling LGB clients, a student made a derisive comment about those in the LDS community, claiming them "the most homophobic." I responded that many religious communities are challenged by homophobia; not one has an exclusive hold on it. Later, the LDS student sent me an email thanking me, sharing that no instructor had ever stood up for his faith.

I listen to individual students. I build each class incorporating the feedback from the last class, and from the outcome of their assignments, what they do and do not do well. If they don't do well, I ask myself what I need to do better. Sometimes I am tempted to blame them first, but in actuality failures are often rooted in how I structure the course, and it is too easy to forget humility.

> I ask students to bring in a question or comment on readings at the beginning of each class. A semester later, a student reveals she "just wrote anything" to comply with my request. I clearly had not communicated the intent of the exercise, which was to encourage deep discussion of the reading.

I believe teaching is a spiritual covenant. I sometimes take summer breaks from teaching, recognizing when my spirit is tired. I try to offer myself the same gentleness in how I work. I am not always successful, but I know that if I do not offer it to myself, I will forget to offer gentleness to students. Staying gentle helps me remain focused on their learning. I return papers and other work and will accept as many revisions as students will submit—I do not give poor grades when they keep revising. The point of teaching is learning.

Another way that I attempt to show compassion is in challenging, an act of caring to tell people the truth. I learned this articulation recently from a conservative friend, who claims confronting is an act of kindness. For example, I recently sat down with a White male student who was concerned about finding a job relative to students of color. I advised him to focus on doing well himself, not to worry about others finding work before he did. I needed courage to invest in him with honesty. The student subsequently relaxed, focused on his unique strengths, and found a good position. Others have done this confronting for me. I will continue to try to extend myself in these ways through compassion.

THE DREAM: INDIVIDUALISM AND COMMUNITY, BLENDED

In my focus on ambition, education, and achievement, all in low context, unconnected to others, I got the message I could be whoever I wanted to be. Sometimes that sense of individual striving, of ambition, still comes through—often for students. I urge them to reach for the stars. I root them on, knowing they will find their own way, individualism in the service of their wide-open futures. And still now, I know we make choices for our families, and I encourage those choices, as well, just as I have made them in my own life. I do not wish for anyone the vast empty, internal space of rootlessness. Many of us need the gentle tether of place.

I find that it is easy for me to put students first, seeking to put them at ease. Here is where I put individualism to good use, remembering each of them as individuals. Now I focus on strengthening individual students and facilitating community. Working with every individual is rooted in how I was treated compassionately by my parents and mentors. They cared for me, and I pass it on. The individualism of my cultural heritage becomes a strength in working with students. I also focus on creating peer community, knowing through my own research the powerful impact of peers on learning. I extend this research in the classroom by creating multiple group activities.

My value of community reflects in my teaching. I routinely encourage conversation in class and group work both in and out of class. I explicitly ask students to support one another. I acknowledge some feeling of competition is normal, but I do not chase that drive; it is partly how we have been educated in a lifetime of education. Instead I ask: Are you being good to one another? My expectations of them now are to take care of one another, and the future, and to give back. I have had so many good mentors. They taught me community, and they showed me the heart of my cultural artichoke—and that is what I seek to give back now—a sense of community for each individual.

REFERENCES

Hall, E. T. (1976). *Beyond culture.* New York, NY: Doubleday.

Helms, J. E. (1990). *Black and White racial identity: Theory, research, and practice.* New York, NY: Greenwood Press.

Rogers, C. (1961). *On becoming a person.* Boston, MA: Houghton Mifflin.

In Service to Students

Developing New Ways to Teach

In this section, faculty authors share a wealth of pedagogies developed from both their own and through contrasts with other ways of being.

CHAPTER THIRTEEN

Lessons FROM My Family

Understanding College Teaching Through Cultural Introspection

ALICIA FEDELINA CHÁVEZ

Educational Leadership
University of New Mexico

I'm not sure of the exact moment I realized college professors taught mostly in ways different from how I learn. Lecturing and multiple-choice tests in most of my courses led me to skip classes, study on my own, and show up only for exams. Because academics come naturally to me, this was not only possible, but I also found most classes confusing and distracting to my learning. Instead, I read widely and incessantly, wrote much on my own, and explored ideas with siblings, cousins, and friends. I became a student peer advisor in part so I could sign my own registration forms and in my senior year did independent study, research, and internships with professors from whom I wanted to learn.

I learn most naturally through applying things in real life, often through trial and error; through visual processes (including observing, reading, models, and images); through reflection; through stories, examples, and metaphor; and through comparing and contrasting my sense of things with others, usually one-on-one. Common lecture modes of teaching in college don't engage my curiosity or match my natural ways of learning. In college I longed for deeper, more complex, engaged academic learning. Graduate school was somewhat better, yet even in small classes was made up primarily of lecture with some professor-led discussion.

Many years later I became acutely aware of ways I teach differently from most other professors. When I finished teaching my first class session as a professor in an eastern university, I noticed a group of students whispering together. They approached me and asked, "Dr. Chávez, how is it that you teach so much like our Mothers, Aunts, and Grandmothers when you are Apache and Spanish American from rural New Mexico and we are Jewish from New York City and Chicago?" This question led me to my research on intersections of culture, teaching, and learning.

I taught that first class session in ways natural to me, facilitating students sharing narratives of their lives and educational leadership experiences in relation to subject matter, relating my own experiences and family stories to explain concepts, having students discuss and apply theory to practice, and weaving in visual means including drawing, charting, writing, and then sharing. I often use a somewhat Socratic method of asking students increasingly probing questions, prompting to complexify and deepen understanding. I use a variety of reflective and discursive techniques to involve every student whether in large or small classes, knowing that we will all develop greater understanding through a collective of insights, interpretations, perspectives, and wisdom.

I design so students learn through a combination of private and public assignments. Usually two out of three papers and projects become readings or presentations we all review and discuss. I intersperse silent reflection to gather thoughts and process ideas, with animated discussion among partners, trios, small groups, and the whole class. I push and tease and encourage, thank and commend and laugh, not letting students remain disengaged. Like my own best family teachers, I am more than a bit intrusive, teasing students to "dig deeper" when they are clearly sharing a less than complex interpretation; asking a late student if they are OK, tracking down absent students to see what they need, and approaching students who seem in distress to offer a listening ear or a referral for assistance to campus resources. I talk with recalcitrant students to let them know in no uncertain terms that they are needed in the world; I know they can do better, and expect them to do so, something one of my former students describes as my "come to Dr. Chávez talk."

There are many foundational aspects of my teaching that originate in underlying cultural frameworks within my heritage as Mestiza. I am from Taos, New Mexico. My Spanish ancestors immigrated to this area in the mid-1500s, intermarrying with Jicarilla and Mescalero Apache Peoples and forming a simple life of sheepherding and farming. Life consisted of whatever was needed to take care of family and extended families collaborated in daily responsibilities.

Children are still guided in my family by everyone around them, receiving teaching, scolding, teasing, affection, and protection in equal measure. Learning in my family involves equal parts quiet contemplation and boisterous interaction, both rote aspects and inspiring creation, harsh discipline and compassionate encouragement. In my family learning is much like nature—learning by observing, doing, collective exploration, long periods of reflection, and from both the harsh and wondrous. Learning within our family and of our own individual gifts was not only nurtured and expected; time for this learning was protected. We were only allowed to be involved in one school activity outside of academics (and only if we could be home for dinner every night). My parents made clear to us that we needed time to pursue our individual interests through reading, music practice, art, horseback riding, sewing, woodwork, cooking, time learning with and from family, and immersing ourselves in developing our own gifts. I continue to learn from the lessons of my family and realized through cultural introspection that most of my teaching originates from the lessons of my family.

LEARNING THROUGH REFLECTION, CONTEMPLATION, AND INTROSPECTION

> Go out by the river and think about life.
>
> —JOSEFITA GONZALES CHÁVEZ

I hold distinct memories of my mother, Josefita Gonzales Chávez, encouraging us as children to make time for contemplation, reflection, and introspection. Purposeful time for going inward is an important responsibility in my family. Contemplation to listen for our place and purpose in the world, reflection to consider the meaning of our choices and actions, and introspection to search for understanding and empathy are all a real part of our daily lives and learning.

Going inward plays a deep role in my facilitation of learning among students. One of the three or four assignments in each of my courses is wholly introspective, guiding students to immerse deeply and learn from their own lives, their own insights. Other assignments include reflective components. Discussions are designed with time for reflection prior to sharing. I believe that learning from ourselves and making meaning of what we are learning in relation to ourselves is critical to our development as human beings, as educated people, and as professionals. It is not enough to absorb, critique, or even apply knowledge. Knowledge is not the end goal of learning; wisdom is, and that requires deep, ongoing reflection both within and outside of ourselves. It is essential to make sense of what we are learning through our own ethical frameworks and in relation to our families, communities, and cultures. It is far too easy when knowledge remains abstract to use that knowledge in ways we regret later. I believe that within my role as teacher lies a sacred duty to facilitate contemplation throughout learning processes.

Facilitating contemplation, reflection, and introspection is fulfilling work yet can also be exhausting and emotional. In the busy techno-filled lives of our students, purposeful reflection is often rare and for some new. It can be frightening or even taboo as some individuals are taught that going inward is dangerous and what lies inside us is not to be disturbed. I have grappled with all of these things in relation to teaching and I am at peace with requiring this kind of practice from students. It is a hallmark of my teaching and of my family. Students in my courses often remark in evaluations that by going purposefully inward they find strength and insights within themselves that are invaluable to who they are becoming as human beings and professionals.

LEARNING THROUGH RESPECTFUL WONDER

> Sit still; slow your breathing … what do you hear, see, smell, feel?
>
> —GABRIEL VENCESLADO CHÁVEZ

Growing up, we spent much time as a family in wilderness places—mountains, deserts, isolated rivers, lakes, and beaches. Always my Father, Gabriel Venceslado Chávez, served as our guide, mentor, teacher, introducing us to wonders of the world around. We learned to still ourselves to watch, listen, and learn. We became enthralled with the beauty and the harshness of the world. My Father encouraged us to observe, ask, question, suspend belief, and learn about complex relationships in nature.

As a teacher, I am not content with students learning only from books and removed consideration of knowledge even with added practica and internship courses required in academic programs. In *every* course, I send them into the field of their own lives and professions to learn through purposeful observations, discussions, asking, and exploring. I encourage them to suspend judgment and "make the familiar strange" (Whitt, 1993, p. 81) so they can experience it anew, from its strengths, and with wonder. It is easy to interpret things only from our first impressions, and though these are invaluable, it is often by engaging in a sense of new wonder that we move more deeply toward multifaceted understandings. It doesn't occur to me to lament students' lack of engagement because it is *my* responsibility to engage their wonder, inspire their curiosity, and help them situate learning in their lives (Baxter Magolda, 2001). I often ask students to apply theory to issues and opportunities in their own educational contexts, to current needs and challenges within their professional positions. I urge them to engage, to become involved, and to care. I call them to be present in the world and to make a positive difference, to live a life of purpose, and to find and create wonder in life. I call them to become transformative educators, leaders, and human beings.

INTERCONNECTEDNESS OF LIFE AND LEARNING

> Unto you I give my blessing. … Go out and do what you were meant to do …
>
> —FEDELINA MARTINEZ CHÁVEZ

My Grandmother, Fedelina Martinez Chávez, never allowed us to leave her home without a formal blessing, even though we visited daily on our walk from the bus stop. Kneeling before her, we received her blessing with her hands cupped to our forehead.

Her blessings always included a call to stewardship, to responsibility, to vigilant awareness of profound connections in the world. Perhaps no one can call as fiercely as a Grandmother for us to be who we are meant to be and strive toward meaningful purpose. Among many Indigenous Peoples, a Grandmother's role includes instilling a sense of personal responsibility for and connection with past and future generations, not just of human life but of all life and the earth that holds us.

I am in some ways as fierce in my teaching as my Grandma Fedelina. Perhaps it is fitting that I carry her name. I call my students to engage strongly in education, to identify and cultivate their gifts for the benefit of others. I tend strongly toward larger lessons, as one student described: "I think I get it now, Dr. C.; you are teaching us learning as a way of being." Developing as human beings underlies everything in my teaching design and facilitation. This means that I constantly push and cajole, inspire and challenge students to see and understand our connection to all that surrounds us. I make constant connections to larger lessons in life and ask students to identify connections to current and future professional responsibilities. I do this hoping they will ripple through generations and me through them. This is how I was taught, how I see my responsibility and connectedness through teaching.

I facilitate connections in many ways by designing meaningful, multifaceted assignments and class activities for them to choose and then delve into issues that matter to them in education and society. I share my own leadership stories as well as others' to inspire transformative professional practice by facilitating connection through narrative. I design many activities to integrate connections between their minds, hearts, bodies, and spirits. Offering professional suggestions, respectful critique, resources, and support to peers is encouraged and rewarded so students continually connect with and facilitate each other's development. I facilitate their deep connections between theory, research, and practice. I ask them to connect with and learn from each other through deep discussion and sharing of experiences and stories. And three of the four projects and papers in my courses become class readings for everyone so that all may learn from and connect through our collective wisdom.

LEARNING FROM EACH OTHER ...

> Take care of each other out there!
>
> —JOSEFITA GONZALES CHÁVEZ

My Mother, Josefita Gonzales Chávez, never failed as we were running out the door to call out for us to take care of each other. I was protected physically and emotionally many times especially by one of my sisters and several first and second cousins throughout my schooling when so many around me experienced bullying, fear, and sometimes violence. My older sisters guided me through college, making sure I had what I needed and never gave up. We all found our ways from the far reaches of the world and our professions to build homes and raise families as neighbors to each other along the Rio Pueblo in Taos, New Mexico. My Mother still reminds us often to take care of each other, and we do.

I think of this often as I facilitate learning among students. How can I guide them to connect, care for, and learn from each other? And how do I call them to connect with and care for their own communities whether they travel far or remain close to home? I know in my deepest spirit that what is needed is within the collective. So in my courses, students are graded for their contributions to each other's learning, not just their own. In my online courses, written discussions are guided by criteria that include illustrating with examples from their professional roles in education and require substantive responses to peers in relation to the topic. Extra credit points are available for respectful critique and alternate perspectives as well as for providing professional suggestions or resources to peers, because I learned long ago that these become common practice more through reward than requirement. I ask students to take care of each other and guide them in this through the design of courses and my facilitation of their learning.

Almost immediately as a teacher I became uncomfortable with the normative practice of papers and projects in which only the student and I learned. This felt incongruent with the collective good, care for each other lessons of my family. I soon found ways using online course sites and library electronic sites to make student assignments available as course readings. My syllabi clearly state which assignments will be shared and which will be private so students can decide for themselves what to include. The quality of work improves significantly as students realize our community will learn from their insights. Students often comment in amazement at how much they learn from peer insights, examples, and meaning making of theory and educational situations. They find that they learn even from very disparate educational contexts, roles, and experiences. My hope is that they will also learn to collaborate and seek insights with professional colleagues as educational leaders.

EQUITY AND BALANCE

> Lift up your head, Mijita; we worship only God.
>
> —RAMONA BACA GONZALES

Such were the words of my Grandmother, Ramona Baca Gonzales, who with her humble beginnings and education refused to bow to others and often stood up for those in need of protection. She lived to the age of 100 and taught me to know in my deepest self that no one person is better than any other. From my Grandmother,

I learned that we must not bow down to others, and we must also stand to protect others. Much of what I do in my teaching comes from a foundation of equity and balance. I do many things to facilitate a learning context that includes each student's natural ways of learning and honors each student as a source of knowledge and wisdom. My job is student learning, and this requires facilitation of many perspectives, many interpretations. A former doctoral student described me as a social constructivist teacher who believes cultivating the collective and individual wisdom of students will enrich education and improve the world for future generations.

I was taught early on that sameness is not equity because we each have different needs and ways of being in the world. This means that as teacher in a learning context, *I must be the one who is most flexible.* I must be the one who designs many ways for students to learn so that each is able to negotiate and balance the many responsibilities and realities in their lives with their academic and professional learning. I must create a learning context and community where no one has to bow down to rules and deadlines that require them to make impossible choices harmful to their health, spirituality, families, tribes, work, or other responsibilities. I encourage students to take the time they need to learn and to let me know ways I can make the course and learning experiences helpful to them. This also means that I mentor through extensive amounts of feedback and connect most of my suggestions directly to their current and future leadership in education. Students are fond of teasing me that they turn in a 20-page paper and receive a 40-page one back from me. My hope is that they learn from my actions how to lead, teach, and mentor others individually in flexible, diverse, and needed ways.

COMPASSION AND FIERCE CARE

> Offer a gentle hand and your fierce protection …
>
> —BLAS CHÁVEZ

My Grandfather, Blas Chávez, was an imposing man—six foot four with very dark skin, piercing blue eyes, a hawk nose, an often imperious expression, and extremely high expectations of himself and others. Yet most of my experiences of him were of a kind gentleness and endless patience with me, his affection for the 20 cats who lined up around the edges of the barn for a squirted taste as he milked the cows, the many dogs who adored and followed him everywhere, his fierce care and stewardship of our family, and the healing hands he consistently offered the lambs among our vast flock of sheep. I remember him often reminding us to take care of the little animals because they take care of us.

Inherently I have always known that much of my work as a teacher is to provide a challenging yet fiercely caring environment for learning. One student recently shared with others in one of my classes, "Last semester when my Father was dying, Dr. Chávez, without lowering her rigorous academic standards, provided me needed flexibility and support through finishing the course, being with my Father in his last days, and urging me to care for myself through it all." I have been known to track students down to make sure they are OK and offer flexibility so that learning and well-being are the priorities. I believe that we must be active agents "who actively reach out, extending a hand to reach an outcome, to fix a problem, putting the human situation first and protocol second" (Rodriguez & Longerbeam, 2015, p. 24). Care and compassion are in no way counter to academic rigor. Student learning and success benefit from a blend of both.

HARD LESSONS

I learned many lessons from those who raised me. Most are positive and I share some of those here. Some are not, some even horrific, and though I do not yet share them in writing, they too influence my teaching. Some of my fierce care and protectiveness originate directly from things I survived in my family. Growing up with few resources, necessitating constant innovation in my life, sometimes causes me to feel impatient when a student becomes overbearing, entitled, or especially demanding. This challenges me to empathize when students do not give their best or show resourcefulness in the face of setbacks. Fortunately, in my online courses there is always a chance for me to purposefully reflect and then revise my first written response to a student whether in email, discussion, or feedback on an assignment. Sometimes this helps me process my initial reactions through a first draft, then, because I have first processed through my initial negative feelings, and I am able to find within myself a more empathetic, helpful, learning oriented response. In face-to-face courses I sometimes need to take a deep breath before responding, to discuss with a student during a break or after class, to offer the benefit of doubt and an ear tuned toward understanding, and to make sure I am well rested so I have greater patience. Over time I develop strategies to facilitate through common situations, issues, and feelings that arise.

LEARNING THROUGH CULTURAL INTROSPECTION

We are, as teachers, our cultured selves. Much of who we are manifests in our teaching, and it is up to us to purposefully reflect, observe, and transform when necessary. I am continually discovering underlying lessons and experiences of my cultures and family through introspection and through the catalyst of working with a diversity of students as people, learners, and professionals. This is a sacred responsibility and humbling reality of teaching. Through teaching we ripple out through generations.

REFERENCES

Baxter Magolda, M. B. (2001). *Making their own way: Narratives for transforming higher education to promote self-development.* Sterling, VA: Stylus.

Rodriguez, E., & Longerbeam, S. (2015, July/August). Encounters with angels: A struggle to return home from study abroad. *About Campus, 20,* 22–26.

Whitt, E. J. (1993). Making the familiar strange: Discovering culture. In G. D. Kuh (Ed.), *Cultural perspectives in student affairs work* (pp. 81–94). Lanham, MD: American College Personnel Association.

CHAPTER FOURTEEN

Teaching Development

MATÍAS FONTENLA

Economics
University of New Mexico

I was born and raised in Argentina and brought up in a Catholic household. The father in our local church, Padre Pablo, was a wonderful human being with a genuine love and commitment to others, and especially to those in need. Probably because of this influence, growing up I wanted to be either a teacher or a priest. Teachers were not paid well enough, and priests had to be celibate, so I became a professor. As a professor, though, my commitment to teaching and serving others could perhaps be traced to my early formative years.

I love teaching. I care about my students. I am passionate about economics. My area of study, development economics, is about improving the quality of life of human beings, and education is a fundamental component of it. I find that easy to be passionate about. Everything else flows from there.

In the mid-1990s I was a first-year student in college in Argentina when I started a backpacking trip through the Americas. What was supposed to be a summer trip became a yearlong journey that brought me to the United States. Just about everything I experienced on these travels was fascinating to me. But what perhaps struck me the most was the deep levels of underdevelopment and poverty. I grew up in an upper-middle-class family, went to private schools, and certainly never had any needs unmet. I had seen poverty and underdevelopment before but had never seen and coexisted with it for long periods of time. I saw many people devoting their entire focus and energy to basic subsistence, living one day at a time. At that time, I wished I had somebody to put things into perspective and discuss these things with me. After that trip I decided I would become an economist to understand and help solve the economic problems of developing countries.

A few years back, I set out to re-create for my students what was a life-changing experience for me. This, while adding what I had wished for in my travels: deep discussions to try to understand social phenomena. I partnered with then graduate student Ben Waddell, and after lots of planning and contacting people, in the summer of 2010 we took 18 students from nine different majors to Nicaragua. Over the course of four weeks, we took a hands-on approach to understand failed development, poverty, and the deep social inequalities that affect our world and, most importantly, to understand solutions to these social problems. During the day we would visit and work in coffee co-ops deep in the northern mountains, housing projects, microfinance organizations, urban slums, medical outposts, hospitals, and rural schools. We would talk to, and get lectures from, community organizers, Nicaraguan scholars, and international aid agencies. At night we would get together to try to make sense of it all.

Since our goal was for students to "live and learn" economic development, they were expected to keep a journal to foster the development of their own thoughts, to express their feelings, and to take notes. Rarely did we lecture, more often we would just moderate lively discussions. We did not give out answers, but we would pose questions. Then we would lean back and observe how they figured things out on their own, based on what they did that day. It was a wonderful, fulfilling experience seeing them "get it" on their own, their eyes sparkling with excitement. Students learn on their own; teachers are just facilitators. After the trip students would write a reflection piece based on their journals and try to make sense of it all, to bring all of their experiences together.

How do I assess whether my goals for this nontraditional class are met? My ultimate goal is impossible to measure in a quantitative manner. My ultimate goal is to help them develop into better, more caring and educated human beings, and for the class to have a positive effect for the rest of their lives. And further, that they use those experiences and knowledge to positively influence the lives of others. Perhaps a survey asking them about it 60 years from now would work.

A more immediate way of observing the impact of this course is what my students did after it ended. They took action, participating in development solutions. They started a UNM chapter of Nourish International, an organization where students raise funds during the academic year and then lead development projects during the summer session. That summer they built a school, built a well, fixed a road, and repaired roofs for women and their children in an urban slum in Granada, Nicaragua. Since then, my students returned to Nicaragua to build a health clinic in the jungle and have gone to Peru and Ghana on other projects. These are amazing young women and men and already are great leaders. They are applying what they learned and positively influencing the lives of others.

Another outcome of my Nicaragua course can be seen in the story of another student, of Native American descent. He decided to stay an extra five weeks after our class volunteering in a small rural hospital in northern Nicaragua. This gave him an invaluable experience that solidified his passion for medicine and helped him in his application process for medical schools. He is now in medical school at the University of New Mexico, which ranks second in the nation for his focus, rural and Native American medicine.

So far, I have led five Nicaragua and one Cuba study abroad course. Student evaluations include comments such as "a life changing trip," "the most important learning experience ever," and "This course expanded my knowledge of the subject matter, my knowledge of who I am, and the knowledge of my purpose in this world. I found who I was as a person through this course, and I recommend it to anyone and everyone." This last statement nicely highlights the additional benefits beyond the specific theme of any good study-abroad course. Experiencing a different culture prompts the student to compare it to her own culture, perspectives of the world, and personal choices. This leads to personal growth and turns students into more open, better world citizens.

When I first started teaching, I asked myself, "What makes a good professor?" and "What do I really want my students to learn?" Many years later, I am still updating those questions, and I hope to continue my learning process on it for years to come. At that time, it made me realize that I was a product of basic chalk and board, and the professors I admired in college were horrible teachers, rushing through equations while talking to the blackboard, never turning around to see our glazed "I was lost 50 minutes ago" faces. We know better now—we are making progress on understanding the learning process.

Learning is a process undertaken by the student, where knowledge is expanded and changed, with the ultimate goal of that person becoming a better human being. I sincerely believe this and keep it at the forefront of my objectives whenever I design a course, a lecture, or when I am in front of students.

When I am in front of students, as I am setting up for class and powering up the computer, I do an exercise I came to develop over the years. I casually look at the class, smile at them, and in my inner voice I repeat a few times: "Forgive me, I am sorry, I love you, thank you." I ask them for forgiveness for my shortcomings as a teacher, human being, and the role-model role I am being thrust into by standing in front of them. I am asking for their compassion toward me. Also, I apologize. By expressing my love for them, I am shifting the center of my being away from my mind, toward my heart. I have seen many people do good things while being without love, being tense, unhappy, and in their minds. I don't want to be that person. Finally, I thank them for being there. I think the precursor for this exercise was watching Padre Pablo praying to give a good mass at the beginning of each service. Regardless, the exercise grounds me, makes me be present, allows me to acknowledge my students' presence, and makes me smile.

In the fall of 2010, I taught Economics of Poverty and Discrimination. Beliefs on poverty in the United States are highly correlated with political beliefs. If you are on the right of the political spectrum, you are more likely to blame poverty on the individual "People are poor because they are lazy." If you lean left, on the other hand, you may blame poverty exclusively on the system and society. These simplifications are so ingrained in people's minds that it becomes hard for them to open up and consider a more complex, messy picture. My objective was for students to allow new information that may challenge their deeply ingrained beliefs and learn. Part of my strategy involved requiring students to volunteer in a poverty-related organization, keeping a journal, interviewing people, discussing their experiences in groups, and writing a paper, all as part of their main class project. Only after having a hands-on, personal experience, talking to people whose situation did not fit neatly in a box, thinking about it themselves, could we refute those simple misconceptions in the classroom and build a more sophisticated story on the causes of poverty. Our discussions in class, their journal entries, and their final papers showed me that most of them got it.

This positive pilot experience with a service-learning component course prompted me to develop a Financial Literacy course in spring 2012. The course was a dual enrollment for UNM and the Native American Community Academy (NACA) High School. We developed an understanding of financial institutions, life planning, budgeting, student loans, debt management, title loans, payday loans, credit cards, etc. The main project of the course was a service-learning component. That is, students developed a workshop, presentation, games and activities, and then presented this material at their high school and at UNM.

I also often teach large introductory courses. I approach these courses with the goals of inspiring them to develop a passion for learning and to realize the value of their education. To do this, I emphasize the basic economic principles I believe will help them be more sophisticated in everyday choice making, and become better informed world citizens. I often loudly announce, "This you need to remember for the rest of your lives!"

At the beginning of each class, I write down the objectives and say, "This is what we are going to do, this is why it matters, this is why you should care." Then we move on with a mix of discussion, teaching aids, and students working on examples. I bring in examples that they can relate to, and I use humor to keep them engaged. And at the end of class, I stress, "This is why we did this today, and this is why it matters to you."

During the body of the class, I use a variety of strategies to keep first-year students interested and active. I understand that they can, at best, only take 20 minutes of traditional lecture format. I plan class time with that in mind. I pause often and ask questions to the class, not only to activate their brains but also to gauge understanding, and I adapt the lecture accordingly. For the same reason, my slides often include multiple-choice questions at regular intervals. I encourage them to take five minutes to work on the problem by themselves, after which they should discuss it with their neighbor. Then we go through the problem together as a class.

I also make sure to add questions on these non-textbook materials to our weekly quiz. I use weekly online quizzes to keep them up to date with the material and to get additional feedback on their understanding.

Another strategy to keep first-year students interested and coming to class are short video clips that emphasize, sometimes with humor, the main lecture objectives that I try to get across. Over the years, I have amassed a battery of what I call "YouTube Learning Aids." There are parodies and musicals on the different schools of economic thought, stick-figures explaining concepts, Homer Simpson's brain explaining to Homer the functions of money, the Stand-up Economist explaining the 10 main principles of economics, among others. Not all are funny: I have brief PBS documentaries on microfinance, on poverty, on the Great Depression, etc. In addition to presenting the same main points of the lecture in a different form, and from a different source, they break up lectures and are a great precursor of "So, what did *you* get from this video?" discussions.

My favorite learning aids, though, are interactive data programs, such as Gapminder World (www.gapminder.org). There we can ask and get answers from the data instantly, on questions such as the relationship between income and health across the world, income and education, and how they have evolved across time. Students really enjoy these and often tell me that "I went home and played with that website for hours!"

The feedback I get from students often mentions how large sections feel like small classes when it comes to student engagement, their changed attitude toward economics, and how they now understand why and how economics matters to them.

In my intro classes in the years 2008–2009, we were in the midst of the unraveling of the U.S. "great recession." These events hit close to home, as Argentina experienced three major crises during my lifetime, the last one being more severe than the U.S. Great Depression. I wrote my dissertation on financial crises. Every class we would start by reading the *New York Times* headlines, discuss what they meant and how they might affect their personal lives. Very lively discussions ensued. Common student feedback that semester mentioned how much they valued this, and how it was a great time to be taking an economics class. Often, I get feedback on how they will keep and apply some fundamental economic concepts throughout their lives.

After all is said and done, though, what I care about most is motivating them to be the best human beings they can be. And to live a good life filled with passion, and love.

CHAPTER FIFTEEN

Transformed BY THE Learners

GARY SMITH

Academic Professional and Organizational Learning
University of New Mexico

On the first day out of Cape Town, South Africa, my father looked toward me across the sedan roof and said, "If we were in the United States, we'd probably get back in the car and keep on driving, wouldn't we?"

What prompted his statement? We had not seen another White person since we entered the town. The sidewalks were crowded with people, mostly Black men sitting against the building walls and carrying on conversations—mostly with jovial gesturing, touching, laughing. My father was not racist. He possessed, and instilled in my brother and me, a Christian sense of fairness and a strong regret for how African Americans and other minorities are treated in America. However, his disdain for inequity didn't keep my father from associating the view on that South African street with the anxiety he would feel if driving into and parking in an all-Black neighborhood in the United States—very unlike his European-descendent farming community hometown or the affluent and virtually all-White Cincinnati suburb where I grew up.

And, yet, this thought that my father voiced was not in my mind. What I saw was a lively group of people who, while clearly different from me in at least one obvious way, posed no threat to me. I was simply enjoying the experience of being somewhere different with different people and not thinking at all of how another White American might have reservations about getting out of the car on *that* street.

I found myself asking several questions ever since that day. Why is it that I didn't have the same reaction as my father? What experiences have made me view people differently than some other members of my family? *Why is it that I have come to cherish knowing and learning from people whose formative experiences were so unlike my own?* By formative, I mean those experiences, typically early in life, that frame our self-concepts, identities, and values. Whatever my formative experiences were growing up in an affluent suburb with family roots divided between urban blue-collar and rural/small-town "Americana," they aren't what I see as forming my values and self-concept today. Why is it that I feel some level of discomfort in homogeneous settings despite the fact that was the comfortable, supportive environment of my formative years? Lastly, how does this transformation in human awareness frame my teaching and my appreciation for students, especially for students of color or from more economically challenged homes than I benefitted from? It makes me wonder what "formative years" really mean.

"Why did you decide to be a teacher?" It seemed like a fair question. The Native American student was making her first visit to my office and, as usual, I had taken time to explore her aspirations for college, her major, and the course. She continued, "You're different than my other professors. The way you teach, the assignments, the way you have us work together, and the way you interact with us all tell me that you really care that we learn and that you care about us." This was not a question or an observation on my teaching that any previous student had raised with me. My pause in responding was further exaggerated because the question came on the heels of her sharing intense stories of her life and what she was trying to rise above in a challenging family history. Many students have confided delicate problems with me, sought my advice, or relied on me as a listening post to emotionally unload, but not at our first individual meeting, and not in only the second week of the semester. Her reflection on her past life and future vision had come from deep inside, and I owed it to her to be just as sincere and vulnerable. And so, for the first time, I assembled on the fly the following narrative of experiences and reflections that had lingered just below the surface of my thoughts for some time—perhaps since that day with my father in South Africa 15 years before.

Although my life goal of being a geologist originated when I was only 12 years old, I had not seen academia as my destination. The seed to be a professor was sown when I was a graduate teaching assistant at Oregon State University (16 years before the trip to South Africa). In hindsight, I'm certain that some of that passion for teaching arose from ego—being a sage on stage. I also enjoyed thinking about how to engage students to learn, not just hear about, concepts that I felt were important or interesting. I was trying to cultivate a passion for learning like my own.

However, my role as a teaching assistant also brought to view who students really are. I had been a student for 17 years (an appropriate apprenticeship for teaching, perhaps) but I now found myself wondering—from my fresh perspective as a teacher—what I had potentially missed in my experiences with classmates. As I came to know the students I was teaching, I realized that they mostly brought life experiences to their education that were different from mine and the peers that I associated with as an undergraduate. I realized how I had benefited from the privileges of a superb high school education, a supportive and stable family climate, and monetary resources that permitted me to be a truly full-time student. However, as a TA I saw many nontraditional-aged students, some returning to school after losing employment in the 1980s timber recession, and veterans suffering from what was not then known as PTSD, and students who were intensely juggling jobs and family along with school that led to distractions not only of time away from scholastic excellence but also of cognitive energy (Mani, Mullainathan, Shafir, & Zhao, 2013).

I started to realize that teaching was not about the ego-pleasing "sage high" demonstrations of amassed knowledge and public presentation; it was about advancing the learners. I was disheartened by how many of my students told me that they did not have comfortable access to professors for help with their learning. I was dismayed by those who were discouraged that they weren't learning much if anything from some courses. In the summers they undertook back-breaking work in the vegetable harvesting and processing industry, sleepless work on fishing trawlers off Alaska, and perilous work fighting wildfires, among other vocations. Now, they watched their hard-earned money spent with little perceived return on learning, but with abundant accumulating frustration and debt. The education system owed more to these learners. I needed to respect each one as a person with varying life experiences and approaches to learning, support their learning, and challenge them to higher-order learning tasks of value to their futures while providing the necessary scaffolds for their confident achievement. Increasingly, in later years as a professor, I focused on the needs of the learner expressed by a desire to know the individual person behind each name on the roster, and appreciating the roles of value-forming life experiences—the essence of culture—different from my own to determine the passions for and approaches to learning.

> Who dares to teach must never cease to learn. (John Cotton Dana Platt, 1989)

Dana's quote represents the 30,000-foot-view of my teaching philosophy, although it held different meanings at different times in my transformative learning as an educator.

If I had known Dana's statement when starting out as a graduate teaching assistant, I would have thought that "never cease to learn" meant remaining knowledgeable in my discipline so that I know the content to teach. However, as recounted above, I rather quickly in my TA experience found myself learning mostly about students. In the close-interactive setting of teaching geology labs I came to appreciate students as people, not pupils. I felt an obligation to be a champion for the learners.

Years later I realized that beyond never ceasing to learn my discipline and learn about my students, I also needed to learn about learning. Like most academics, I taught as I was taught: lecture, homework, lab exercises. Although content (complacent?) with strong teaching evaluations and enjoyment for teaching, I increasingly found myself asking, "What do I really know about teaching?" I was energized to discover research on learning that I never knew existed. I became aware of the contrasting teacher-centered and learner-centered approaches to course design and pedagogy, and I realized that my *people-centered* passion as a teacher was better served by further shifting my attention from being a better teacher to helping my students become better learners. Growing curiosity about learning and passion for students led me to a second career in faculty development and a shift of my academic home from geology to learning sciences and human resource development.

In light of Dana's motto, my career tracks my transformative learning as a teacher. From seeing my ceaseless learning as a teacher evolve from being about learning the content, to learning the students, to learning how to teach diverse students to activate their learning. Along the way, my values and self-concept also transformed.

Ultimately, our actions are based on our values. My passion and vocation as a teacher are rooted in two values that are founded in life experiences that range from childhood to ongoing transformative insight: *hard work* and *respect and caring for others*.

The first value that guides my approach to teaching is the importance of work, and by extension, learning requires hard work by the learner, not rote memorization of what one is told. This value is rooted in my strong work ethic that evolved from watching older family and community members. I grew up in a nearly all-White, dominantly Protestant, middle-class suburban community, and in a family of mostly German heritage on both sides. "Work ethic" was promoted constantly and attention to household chores and homework before (and commonly at the exclusion of) play was a part of growing up. I grew up immersed in the Anglo-Saxon mantra that America is a land of busy people who stress disciplined, productive activity as a worthy end in itself and that hard work is rewarded by advancement and success (Wlodkowski & Ginsberg, 2003).

Hard work is also part of my experience as a learner. I learned more, and retained that knowledge, from the teachers who expected more from me than I at first thought I could give. I learned the most when I went beyond what was expected to ask additional questions and seek those answers through my own research or closer work with teachers. I was a self-directed learner at an early age, designing inquiries driven by my own curiosity and researching solutions that led to me being welcomed into conversations with university faculty while I was in high school. That initiative and the opportunities that they provided frame much of my thinking about the learning process. However, I continually remind myself that the circumstances and experiences that frame my value for hard, self-regulated, self-directed work at learning are not shared by many of the students who sit in my classes. Nonetheless, I believe that I must push students to think and reason deeply about the topics of the courses that they complete and to think more about their own thinking along the way.

Therefore, I set high but realistic expectations in my classes, discuss these expected outcomes with students, explain the purpose for every assignment, and provide time, assistance, and encouragement to help students reach their potential. I use value-expectancy strategies to motivate attainment of the course objectives. Early in the semester the students write about the stated course outcomes that are of greatest interest to them (value) and to advocate for additional outcomes. I sometimes ask students to write briefly and reflectively about their attitude toward learning in the course and how they and I can adjust to maintain positive focus (expectancy) on achieving mutually desired objectives. Example prompts include: What do you think was the most important thing you learned this week and why? What aspect of pursuing mastery of the course outcomes is most challenging for you, and how can you and I work together to improve your confident progress? How is your team functioning, and what can *we* do to improve your learning together?

At the intersection of working hard and being motivated to undertake that work is anticipation that one can succeed. Therefore, I know that building student self-efficacy is a central feature to their successful learning. A teacher cannot build learner self-efficacy from applying knowledge of the course content; building self-efficacy requires knowledge of the learner, and that relates to my second value.

My second value is respect for individuals and their values, experiences, accomplishments, and challenges. This value translates to teaching through acknowledging and validating students' identities, recognizing that each person encounters varying life challenges beyond obtaining a degree, and that new learning takes place in the context of what is already known and how the prior learning happened.

The source of this value is complicated, as implied by recounting my experience in South Africa with my father. The value was inculcated by how I was raised but it did not become a significant part of my intentions and actions until I began teaching as a graduate student. Why the delayed enactment of a personal value? It is one thing to learn about ethical Christian treatment of other people and respect for other cultures and religions, but how can a person really enact such values in a homogeneous community? There were no Hispanic peers in my 408-student graduating high school class; no students of Asian or Middle-Eastern heritage; only nine African Americans. Exchange programs were with schools in Western European countries—the roots of the cultures that already dominated the student body. The vast majority of my social and academic interactions throughout college were still with students like me: White, from families of sufficient means such that work was something done only during the summer for spending money, from schools that offered many privileged opportunities to prepare for college success.

Students choose their peers and, to some extent, their teachers, but teachers do not choose their students, and I have come to realize how that changed my life. When I first started teaching I realized that these are the people to whom I have a responsibility. Some are like me and have led lives like mine; most have lived and are living lives that I cannot easily relate to. If I had chosen the students in my class, they would have been chosen like the friends that I had before then—people like me. Who was sitting in front of me was not my choice, but I had chosen a job that required that I teach them, provide opportunities for them. This choice to guide students to learning along a path to their future success gradually came to supersede my enthusiasm for teaching the subject that I had devoted my intellectual energy to since the age of 12.

The experiences I had, primarily after beginning to teach as a graduate student, account for the different perspectives that my father and I had on the South African street. He and I shared a value. But, I had not really acted on the value of respecting and honoring people unlike me until I lived with them, worked with them, entered their homes, married a woman from a different heritage, and—most importantly—had the opportunity to be teacher, mentor, and coach to students unlike me with so many opportunities to learn from them at the same time.

As a people-centered teacher, I care about my students. I am strongly influenced by the writings of retired history professor Louis Schmier (2015), whose blog focuses on the importance of giving unconditional love to students. Many readers react strongly to Louis's advocacy of love, feeling that holding such a view of students is inappropriate. But, is it really any different than the philosophy of agape, rooted in Judeo-Christian traditions, that focuses on love as an agency for having the courage to grow, with learning being an essential part of personal growth (Anderson & Ventiglia, 2006)?

I understand, starting with my Oregon experiences and honed by 28 years of teaching at UNM and time spent in New Mexico communities, that there are many competing needs for time, energy, and commitment to others that I must honor and endeavor to understand fully, despite not being part of my college years and earlier formative experiences. For instance, I tell students that I admire their dedication to degree attainment while working and raising children and negotiate deadlines with students to respect competing commitments to family, jobs, and communities. Negotiating the learning process with students is a transformative change from the values I maintained when I was a student—an emphasis on the practical value of getting things done, which is likely another mark of my Western European heritage (Wlodkowski & Ginsburg, 2003). Now, I focus on the learning process and affording students opportunity to demonstrate learning within the sometimes inflexible boundaries of their lives.

People-centered teaching requires a commitment to inclusive pedagogy. In hindsight, I now have greater appreciation for the Chicana student who invited me to be her study partner for calculus when I was a college sophomore. I was accustomed to and thrived in a competitive classroom atmosphere that focused on individual achievement. She, on the other hand, was the daughter of immigrant farm workers, accustomed to learning collaboratively with siblings and other family members and, although assimilating the way her college courses were taught, sought the comfort zone of learning with another person. She sought to replicate her experiences of doing homework with all of her siblings assembled at the kitchen table, talking with each other and their mother, who encouraged them while conducting household tasks around them.

I transformed my approach as an educator partly out of a feeling that learning activities should be more authentic of how knowledge is gained and, later, from appreciation of the research on cognition. I also give serious consideration to the cultural roots of learning approaches (Sanchez, 2000). As a result, I appreciate that the adoption of active learning, collaborative learning, individual reflective learning, frequent feedback delivery, and reaching out to demonstrate that I care for students' individual situations improve outcomes for all students while diminishing ethnicity- and gender-correlated achievement gaps (e.g., Haak, HilleRisLambers, Pitre, & Freeman, 2011). I now realize that these differences between my approach to calculus compared to my Chicana classmate is just one reflection of my cultural context for individuated, low-context approaches to learning whereas others follow integrative, high-context approaches (Ibarra, 2001; Ke & Chávez, 2013). I find myself increasingly drawn to learn from and alongside people who are unlike me, to celebrate difference so as to make classrooms feel comfortably inclusive and to make my life richer. Along the way, I find myself not simply willing to accept learning and cultural differences in my classroom, but I increasingly embrace more integrative, high-context approaches to my own learning, interactions with people, and living.

Returning to the thoughts that were inspired by the frequent recollections of the morning in South Africa with my father, I realize that values are not static. My formative experiences as a child were insufficient to account for all aspects of the core values that I have today. I have had transformative experiences as an educator among diverse students that took two critical values—hard work and respectful caring for people—and built them into intentions and actions that would otherwise have been impossible.

REFERENCES

Anderson, D., & Ventiglia, M. (2006). Learning and teaching: Gambling, love, and growth. In D. R. Anderson (Ed.), *Philosophy Americana: Making philosophy at home in American culture* (pp. 167–187). New York, NY: Fordham University Press.

Haak, D. C., HilleRisLambers, J., Pitre, E., & Freeman, S. (2011). Increased structure and active learning reduce the achievement gap in introductory biology. *Science, 332*, 1213–1216.

Ibarra, R. A. (2001). *Beyond affirmative action: Reframing the context of higher education*. Madison, WI: University of Wisconsin Press.

Ke, F., & Chávez, A. F. (2013). *Web-based teaching and learning across culture and age*. New York, NY: Springer.

Mani, A., Mullainathan, S., Shafir, E., & Zhao, J. (2013). Poverty impedes cognitive function. *Science, 341,* 976–980.

Platt, S. (1989). *Respectfully quoted: A dictionary of quotations requested from the Congressional Research Service*. Washington, DC: Library of Congress. Retrieved from http://www.bartleby.com/73/

Sanchez, I. M. (2000). Motivating and maximizing learning in minority classrooms. *New Directions for Community Colleges, 112*, 35–44.

Schmier, L. (2015). *The random thoughts of Louis Schmier.* Retrieved from http://therandomthoughts.edublogs.org/

Wlodkowski, R. J., & Ginsberg, M. B. (2003). *Diversity and motivation: Culturally responsive teaching*. San Francisco, CA: Jossey-Bass.

From Oppression FOR Difference TO Empowering Through Teaching

In this section, faculty authors write about negotiating their identities in contradistinction to dominant culture and finding ways through their teaching to empower students, their cultural intersections, and their individuality.

CHAPTER SIXTEEN

Family AND Geopolitics IN A Culturally Alienated Society

R. A. KASHANIPOUR

Latin American History
Northern Arizona University

> The culturally alienated society as a whole is dependent on the society that oppresses it and whose economic and cultural interests it serves. At the same time, within the alienated society itself, a regime of oppression is imposed upon the masses by the power elites which in certain cases are the same as the external elites and in others are the external transformed by a kind of metastasis into domestic power groups.
>
> —FREIRE, 1970 (PP. 2–3)

> Culture not only mediates history, it shapes it. [Culture is] the primary terrain for realizing the political as an act of social intervention, a space in which politics is pluralized, recognized as contingent, and open to many formations.
>
> —GIROUX & GIROUX, 2004 (P. 95)

The first vivid memory of my childhood came with the beginning of the Iranian hostage crisis when I was five years old. My small family transformed from being seemingly insular and operating on its own terms, to being immersed in local ethnic bigotry, national cultural animosity, and a world of global geopolitics. While my earlier experiences rest in a cloud of conflated people, feelings, and events, the details of that period are vivid. The days were short, the nights cold, and the air in and outside of my household wrought with tension. I remember countless newscasts showing dual angry mobs of Iranian and American protesters. I recall an anxious President Carter coming on national television to recount the perils of American embassy hostages in Tehran. Most of all, however, I recall what matters most to a child—my immediate experiences. I was five years old in the winter of 1979 when I learned that my family was marked as distinct, foreign, Iranian outsiders living in the community.

Late in 1979, my small family suburban home on the outskirts of Houston, Texas, developed into the center of community strife. The front lawn of the home became a site that marked our unwelcome presence in the community. Two noteworthy distinctions came from the months turned into years of that crisis. For one, the dozen or so cypress pine and Texas oak trees that lined our manicured yard were draped in yellow ribbons. The yellow ribbon served as a folk symbol in honor of prisoners. During the hostage crisis, however, the jingoist song, "Tie a Yellow Ribbon Round an Ole Oak Tree," played seemingly nonstop on local airwaves, and yellow ribbons appeared on trees to mark solidarity with the political hostages in opposition to the revolutionary regime in Iran. In our yard, however, the yellow ribbons served as messages of solidarity of our neighbors *against us*, a family of supposed outsiders. Night after night, under the cover of darkness, anonymous neighbors tied massive yellow ribbons around our trees. The first ribbon was a soft satiny cloth that seemed to me to be a beautiful decoration. As a household comprised of a practicing Muslim, my father, and an ethnic Jew who practiced an odd strain of evangelical Christianity, my mother, we never celebrated nor decorated for Christmas, which was highly unusual in suburban Texas. The sudden appearance of a massive yellow ribbon I imagined was some sort of beautiful but odd Christmas ribbon. Ribbon after ribbon after ribbon appeared until there were literally dozens. Under the cover of night, neighbors tied ribbon after ribbon around the trees. Within days, there were literally dozens of ribbons, on each tree—from sturdy old oak to wispy young sapling. Our yard became a yellow-streaked spectacle that not only protested the contention of the Middle East but also our presence in the community. I am not entirely sure why, but my parents never took down the ribbons. Quality soon dissipated. Plastic tape replaced cloth. Florescent and harsh yellow replaced the gentle hues of citrine. I suppose taking down the ribbon would have meant that our family did not support the hostages and, therefore, did support the revolutionary regime, which could not have been further from the truth. By leaving the ribbons, however, our yard served as an obvious public reminder of the distinction of our household in the community.

A second issue marked our home with less decoration. As if the subtlety of seeing dozens of yellow ribbons was not enough, someone with a more obvious sense of messaging blazed the words FUCK YOU! in gasoline across our finely manicured lawn. By the way, in the suburban South of my childhood, lawns are highly praised endeavors. Our neighborhood awarded monthly awards—in the form of a sign erected next to the mailbox—to the best-kept lawn. At five years old, I remember marveling at the massive letters of that FUCK YOU!, each one longer than I was tall. I could not read the words, but I knew the message was not friendly. My father, embarrassed by this and all forms of profanity, resodded the grass by carefully replacing the poisoned letters and toxic soil with new plants and earth, and the words mysteriously appeared again. After a second resodding, the words yet again appeared. It was never clear to me whether a malicious and determined neighbor vandalized the yard repeatedly or whether the damage was so deep that the words just reappeared. I must have been eight before the last vestiges of the scorched letters finally gave way to green leaves of grass. In any case, the symbolism was profound—the substrate of the community poisoned by bigotry and hatred—and the message was clear—cultural difference could be toxic.

I awakened to the world around me to find cruelty, hatred, and animosity displayed outside my home. The neighborhood portrait of my family, the front yard, was marked as unwelcome, foreign, and other. Friends, classmates, and neighbors over the years prescribed similar foreignness to me. In fact, an early and durable nickname reaffirmed my otherness. In the 1980s, the name *Ryan* was popular enough that there was another in my first-grade class. The other children labeled me *Ryan-the-Iranian*, seemingly to avoid confusion. This name endured and followed me through high school, but it became a part of the broad mix of monikers affixed to me.

Unlike in the outside world, I found few such sharp edges within my household. While we were defined as generically foreign, specifically Iranian—the self-described enemies of the United States—our family embodied the great diversity that is only possible in the United States. Present in my small nuclear family were seemingly massive ethnic and religious divisions. My Persian father was a practicing Shi'a Muslim and my German Jewish mother a devout evangelical Christian. Between my parents, there were five languages in my household: Farsi, Arabic, German, Yiddish, and English, the last being the only common tongue. In oddly accented English, my parents taught myself and two siblings patriotic songs and told stories of founding fathers. We celebrated summers at the community pool and made periodic voyages to the American Jerusalem of Las Vegas and Disneyworld. We played weekend softball. My mother hosted regular Bible studies, while my father was a regular at the Indian casinos. All of this was the norm of life in suburban America.

My parents were immigrants to the United States and came from strikingly different backgrounds. My father, Hossein, is from a large and old Persian family. In Iran, Kashanipours are a family known for convention and conservatism. We are the people of Kashan, the home of the Persian carpet tradition since the 18th century. The Kashani name is not an old one as Persians did not start using surnames until the early 20th century. Nevertheless, the family is large, established, and prominent. Notable members of the family are not hard to find and include high-ranking members of civil society and the government. Today, Kashanis have carefully navigated national and international controversies to become prominent secular leaders in and outside of Iran. I have more relatives than I can count, most of whom I have never met. My mother, Steffania née Müller, is from less transparent lineage. She was born during the last days of World War II in Poland as a German refugee. While the identity of her father is a mystery, her mother was from a family comprised, in part, of Jews. My great-grandfather and his siblings died anonymously during the war, presumably in camps across the Reichland. These two families—one rooted, prominent, and wealthy, one rootless, anonymous, penniless—came together to forge my own.

Both of my parents immigrated to the United States in the 1950s. My grandmother and mother immigrated to the United States when she was nine years old in 1954. After a two-week journey by ship to New York and a weeklong bus ride to California, they settled in San Francisco where, as my grandmother would say, everything is new and everyone is free. My father came to the United States in 1959, some two decades before the revolutionary fervor of the Islamists seized the country. As the middle son of a wealthy Persian family, his responsibilities were to manage the family wealth and property. He immigrated to the United States for an education so he could, in part, transform the family estates from feudal-style sharecropping endeavors to full-fledged modern farms. He came, in other words, out of duty. He stayed, however, because of independence. My father claims he found the clichéd land of opportunity, by which means opportunity came to be whatever he desired.

My childhood outside of my household began as I witnessed the importance of ethnicity, culture, and history in everyday life. I believe those moments helped instill a sense of distinction and difference within my attitude and perspective, issues that were reinforced by the overall structure of my family itself. I learned at that young age that culture, ethnicity, and politics were intertwined relationships of power—all of which were subject to change. Emblazed across my yard, I saw that representations of power served to create divisions, all of which were based on little more than transient, naïve perceptions. Most likely because of my immature ignorance of their significance at my age, I embraced the distinction of those yellow ribbons. The threats fell flat on my childish perception. I found that they marked my family as outside the mainstream, sentiments that greatly appealed to me. What I experienced at that early age was what Paulo Freire (1970) described as the "culturally alienated society" that persecuted a family perceived to threaten local cohesion and uniformity. In isolating our family, those who tied ribbons and defaced our lawn created distinctions where there were none. Within the Persian community of Houston, my father was among the first to stand against the Revolution because it celebrated nationalism and religion, a toxic mix, above all else. This was obviously an irrelevant nuance that was lost in the ignorance of our neighborhood community.

The importance of ethnicity, culture, and history was constantly reinforced within my family household. My heritage—as Persian and as Jewish—was a marker of pride. They framed my life. To be Persian, as my father would say *ad naseum*, is to be a member of "the oldest civilization on earth." Persian-ness was framed as an identity that celebrated the past as lived experience. Alongside accented stories of great Americans, I learned ancient tales of my great fictive kinsmen. Darius's and Xerxes's exploits of empire mingled with my *Pedar Bazork's* (Grandfather's) gifts of gold. To be Iranian was to be a short-sighted modern nationalist in the model of the Revolutionaries or the Shah's supporters. To be Persian was to be tied to ancient traditions that valued family, convention, and conservatism. Kashanipours are Persians and we did not mind a few yellow ribbons because we are part of ancient traditions. My Jewish ancestry served as a remarkable contrast to my Persianness. While the past as lived experience transcends Jewish culture, our connections had been severed by the cruelty of humanity. Conversations of my maternal family rarely extended beyond the savageness of the 20th century. Those yellow ribbons, like so many other markers of otherness, harkened back to past markers of distinction. From my mother, I learned to embody distinction as a means of survival. From the internal structure of my family, I learned more practical matters about distinction. Muslims and Jews, we know from popular depictions, cannot coexist. However, in my household, a practicing Muslim and an ethnic Jew who practiced Christianity created a tightknit family that celebrated our differences. In the day-to-day relations of my family, I witnessed that individuals forge relationships regardless of supposed boundaries. I learned of the malleability of culture and that distinction was always made. In this vein, I always experienced identity as fluid and subject to change. To outsiders, my parents could not have been from more distinct traditions, which in many ways was true. Nevertheless, their lived experiences involved forging and maintaining relations at an individual level. They were not a married Muslim and Christian-née-Jew as outsiders stressed, but a husband and wife, father and mother. Likewise, I was not simply Ryan-the-Iranian, but a Persian kid living in America.

From these experiences I can see three expressions in my research and teaching as a historian. First, I stress that history is a product of the intersection of power, perception, and experience, which are central to Freire's theory of critical pedagogy. The past exists not as a value in itself, but as a direct extension of structures of meaning as they related to institutions of power. In other words, while economic, political, and social forces create contexts of the world over time, cultural perspectives and understandings frame individual experiences. As such, I believe it to be vital for students to reflect on the particulars of their own conditions to identify the relations of authority and power that shape their world. For instance, in many of my courses I require students to collect and reflect on the presence of issues raised in the class as they appear in the world around them and shape their perceptions. In a course on modern history, one such assignment starts with a long scavenger hunt for local items from Latin America, which, as students discover, are often hidden in plain sight in the community. The assignment ends by asking students to reflect on how these items reflect the economic and social position of Latinos in their community, who are also often hiding in plain sight.

Second, borrowing from Henry and Susan Searls Giroux, I believe that culture and identity, like history, are malleable. Individuals are always immersed in distinct and varied social groups. While the groups may display hard demarcations, the individuals within them do not as they live across social boundaries. Everyone holds multiple, rather fluid identities simultaneously. One can be both in a position of prestige and authority in a professional setting and the subject of discrimination and suspicion in the social sphere. For instance, the Black Lives Matter movement that emerged in 2015 protests excessive police violence and the targeting of young African Americans. Likewise, family groups and ethnic communities frame perceptions, but individuals constantly exist as arbiters and mediators of different traditions. As individuals wrestle with beliefs and practices, they borrow widely from their unique and distinctive backgrounds. In this way, culture is constantly re-created to meet individual experiences and needs. Third, alienation and oppression can come in various forms. The process of creating one group can come as a process of perpetrating violence on another. Violence comes in a variety of forms, not all of which involve physical aggression. Symbols, in fact, can carry historically significant meanings for individuals. In less abstract terms, I believe those early experiences taught me to value the individual distinctions of everyone, to recognize that divisions are often products of broader social and political forces, and celebrate those who stand in opposition to injustice of the dominant norm, which is what I try to impart to my students.

I take great pride in my teaching and constantly try to find new ways to connect students to the world around them. My aim in teaching is multifaceted. First, I seek to push students to confront stereotypes, inequities, and obfuscations in the contemporary world by exploring their historical roots. As a Latin Americanist interested in cooperative ethnic interactions, my courses often examine underrepresented histories of social exchange and collaboration alongside more conventional narratives of conflict and division. As such, I encourage students to challenge common perceptions and popular approaches. In one recent course on the U.S.-Mexico borderlands, for instance, my students examined the development of bi-national, conjoined towns divided by the border. While the overwhelming public discourse about the contemporary border stresses violence, upheaval, and disorder, my students and I explored the deeper history of collaboration in the borderlands. Second, I encourage students to move beyond their everyday world to critically examine the past. The focus here is teaching historical content by stressing interpretation rather than simple retention. My students, for instance, only write comprehensive, essay-based exams because I value that knowledge is both cumulative and analytical. In these essay-based exams, students must marshal and organize information to produce conclusions. The emphasis here is not on information—dates, people, or events—but rather on production of knowledge through interpretation. Finally, I teach the methodology of history as a method of skeptical analysis. History, therefore, serves as the mechanism to train students to learn to question, research, and interpret complex processes. My approach is inspired by the pedagogy of secular humanism, or what Freire described as critical pedagogy. Obviously, while most of my students will not become professional historians, I hope that they will become constructive citizens with knowledge of the past and tools to build a humane and equitable society.

REFERENCES

Freire, P. (1970). *Cultural action for freedom.* Cambridge, MA: Harvard Educational Review.

Giroux, H., & Giroux, S. S. (2004). *Take back higher education: Race, youth and the crisis of democracy in the post–civil rights era.* New York, NY: Palgrave-Macmillan.

CHAPTER SEVENTEEN

Being Multicultural Is Not a Luxury

A Strategy for Teaching and Learning in a Racist Society

RICARDO GUTHRIE

Ethnic Studies
Northern Arizona University

"BLACK HISTORY IS MY HISTORY..."

The experience of growing up Afro-Latino in the 1960s reminds me that being multicultural is not a luxury—even today, in the "twenty-tens" and the post–Civil Rights era of inclusion, diversity, and equity. In the classroom, as in the larger society, however, the racial and cultural dynamics of exclusion and division remain. Students, faculty, and staff still use simplistic racial dichotomies to instruct and mentor learners; too often, students are urged to ignore their racial and cultural heritages to support a fictive, colorblind environment in which everyone is supposedly equal. However, when I was growing up, I learned the value of celebrating dual heritages of being Black and Latino, as demonstrated in the following dialogue between my mother and me.

I was a 20-something graduate student, visiting my parents in San Diego, California, for Christmas break in the mid-1980s. I was fastening a button featuring the image of Harriet Tubman, outlined by the slogan "Black History Is My History" on my denim jacket, and stepped into the kitchen to cook breakfast. My mother, who was watching television, scanned my jacket and scoffed: "You have another history, from Guatemala, you know?" I began to respond that "Black history is everyone's history," but I paused, considering my mother's comment—she had migrated from Guatemala in the early 1950s and had married my father, raised five African American kids in Biloxi, Mississippi, during the Jim Crow era, before the family moved to San Diego in 1960. Black history was *her* history, too, but her point was that Latino history was important to her—personally and politically.

She was proud of being Guatemalan and carried a green card for nearly 50 years before finally applying for U.S. citizenship in the 1990s. She was quick to regale us with tales of Guatemala and Belize, where she had grown up and attended Catholic School—St. Catherine's—during the 1940s. She was an ardent critic of American imperialism in the region, having worked on banana plantations and shared many stories about land reform under progressive Guatemalan presidents who had, nevertheless, been removed from office by U.S. CIA operatives.

Yes, there was another history that had to be told—a family history stretching back to the Afro-Latino Caribbean coast of Guatemala and Central America; of Puerto Barrios—my mother's hometown; of "Caribs" (dark-skinned natives who reflected trigeño heritages of Indigenous peoples, Africans and Spaniards); of U.S. invasions and corruption, greed, violence, and class warfare among Ladino elites; of migrations to El Norte by my mother and countless others who sought education and better fortunes in America. But it was a missing history, for my mother was largely silent about her family, and the push-pull factors that led her to upstate New York, to go to nursing school, to marry a Black American, and to, ultimately, give up hope of ever returning home to Guatemala.

It was an ironic comment by my mother—"You have another history…"—since she was so reticent to talk about it. My father understood but said she would tell us more, on her own terms, in her own way, over time. And surely she did: describing how bananas, mango, and platanos in her country tasted better! How Americans were delusional about foreign countries and their place in the world. And how she learned about life from her Mayan grandmother, her Boston-born father who worked for the United Fruit Company, about struggles in St. Catherine's and the Catholic convent in Belize, about Esquipuljas—the patron saint who was Black ("You Americans are so fixated on race!") and who could perform miracles for those who believed. And about the need to ignore racism while proclaiming pride in yourself and your cultural heritage.

These were the home values, stories, and ideals imparted by my mother as I was growing up; I contrasted these stories with those of my father and his cousins. Since we lived in African American communities under segregation—even during the Civil Rights era in San Diego of the 1960s and 1970s—I grew up Black. Being *diverse* was not an option; we didn't have the experience of being called *multicultural*; you were either *White* or not-*White*. This lumped all Asians, Mexicans, Jews, Africans, Arabs, West Indians, and Afro-Americans into one category—we might not all agree to be *Black*, but each of us knew that we were not *White*, and that our cultural values were not always welcomed by the dominant society. It was a hard lesson to learn, but ultimately I understood that being *Other* united me with more people who shared dual heritages in settings that were often hostile, intolerant, and unforgiving. The experience of growing up Black and Latino reminded me that being multicultural is not a luxury.

The two ethnographic poems that follow articulate the erstwhile "gamble" involved in celebrating dual heritages—as exemplified by my mother and my father.

KEY VALUES AND CHARACTERISTICS THAT INFLUENCE MY TEACHING

Growing up understanding my dual heritages has caused me to value the strength of different ways of thinking and feeling in a White-dominant, racially stratified society. These are the ways of thinking and feeling that students can bring to the classroom—that people embody different means of comprehending the world, and that their personal histories exceed simplistic stories or ways of learning. In my case, my mother reminded me that the history of her home country has a direct effect on my identity, on how I was raised, and on how I might use that history to navigate, instruct, and inspire others in the classroom and in daily life.

So, a key value from my personal history is that I learned I am a citizen of the world, as well as a citizen of America; the characteristic that follows is that we all have multiple identities and resulting consciousnesses that influence what we know and how we learn.

In the classroom, I provide exercises for students to evaluate modes of expressing themselves, and how their knowledge compares with others. I teach film and media analysis, as well as the history and politics of race, ethnicity, and culture. When viewing films, I have students work in small groups to examine two or more elements of film: literary design, visual design, cinematography, editing and montage of scenes, and sound design. Collectively, students evaluate film elements and then discuss agreements and different ways of explaining particular scenes or the film overall. The groups report back to the larger class, share their perceptual analyses, and then the class as a whole compares and contrasts how the elements work together. In this way, a student who had direct experience working with Navajo communities could share her perspective on the images and ideas reflective of her culture—compared to others who had little or no interaction with Indigenous people before. Others, who were asked if they could identify with certain characters of different races and ethnicities, could see how similar or different their lives really were. As a final project I ask students to portray their own lives and views through the experiences of fictive characters in a variety of films screened in class. Men can identify with women; Whites can reflect on Asian or African American lives, and so forth. The unifying themes emerge in auto-ethnographic narratives coinciding with racial and ethnic characters from *Real Women Have Curves*, *Dragon: The Bruce Lee Story*, *Akeelah and the Bee*, and *Smoke Signals*, for example.

This approach demonstrates how Vygotsky's zone of proximal development (ZPD) works in the classroom: Under my guidance, students can learn more together than they would have been able to learn on their own, as they apply different levels of analysis to answer a similar set of questions or concerns. It is often uncomfortable, because few students have been trained to analyze films or culture in several dimensions, and few are encouraged to offer more than an individualistic assessment that might run counter to dominant ways of knowing and experiencing film/culture. Second, there are few incentives to abandon competition for grades; thus, it is important that I, as the instructor, provide safe environments and support for students to cooperate, collaborate, and to express vulnerabilities in completing their work.

These exercises are microcosms of the larger society, in which the *many streams* of consciousness experienced by people of color are often submerged beneath a presumptive *mainstream* of White American culture. These exercises—and the history and culture offered through my film courses such as Race, Identity and Film, Immigrants and Alien Others on Film, and Black Cinema—reflect the values I learned while growing up Afro-Latino. I seek harmonious resolution of tensions between dominant and subordinate experiences, and in so doing, provide learning contexts that challenge monochromatic ways of understanding. These exercises highlight a multiplicity of experiences shared within a presumptive collective.

Try this exercise: View a scene from *Dragon: The Bruce Lee Story* in which Bruce and his date, Linda, go to see a movie, *Breakfast at Tiffany's,* starring Audrey Hepburn. Bruce and Linda settle in and watch as Mickey Rooney, an Irish American actor, plays a Japanese caricature in "yellow face," with buck teeth, broken English, and slapstick, comic mannerisms. Bruce is clearly upset, but Linda giggles and laughs along with the rest of the theater audience, until she looks over at Bruce and notices that he isn't laughing. The camera pans from her face to Bruce, and back, while her whole demeanor changes. She returns her gaze to the movie screen and sees—for the first time—that the yellow-face caricature played by a White actor is demeaning. I ask students to review the scene based on two filmic elements, and then explain how the filmmaker exposes Linda's epiphany about the harmful effect of racial stereotyping. I ask them to explain what happens when Linda learns to see the world through Bruce's eyes; how do cinematic elements show viewers that the visual culture of race and racial exclusion within American society often enforces cognitive dissonance for non-White *Others*, while reinforcing White dominance and superiority? At the end of the scene, how do we comprehend that Linda *knows* what Bruce Lee *knows*—even though he is not Japanese, he is not amused by Rooney's portrayal of the alien Other?

By the end of the film, Linda marries Bruce, over her mother's objections, and becomes a proponent of Chinese-American culture, martial arts, and interracial community (even against the challenges of Chinese elders who condemn Bruce for teaching Kung Fu to *gwailo*/Americans). I ask the students how her identity changes—does she acquire the same dual consciousness as Bruce Lee? Is she still

White in her consciousness and identity? How are we, the viewing audience, replicated on screen and in society? Are we dominant or oppositional viewers who are able to shift perceptions and privilege, armed with the new consciousness embodied by Linda and Bruce? What happens when the film ends and we return to daily life?

"NOT ONE OF US KNOWS AS MUCH AS ALL OF US"

My teaching philosophy—in these assignments, and in each of my classes—focuses on the needs and interests of students, and developing collaborative learning that builds upon shared responsibilities between students and the instructor. My teaching is based on the belief that students and instructors working together create the most conducive learning environment. I believe that "Not one of us knows as much as all of us together," and I employ group practices to extend each student's learning capacity. For example, in most class environments students typically learn how to speak up and to write responses to questions and lesson plans, but other modes of interaction are rarely emphasized, such as listening, using art or music, performance and play, or using expressive culture in small groups. By contrast, in my classes, students are encouraged to model different ways of learning, and to teach others what they have learned—sometimes in front of the classroom, but more often in homework assignments and group work outside of the classroom.

I encourage dynamic learning that emphasizes contributions from everyone in the class. These collaborations are developed in addition to individual achievement and active engagement of each student—they are not intended to replace individual achievement but to augment and highlight the benefits of group engagement. I discourage rote memorization or ritualized regurgitation of preapproved answers to test questions. I believe that the ZPD can be enhanced by expert facilitation of the instructor (myself) who is attuned to the individual and collective needs, strengths, and relative abilities of students in the classroom. I also believe that students on predominantly White campuses need and deserve quality engagement and instruction in analyzing race, class, and gender diversity in today's increasingly multicultural society.

Throughout my teaching career, I have encouraged students to develop a multimodal approach to learning: they are expected to come to class having read the material; to take notes from the lectures; to engage the concepts by conversing and asking questions during class; to present the material to other students; and to undergo exams or quizzes that allow them to measure what they have learned. In this way, students from different disciplines and backgrounds might learn the structure, purpose, and philosophy of Ethnic Studies as a coherent field of analysis. We emphasize the history and cultures of racial and ethnic minorities in America, while elevating the knowledge practices of these groups.

The experience is not always easy. For example, when analyzing the film *Pow Wow Highway,* one student derided the film depiction of uranium poisoning on a Cheyenne reservation—suggesting that uranium occurs naturally in some areas, and that many Native Americans have a choice in how they decide to use the land. She based her assessment on individual research she conducted as part of a national research team. In her online remarks, she reiterated her views, which most of the students in the class vehemently disagreed with. They said she was generalizing and blaming the victim in her remarks. I provided students room to debate the issues and discovered that the class was polarized. During the debate, students fell back on their own experiences, which highlighted divisions among dominant to subordinate learners. I reminded everyone that the greatest opportunity for learning occurs when divergent views are shared, and information evaluated within social, cultural, and political contexts. Moving beyond opinion to embrace critical analyses for selected issues, I asked each student to consider more than one way to analyze the depiction—not just pro and con, but to evaluate the film along several dimensions. Although the individual student's assessment of the effect of uranium mining on Native Americans was inaccurate (because she generalized from one research site and anthropological analysis to the Cheyenne nation, and the film depiction), she insisted that her research experience qualified her to offer an expert opinion. The overall discussion was fruitful, however, because it provided an object lesson for others who were reticent to raise their own analyses, for fear of being insensitive or intolerant. I told the student that her views were inconsistent with the experience of the Cheyenne people, and that it was important to contextualize her knowledge and experience while offering analyses.

It is clear, in this example, that sometimes students are not willing to give up or change their perspective—based on their own experiences—but they have the opportunity to begin a lifelong commitment to learning beyond their individual experiences, and to value subordinate or subjugated knowledge practices that inform a multicultural society.

In another class, we debated the use of reclaimed water on the Sacred Peaks near Flagstaff and asked students to evaluate perspectives of several different groups affected by the decision: Native Americans, tourists, city residents, federal agencies, businesses, and university members. Again, as in the earlier debate, a small segment of students felt the discussion was *biased* against White experts, and that Indigenous rights had to be balanced against the needs and rights of tourists, businesses, and the federal government. They felt that films and websites were skewed against opponents of Navajo and Indigenous tribes, that fair debate was impossible, and that an equitable solution was unavailable. I noted that the purpose of the exercise was to raise consciousness about the problems of development on sacred sites—even as everyone agreed that such sites should be protected. I also emphasized that competing interests and tensions remain unresolved in the real world, even as we strive to do the right thing. Finally, students were instructed to apply the strategic analyses from the Sacred Peaks exercise to other examples: the siting of professional sports teams and stadiums, the use of public dollars for infrastructure and educational facilities, medical centers, housing, and prisons—to see if there were other sacred sites that extended beyond Indigenous vs. White rights. In this way, I demonstrated that race, ethnicity, and culture affect many of the rights-based decisions we make every day. In other words, to comprehend Indigenous ways of knowing can provide insights into other realms of society that we might not immediately view as *sacred*.

CONCLUSION: TRADING TRADITION FOR COLLECTIVE HISTORY

These personal experiences—in the classroom and in our lives—allow people to learn to tell their history while building a ZPD that strengthens learning for everyone. I have since discovered research that the ZPD approach works well for non-traditional learners, but I've also found that it seems to threaten others who cherish individualism, or who are uncomfortable being a White minority in multicultural classrooms. I adapt lesson plans and learning opportunities to allow growth and expression, but I do not believe that individualistic learning benefits those who need more support and engagement in public schools. Those who cannot afford a residential college experience, for instance, will be pushed to take online education that may earn them a degree and some of the lessons/learning from academic disciplines, but they will miss out on the lived, interactive experience that makes a ZPD, and culturally based instruction, so compelling—and so essential—for today's society. And for me, that story is the most difficult one of all to accept.

For these reasons, cultural approaches to teaching and learning are fraught with difficulty—both for those who need it and for those who don't know they need it—but it's a valuable method for increasing learning for all. Based on the lessons from my mother and father, I've learned to embrace nontraditional ways of knowing and acting, and for creating space for others to explore for themselves how their culture informs and validates our collective existence.

ETHNOGRAPHIC POETRY FROM MY CULTURAL BACKGROUND

Hot & Cold Blues (dedicated to my father, Robert V. Guthrie)

My paintings and collage demonstrate poetry as ethnography: How collective memory reflects social, political and cultural dimensions of growing up Black in Jim Crow America.

The artwork below references a photo of my father playing the saxophone in the backyard of his Kentucky home in 1947. As an African American teenager growing up in the South during segregation, he lived under a system that questioned his humanity. *Hot & Cold Blues* describes how my father, Dr. Robert V. Guthrie, and many other African Americans focused on art, music and culture to overcome social conditions which might have hindered them.

Indian Gaming (dedicated to my mother, Elodia Sánchez Sexton)
She was the one
who
left her home, her country,
her way of life
to go to school in the U.S.
of A.
—upstate New York, Cornell, must have seemed the furthest corner
of the frigid earth
from the tropical jungles of her
native
Guatemala.

She was the one
dating and dancing with
my then–Air Force staff sergeant
father
at Sampson Air Force Base—
eventually marrying and moving
to the deep South, Mississippi.
Learning to speak English fluently wasn't the only obstacle
she tackled: raising five Negro children in a 1950s colored neighborhood without benefit
of Spanish-speaking friends wasn't
impossible (she said)
but somehow all things seem easier once they're over and done with,
huh mom?

She was the one,
pregnant, but still responsible for seeing to our
needs on the trek to San Diego in 1960—getting resettled in the wild-wild-West,
years before being Black
or Latino
was
fashionable.

She was the one
who
took us to school
then challenged teachers and principals
to explain what the hell they meant when they said
we weren't cooperative, didn't fit in, or were "too vocal" in the classroom.

She was the one
who held onto her green card for 50 years
(she said she'd always be Guatemalan), even though, to my mind, she was more "American"
than any one of us
born
here.

She was the one
who helped raise her first grandchild
when my sister separated and then divorced,
and had trouble providing for herself and
the baby.

She was the one
who raised us all, while my father went off to work.
She cooked and cleaned, shopped, shared her dreams, nursed our wounds, rocked us to sleep, beat us when we were bad—and sometimes when we weren't—let us stay up late to watch "Saturday Night at the Movies," or came down the stairs swinging a belt for playing "Monopoly" at 3 a.m., laughed and cried with us through happy and sad times, and never failed to remind us of who we were and what we were
supposed to do
with our lives.

She was the one
who
always had a story to tell
about how she survived Catholic School in Belize,
how she worked the banana fields for the United Fruit Company, before they stole her country and
plunged it into chaos and bloody terror—but she never talked
about the family she left
behind.

She was the one
who,
when we were all grown,
spent her time at the race
track
betting on the horses
(and winning too!),
and now, finds excitement
in "Indian Gaming" at Viejas
or Barona
twice a week—becoming such a
"regular" that the dealers know her by name.

She was the one
who,
I should have realized long ago,
had always
been
a gambler.
—ricardo guthrie

CHAPTER EIGHTEEN

Rage, Courage, Encourage

Citizenship in the College Classroom

T. MARK MONTOYA

Ethnic Studies
Northern Arizona University

A CRITICAL INVENTORY

Who cares about my teaching story? Aren't autobiographies of unknowns, like myself, narcissistic? Even a *well-known* voice has shared similar concerns. Cornel West (1999) writes, "I have great suspicion of autobiographical writing. So much of it reeks of self-indulgence and self-absorption, yet any serious engagement with the world includes a questioning of one's self" (p. 1). West's words resonate. He continues, "A wholesale critical inventory of ourselves and our communities of struggle is neither self-indulgent autobiography nor self-righteous reminiscence" (p. 3). Accordingly, I think of this essay not as an autobiography, but instead as a critical inventory of self *and* of community—one that highlights my cultural ambiguities and their connections to teaching and learning. In another reaffirmation, Victor Villanueva Jr. (1993) maintains:

> But I can't just say nothing about how it is I come to know some things ... and how I come to think the ways I do about racism and ethnocentricity and the class system ... I can't just say nothing. But there's Mami and the Latino ways: private things should remain private. So, play out the tension. (p. xi)

The tension is here. I am not a narcissist, but I play one in the classroom.

The first part of my title is a play on the word *rage*. To write this critical inventory, I first had to make clear that its meaning was not solely based on anger or violence. It is not. Rage is also about passion. My idea is that rage will lead to courage, and having courage allows me to encourage; thus, I create some sort of messy teaching and learning sequence. Inherent in the sequence are a number of assumptions. Most important is that rage, courage, and encourage are *not* neutral concepts. Instead, as indicated in the second part of my title, they involve respect, well-being, dignity, empowerment, democracy, justice, and particularly belonging. There is something significant about what it means to politically, culturally, and socially belong—citizenship; and for most people belonging is often articulated through the complexities of everyday experiences. Here is where I get from rage to encourage, with a little bit of courage in between.

RAGE

A Personal Desire to Learn

It takes a great deal of rage to have courage, and it takes even more courage to encourage. How do I encourage in the classroom? I start with personal narratives. Because I teach Ethnic Studies and because I variously identify as Latino, Chicano, Hispano, Mestizo, New Mexican, and borderlander, my stories are infused with culture. While I have not thought too much about my culture and its relationship to teaching and learning, my culture is always there. I cannot and will not separate it from who I am. In the classroom, I am a storyteller. I did not always think of storytelling as a pedagogical tool; I just know that I usually remembered the stories my college professors shared. Furthermore, the stories of everyday folk intrigue me.

In Nasario García's *Old Las Vegas* (2005), one of the viejitos (old-timers) describes his brief and ultimately unpleasant educational experience. Recounting his schooling, the viejito states:

> I only attended school till I was in the third grade. You were required to go to school. And what little I did learn, I learned speaking with the Anglos. I know how to solve math problems, I know who to write in English and in Spanish, but I believe what I know is simply because of personal desire to learn. (pp. 80–81)

The viejito continues with a diatribe about being bullied, about absent and absent-minded teachers, and about mischief in the classroom. That the viejito's focuses are on the negative aspects of his short-lived formal education illustrates the immeasurable disconnect between culture and learning, particularly in "Hispanic" rural Northern New Mexico of the early 1920s. García writes, "Hispano children went from a cultural environment uniquely their own to an educational setting that was, at best, alien" (p. 76). In spite of, or maybe because of, this disconnect, I too share the viejito's "personal desire to learn." I also share more with the viejito.

The viejito was my paternal grandfather Arsenio Montoya Sr.—"Grampo Archie" to his grandchildren. He died at the age of 86, the year *Old Las Vegas* was published. His 43 grandchildren have all taken different paths. My path was and continues to be higher education; and because of stories like my Grampo's, I remain keenly aware of a continual disconnect that many of my students have between culture and learning—a disconnect that I can only hope I am helping them challenge, confront, and overcome. For this reason I share the story of Grampo Archie with my classes.

Unlike Grampo, my memories of school are fond. Except for what I would consider typical instances of awkwardness and one instance of bullying, I can say that I enjoyed my formal K–12 education. I do have, however, a semi-repressed memory of some snot-nosed kid with dirty ears telling *me* that I had to be an American to be the president of the United States. How dare he! I mean, he was a dirty kid. However, my brown, unlike his, did not wash off. My classes know this story, too, and are able to connect conceptions of citizenship to race and ethnicity.

I especially have fond memories of my second-grade teacher. My tangible memory is my report card. I have kept all my report cards. There are so many stories in them. I have filed them in right after the seemingly never-ending folders labeled "Financial Aid." There are many more stories here. In the report card's "1st Progress Report" my teacher wrote, "Mark's work is improving but he still needs to work at a faster pace. He daydreams quite a lot."

Thank you, Mrs. Hutchins. I still work at a slow pace, I would say deliberate, and I still daydream quite a lot.

Who are you? How do you identify? Where do you come from? Where do you want to go? Take some time to think about it. Be deliberate. Daydream! This is how I encourage my classes. Once we have established these parameters, students are more apt to share their stories and henceforth become more capable of recounting their personal narratives through the lens of Ethnic Studies. They see how learning through culture is a process and not an outcome. I teach how I best learned, and I best learned through my own experiences and daydreams. Perhaps I was daydreaming about *my* path in life.

MY PATH WAS A BRIDGE

When I started in college, I enrolled in an Honors English course. In this class, with 15 or so other first-year students, the instructor gave us the opportunity to choose our final research project on day one—a project we would work on as the class progressed. When the instructor asked me what I was interested in, I said, "identity and culture?" In hindsight, my politics were emerging with my answer. She said, "I have a book for you, it's *This Bridge Called My Back*" (Moraga & Anzaldúa, 1981). Although I do not make my students choose their final projects on the first day, I do give book recommendations. I probably over-share with my classes all that has influenced me. In fact, I do not even own a copy of the book, because I lent it to a student years ago. I hope it is making its rounds.

Teaching and learning are cyclical, communal, and collective. My college learning process, which thankfully was not a linear one, started with feminism, but not any kind of feminism; it was radical women of color feminism. Thanks to the subtitle, *Writings by Radical Women of Color*, this was the only way I could describe it. I read the book, out of order, but cover to cover, because the contributors were speaking to me; they were teaching me. I learned about gender, sexualities, race, racism, and so forth, but with a much deeper meaning than I ever imagined—complex stories and essays for a first-year college student. I daydream about what my path would be today had I said "music and art," but I said "identity and culture."

Throughout the rest of my undergraduate career, I did my best to take as many classes as I could that I deemed as dealing with "identity and culture." I sought out Ethnic Studies types of courses. I did the same with my graduate career, whereupon I was introduced to the Zapatistas, to the U.S.-Mexico Borderlands, and to social movements literature, all of which were often interpreted through the lens of cultural politics. When I read a communiqué from the Zapatistas, one ended with these words: "We need not conquer the world, it's enough to make the world new. We. Today" (EZLN, 1996). I need to learn more, I thought. I need to figure this out. It sounded like the Chicana feminism.

Even now, in my Introduction to Chicana/o Studies class, I start with Chicana feminism. I start with the critique. I start in the middle, and comparing to other Intro syllabuses and texts, I start at the end. Again, I do this by sharing these stories. My learning was not linear. Our lives are not linear, and our classrooms should not be linear. In lives and in our classrooms we have glimpses of opportunities and challenges to see what we will make of them.

COURAGE

Crossing Borders

Today, I have the sacred opportunity to teach—to ask students what they are interested in, and to connect their cultural experiences to their learning. Do you change the system from within, do you become the system, or is the system the problem? In my current research, the "problem" is borders. The "solutions" are challenging the citizenship regime and crossing borders. This takes courage. A larger question is, How do I connect with students who have similar and different cultural frames and values?

I do this by talking about borders. Whether they know it or not, students are constantly crossing borders, and crossing borders is not easy. Nothing about borders is easy. I do not say this because this is my field, but the U.S.-Mexico Borderlands are not easy. In fact, it is a complex and a difficult area to study. My political life is about crossing borders. The same is true for my teaching life. I cannot separate the two, nor do I think they should be. While my scholarly research focuses on alternative citizenships in the U.S.-Mexico Borderlands, my primary focus at the university is teaching, and in particular teaching first-generation, Latina/o, working-class students like myself.

Why? Because Latina/os are the fastest growing ethnic subpopulation in the United States and they comprise more than 15% of the total population—almost 46 million people. Of those 46 million, only 11% are in college, and of that 11%, only 12% will graduate with a college degree (Alonso-Zaldivar & Tompson, 2010). This underrepresentation is shameful, and underrepresentation via push-out is wrong.

Why? Because often unmentioned in all of this is humiliation. "Higher education," writes Laura I. Rendón (1992), "often requires not only that [Latina/o] students be humble but that they tolerate humiliation" (p. 61). Rendón continues, "To become academic success stories we must endure humiliation, reject our old values and traditions, mistrust our experience, and disconnect with our past. Ironically, the academy preaches freedom of thought and expression but demands submission and loyalty" (p. 62). That getting a degree requires humiliation is heartbreaking, and I have a great opportunity to help end this cycle. Our cultures matter, our stories matter, and finding yourself in others matters.

Why? Because of the financial difficulties and hardships associated with higher education. Being in debt is not fun, but being in debt for doing the "right" thing is downright painful. A yearly phone conversation in my house goes as follows: "I'd like to request another forbearance on my student loans." Victor Villanueva (1993) shares a similar story: "He thought the Ph.D. would be the end to suffering of this sort—begging for work with dignity and with meaning and being denied, having to return to menial labor" (p. 139).

I promised my Dad no menial labor. Besides, as my Dad often told me, "I come home with a hurt back, so you can come home with a hurt brain." He cleaned a school. I too clean a school. Oh, have I had to clean some messes.

To avoid these messes, I teach my classes this simple rule: If you have to ask yourself if it is racist (or sexist, or homophobic, or some other intersectional form of oppression), the answer is, yes!

Why? Because having a stomach bug is one thing, but I will not tolerate you vomiting on a people for their differences. Have some courage. Be stronger than that, and do not place cultures in a box!

ENCOURAGE

Think Outside the Box

I have started all my classes with a drawing of a box on the board. I ask the class to identify the drawing, with most of them saying, "It's a cube." I say, "It's a box." I then say, "Some classes want you to think outside the box and other classes want you to think inside the box." I then ask, "And this class?" They usually answer, "outside." "No," I say, "there is no box! To think outside the box is to assume that the box exists. I want you to ask, who/what put the box there?"

Now, I am not trying to suggest that nothing exists, but instead I want to suggest that "problems" exist because we apply a particular meaning or value to people, to identities, to cultures, and so forth. So, let's problematize "the problem." Let us say the problem is racism. In other words, let us challenge the structures that have defined race in the ways that they have and hence created patterns of racism. The problem is not skin color. The structures and institutions of racism are the problem. In other words, the problem is the systemic oppression based on skin color, and the various attributes and oppressions (gender, class, sexuality, and so on) associated with being "other."

This is not as simple an exercise as I have suggested, primarily because power and privilege are often invisible to those who have it. There is also the issue of what counts as evidence. For example, me, teaching Ethnic Studies courses, often perpetuates the assumption—for many, if not most, students—that a Latino would have an easier time teaching the courses. "Is it easier?" I ask. No, because any educated person who has extensively studied the topics can and should be able to teach the courses. Yes, because as an "ethnic minority," I can speak to experiences and can give concrete examples of discrimination. The arguments make sense because they are simple ones. Again, we need to problematize the "problem." I do this by sharing a story of the conversation that led me to ask the "is it easier" question.

Several years ago, an influential mentor, who was known for his work on critical race theory (see Olson, 2004), told me that he, as a White man, had it easier in Ethnic Studies classes because no matter how much he talked about racism, about privilege, and about systems of oppression, he would always be taken as neutral and objective. I, on the other hand, would be another "minority" complaining. No matter my use of the scientific method, which I am critical of anyway, the class would assign a value to me based on my cultural identity—one that would assume an irrational and subjective voice. As Villanueva (1993) writes, "My views are grounded in experience, elaborated upon by theory, and tested in research" (p. xvii). Even so, the bias is there. The bias is this: I am the biased one. Many of the students have already placed me in a box.

HIGHER UNLEARNING

So, how do I reach those students who have put me in a box? I reach them with humor, with active learning, with sharing my teaching thoughts aloud, and with continual support for them as learners. Due to these box constrictions, I emphasize the need to "unlearn." Learning can actually be easy, but unlearning is hard.

This is where and how I reach students culturally. I encourage them to share their stories. We become partners in teaching and learning. I am as much the teacher as I am the learner. The best pedagogical tool I have is when students allow me ways to adapt and adjust my own ways of teaching. When I teach without a box, students learn without a box; they cross borders in their learning and in their lives. They do this by drawing on their strengths, which come from the hardships they have endured. Subsequently, they become student citizens, not because they are members of the class, but because they realize they matter. They exist!

CITIZENSHIP IN THE CLASSROOM

Citizenship is political; as such, politics are cultural. In this critical inventory of self and of community, I was to talk about how my culture influences my teaching and vice versa, but my culture is always there. My culture cannot be taken as a variable that makes me who I am. It is who I am. I belong to the borderlands—the vague and undefined zones in all of our lives. The borderlands are where cultural formations are variable, continual, and ever changing. Who am I? I am a citizen, *and* I play one in the classroom.

REFERENCES

Alonso-Zaldivar, R., & Tompson, T. (2010). 87% of Hispanics value higher education, 13% have college degree. Retrieved from http://www.usatoday.com/news/education/2010-07-30-poll-hispanic-college_N.htm

EZLN (1996). First declaration of La Realidad for humanity and against neoliberalism. Retrieved from http://palabra.ezln.org.mx/comunicados/1996/1996_01_01_b.htm

García, N. (2005). *Old Las Vegas: Hispanic memories from the New Mexico meadowlands.* Lubbock, TX: Texas Tech University Press.

Moraga, C., & Anzaldua, G. (Ed.). (1981). *This bridge called my back: Writings by radical women of color.* Watertown, MA: Persephone Press.

Olson, J. (2004). *The abolition of White democracy.* Minneapolis: University of Minnesota Press.

Rendón, L. I. (1992). From the Barrio to the academy: Revelations of a Mexican American "scholarship girl." *New Directions for Community Colleges, 1992*: 55–64.

Villanueva, V., Jr. (1993). *Bootstraps: From an American academic of color.* Urbana, IL: National Council of Teachers of English.

West, C. (1999). *The Cornel West reader.* New York: Basic Civitas Books.

CHAPTER NINETEEN

Intersectioning Indigenous Teaching Practices AND Critical Pedagogy IN AN Academic Classroom

CARISSA TSOSIE

Library
Northern Arizona University

I am a Navajo woman, born and raised in Arizona, a product of the public school system. I hold two bachelor's degrees, one in anthropology and one in history from Northern Arizona University in 2003. I earned a master's degree in library science from the University of Arizona in 2011. I am currently working on a second master's degree in history, also at Northern Arizona University. I spent my early childhood in Ganado, Arizona, where I attended the Ganado Primary School to the second grade. I enjoyed my time in Ganado. I learned so much from playing in the Pueblo Colorado Wash that wound lazily through my grandmother's land. Ganado is my grandmother's ancestral home, but she did not live there her whole life. She left home at the age of 13 to attend the Sherman Institute in Riverside, California. Since she was an older student, she was trained at this school to do housework so that she could get a job as a maid when she finished her program. She lived in several different states, got married, and had five children before moving her family back to her hometown of Ganado. Starting out as a candy-striper, she eventually worked her way into a nursing position at Sage Memorial Hospital in that town. She worked there until her retirement in 2009.

I tell this story of my grandmother because she was so influential in my academic career. I was born in 1978 to my teenaged parents, Malcolm and Pearl. My parents met while attending Coconino High School in Flagstaff, Arizona, and my dad's sister introduced them one day in the hallway. My parents ended up marrying and having three daughters together. My dad never graduated from high school and did not attend college. My mother earned her GED and briefly attended Clemson Business College in Phoenix, Arizona, but she did not complete her course work. The pressures of attending college full-time and taking care of her family were too much at the time and she dropped out of school. They have both told me on multiple occasions that we struggled so much because they did not have the opportunities that a formal education would have presented.

At the time of my birth, my parents were living with my grandmother in her two-room house. My earliest memories are of playing in the wash from dawn until the early evening hours. I learned and played in the outdoors for the majority of my early years; it was a wonderful way to learn about the processes of nature. I also have many, many early memories of my grandmother telling me and my sisters that we were going to college no matter what. She would say, "You have to get an education if you are going to be successful; you *have* to go to college."

I believe that I learned most when walking and talking with my parents and grandparents in the high deserts of Ganado. The land is dotted with pinon and juniper trees, the earth is red from iron oxide, and sheep graze lazily on desert grasses and shrubs that grow in this area. In the summer, dust is kicked up by whirlwinds and tumbleweeds make their way through the desert and become stacked up in humungous heaps. Ganado sits at about six thousand feet in elevation, so it does get a substantial amount of snow in the winter months. In the late summer, the monsoon winds bring much-needed rain. Dry farming is an important part of daily life on the reservation; from May to October farmers care for and harvest corn, beans, squash, melons, apricots, peaches, and alfalfa.

According to the 2010 census, Ganado had a population of about 1,200. That's down about 300 from the last census in 2000. Many people move away from Ganado to find jobs off the reservation. The unemployment rate on the Navajo Nation soars at 50%. Many young and able-bodied Navajos move to reservation border towns such as Gallup, Farmington, Flagstaff, and Cortez, Colorado, to get work.

I moved to Phoenix, Arizona, with my family when my dad got a job at a welding/fabrication business in that city. I lived there for two years when my parents got divorced. After the divorce my mom moved us to Flagstaff, Arizona, so she could be closer to her family in Leupp, Arizona. I was then placed in several schools in the Flagstaff Unified School District: Killip Elementary, Marshall Elementary, and Thomas Elementary. We moved a lot because my mom could not always afford payment for rent, and we were homeless for a few years right before I went to live on the campus of Northern Arizona University. During this time, I found books and read voraciously as a means to escape my difficult home life.

My past experiences have provided me with a foundation for how I interact with students and how I teach in the classroom setting. I believe that we all have meaningful offerings and we should all be encouraged to use our knowledge not only to teach others but to learn *from* others as well. I consider it my responsibility as a facilitator of learning to bring out the pre-knowledge that all students bring with them to the classroom. In the next section I would like to discuss my identity as an educator and why my past experiences while being a student weigh heavily on how I interact with my students.

MY IDENTITY AS AN EDUCATOR, LEARNER, AND COMMUNITY MEMBER

My dad always had his face in a book, magazine, mechanic's manual, or newspaper. He read insatiably, and I was always jealous of what he was reading because it meant that he was not focused on me. My dad was a quiet man; he did most of his talking during our walks around Ganado. He would talk about history, world politics, documentaries that he'd seen, and the land; medicinal plants, the animals, and trees; and he would throw in a few funny stories here and there. I guess it was during these walks and talks that I began to have an interest in history and geography.

Before I even started attending school my parents, aunts, uncles, and grandparents pushed me to do well in school and to go on to college. "Get your education and get a good job," they'd say to me and my sisters. I listened to their supplications. After graduating from Sinagua High School in Flagstaff, Arizona, I enrolled in the Successful Transitions and Academic Readiness (STAR) program at Northern Arizona University. The STAR program is a bridge program for new first-year students who are also first-generation and/or demonstrate financial need. I received a scholarship to participate in the STAR Program in the summer of 1996. The program consists of five weeks of instruction and orientation to the NAU campus. I was fortunate to have met a STAR representative from Northern Arizona University, Eugene Begay. Mr. Begay is still is a program coordinator with NAU's Educational Talent Search. I am so glad that I met him, as he was instrumental in getting me to attend NAU my first year. Even though I completed the STAR program, my first semester as an undergraduate did not go as well as I had expected. In fact, I nearly flunked out of college. However, I was able to take a semester off to really think about what I wanted, and I decided that I wanted to complete my four-year degree. I set out to graduate and fulfill my family's wishes that I go to college and finish with a degree in hand. I finished my degree program six years later, graduating with two bachelor's degrees, one in anthropology and the other in history. But this success did not come without many failures and starts and stops. I had to learn to be engaged in a place where I felt very uncomfortable. I have always been passive in teaching spaces. Often, I did not ask for help, and I have never felt completely safe in the classroom. I have always believed that the following experiences contributed to my feeling uncomfortable with my teachers and uncomfortable in the classroom in general.

My second-grade class was taught by Mrs. McClanahan, and she was an impatient woman. She was an older teacher by the time I was in her class. I got the feeling that she was tired, tired all the time, and was tired of teaching. I believe that is why she was often so upset with our class. She would grow more and more impatient with the class as the day wore on, and many times several students were held after class as punishment for minimal infractions. One day, I was one of those students; I was so late getting home that day that my mom was on the phone with the police when I finally walked in the door. My mother was furious with me and failed to hear my excuse for being so late. I was grounded for a week. I remember feeling that it was wrong of Mrs. McClanahan to treat her students so poorly, that she was taking her frustrations out on us and that was not fair. I learned quickly to avoid her after lunch and to be invisible so that I would not be held after class. Even then, I knew that no student should be afraid of their teachers.

My third-grade class was taught by Mr. Anaya: Mr. Anaya was a small man; he wore the same thing every day: a cardigan, an oxford shirt, slacks, and dark brown leather shoes. His hair was meticulously parted and combed with hair oil so that it stuck to his head. When he got upset with the class, his hair would come out of its form because he shook as he yelled at us to clean up our desks. He would routinely knock over desks that he deemed particularly messy. He ran his classroom like a drill sergeant. We even had to click our heels and stand at attention when he inspected our desks or our homework. He was an anomaly in the classroom. He should have been a drill sergeant, breaking men and remolding them into soldiers. Instead he was in charge of my third-grade class. Unfortunately, I have one memory/experience that sticks in mind and has confirmed my belief that some people should not ever be let into the classroom. Mr. Anaya would have the class conduct show and tell every week. I had a pretty healthy interest in rocks and minerals when I was a kid. One week, for show and tell, I brought in a selection from my collection of amethyst crystals. When it came time for my show and tell, I nervously got up from my desk and walked toward the front of the class. I was excited about presenting my prized collection to my class. I had spent what seemed like forever trying to get up enough guts to go up in the front of the class in the first place. I did not know that I was about to walk into a minefield! I walked up to the front of the classroom and turned around to face my classmates.

Just as I made my way to the front of the class I felt my face turn red and my palms started to perspire. My mouth was dry and my tongue was so sticky it was hard to talk. After several painful seconds I was able to say my name, though my voice was quiet. As soon as I said my name, Mr. Anaya pounced; he began to make fun of me in front of the whole class because I did not speak loudly enough for his liking. I just stood there while he pretended to be me. I was so embarrassed, I couldn't move or talk. Once he had the rest of the class laughing and pointing at me, he went back to his desk and admonished me for not speaking loud enough.

He then let me proceed. I started to talk about my collection of minerals when I heard him get up from his desk, and then he was standing behind me and mimicking my movements. He was again making fun of me and how I was presenting my collection. The whole class was laughing at this point. I decided then that I would try harder to present in a manner that Mr. Anaya would have liked. So I stayed and tried to talk about my items, but every time I tried to talk, Mr. Anaya would mock me; I was very upset and wanted to leave but I knew that if I tried to leave I would be punished. After Mr. Anaya had grown tired of making fun of me he let me finally sit down. I had tears in my eyes and for the rest of the day I thought of ways that I could have done better. It never occurred to me until right now, as I write about and reflect on my experiences, that this situation was wrong. I should never have been made to feel so small. Mr. Anaya was a bully; he did not belong in the classroom. This incident made me feel like I was not welcome in Mr. Anaya's class. Mr. Anaya fancied himself a tough educator; he always said to our class that discipline was the best thing for us. If we went through school not learning discipline, then we had, in his eyes, failed. These two early experiences taught me a lot about how teachers can sometimes behave badly in their jobs. Since I have begun to teach I have made it a point to not behave in this way, to treat my students with respect and to make my teaching a two-way process.

I have since been exposed to wonderful teachers during my high school, undergraduate, and graduate careers. Not surprisingly, it took me a while to recover from the treatment described above. My experience led me to feel very inadequate and out of place in the classroom. However, when I got into high school, I met the first of several wonderful educators who truly cared about their students and student success. Mrs. Nicholson was my sculpture and ceramics teacher for the last three years at Sinagua High School. I remember thinking that she was different from most teachers because she seemed to be energized by the *act* of teaching. I could tell that she did not feel as though she was keeping tabs on the class; she actively sought out our opinions and thoughts on creating art. In her classes I felt like I was part of the discussion rather than being passively lectured to. I enrolled in my first college-level history class in the spring of 1999. Dr. Avery taught my Women in American History course that semester. I was blown away by her ability to be present with each of her students. She was excited about the content of the class, and her enthusiasm created a fun and engaging environment in her classroom. From this point on, I made it a point to get a feel for a professor's engagement with the information he or she was teaching. It's important for a class to feel as though the professor is not only interested in student success and learning but to know a professor is interested in what he or she is teaching and how the professor interacts with and facilitates the class.

As far as my culture is concerned, I feel there have been very few times in my scholastic experiences that my culture was upheld in the classroom; most times, my culture was viewed as something exotic, something to be studied and scrutinized. I want my students to be able to express their opinions in my class, to contribute the knowledge they *bring* to the class. I want my classes to be open exchanges between me and my students. They are in a position to teach me as well. Using critical pedagogy in my classroom, I seek to build a meaningful partnership with students. To do this, I attempt to engage the students as much as possible. This can be difficult at times, for example, due to varying levels of preparedness, the perceived importance of the session, and the support I get from the professor as I teach her class on the techniques of searching and finding good information. Again, a classroom environment that is respectful and upholds the culture of all students is so important to me as I begin my career as an educator.

My current teaching mostly consists of instructing classes on how to use library databases, the library catalog, and other online information resources. In the past I have taught classes on mapping archaeological sites and gave many presentations on class projects that included instructional aspects. However, I do not have experience teaching a traditional college course. I noticed that in my analysis of my past teaching and the teaching that I am doing now, I am driven by the content of the session. I wish to sort of move away from that to more of an organic discussion and build an environment that fosters teaching and learning as a two-way street with exchanges going from student to teacher and vice versa.

AN ANALYSIS OF MY TEACHING

When I look at culture and teaching, I see my values: family/community, living without competition, and lifelong learning. I see my classroom/space for learning as being a community, a safe place for my students to express themselves non-competitively, and with a mind for encouraging lifelong learning in each other and for themselves. I also see that I should steer away from defining and using false dichotomies in my teaching; for example, I consider myself to be deeply internal and I process information internally. I must be mindful not to exclude those students who are external processors, as they will not only lend to the movement of ideas in the classroom, but they also bring a different prospective on how one learns and uses information. In my discussions with a colleague I made a distinction between being collaborative and being an internal processor. My colleague reminded me that the two need not be at odds, that they can work well together. I will take this teaching into consideration when I am teaching now and in the future.

As a librarian I see how my career path parallels my commitment to my own lifelong learning and my commitment to incite the desire for lifelong learning in others. I have been contributing to the learning of others by my chosen career in the information sciences. I work in an academic library, and I am an academic librarian. I love my job. I show students and faculty how to research and find useful information. I have an opportunity every day to contribute to the creation of new knowledge and scholarship. To me, this is a dream come true. I am excited to work with students who are conducting their first college-level research papers as well as working with seasoned researchers to find that elusive piece of data.

I seek to treat my classroom as though it were a community. We are a community of learners, we all have had different experiences, and we come to the classroom with set of skills and knowledge that can be helpful to the community's learning. I seek to encourage all students to impart that knowledge wherever possible.

The Strength of Cultural Values and Their Influence on Teaching

In this section, faculty authors reflect on their cultures of origin as a substantial and often most powerful influence on teaching.

CHAPTER TWENTY

Pros and Cons of a Cosmopolitan Classroom

K. MARIA D. LANE

Geography
University of New Mexico

Because I teach in a university with high percentages of non-white and minority students, there is more attention to culture and diversity on my campus than I have encountered anywhere else during my academic career. Yet in almost a decade of training on how to recognize and respond to the cultural identities that *students* bring to the classroom, I never considered what cultural identities *I myself* bring to the classroom. Participation in a yearlong faculty institute on this topic has prompted me to account for the cultural values that underlie my behaviors as an educator and, in so doing, to face difficult questions. What does it mean if some of my value-laden classroom behaviors turn out to have negative impacts on students? Does it mean that my values are inconsistent with my work as an educator? Does it mean that my values are wrong? How can I do a better job of accounting for the inevitable cultural messiness that accompanies the process of education, mitigating potentially negative effects where possible? This essay falls short of answering these questions, but it provides a basis for long-overdue reflection.

ROOTS

My cultural identity is based primarily in the traditions and practices of my nuclear family, in which my parents synthesized their different cultural upbringings to forge a set of beliefs and practices that my siblings and I have always (mis)understood as somehow non-cultural or simply "American."

My mother immigrated to the United States from the former Czechoslovakia in grade school and grew up in mid-Atlantic communities that maintained traditional Slovak ethnic customs yet also fostered assimilation. My father, on the other hand, is a sixth-generation Floridian in a small Protestant community in central Florida where culture was defined more in terms of a shared struggle for economic prosperity than in residents' shared English, Irish, or Scottish heritages. Despite these differences in ethnicity and regional background, my parents found common ground in values that are now fundamental to my own cultural identity: the importance of hard work, the moral imperative to act with compassion for others, and the necessity of striving for educational attainment.

In addition to these core values, I learned from my parents' example that individuals and families can "choose" whether to identify with a traditional culture. My parents both changed religions when they married, leaving behind foundational cultural structures in much the same way they had left their home communities to pursue educational and professional opportunities. This always seemed to me a "normal" way of being in the world, and I've therefore always perceived a fundamental difference between myself and those who identify strongly with traditional ethnic cultures, including even my own Slovak grandmother. Despite the fact that her traditional cuisine, sayings, and observances anchored much of our family life, I was always quick to identify my grandmother as "Slovak" but always described myself as "a seventh-generation Floridian."

With culture thus hidden in the background, both in my family and in the 1970s American public school system, I grew up orienting my values first toward educational attainment and, second, toward the application of my talents to activities that would provide individual satisfaction while also helping others. My husband's family also values education deeply (as it provided his parents with a critical path from rural Appalachian towns to financial self-sufficiency), and education has subsequently emerged as the primary focus of life and value in our own young family. Because I value education so highly on multiple levels, I suppose it is somewhat embarrassing that I haven't thought deeply about the underlying values that I bring to my professional work as an educator of college students. In what follows, I have tried to dissect the origins, meanings, and impacts of three primary values that shape my teaching in Geography and Environmental Studies at the University of New Mexico.

I VALUE STRIVING

To me, "striving" means orienting your life toward progress, change, or improvement. It means setting ambitious goals, accepting major challenges, and working hard to achieve excellence. It also means working to build a stable foundation—through education, financial self-sufficiency, career choice, health habits—that allows one to maximize talents and achieve something meaningful in the world. Because I consider myself to be a striver, I gravitate toward others who seem to hold the same value. By contrast, I find it difficult to tolerate negativity, complaining, laziness, nonchalance, or even inefficiency.

Most deeply, this value stems from my parents' teaching and example and is reinforced by a general Protestant-based work ethic that dominates Anglo culture in the United States. My mother came to this country as an immigrant who didn't speak any English, yet she eventually became a successful school teacher, recognized for excellence not only by fellow professionals but also by hundreds of students and their families. This positive impact was built from hard work and a dedication of talents to a profession that makes a great impact on people's lives. Similarly, my father paid his own way through both college and law school, working long nights at a variety of jobs to complete his education and achieve financial security. As a professional, he has been extremely successful and also active in the community, constantly committing time and effort to charitable causes that benefit others.

Although my own path through life has so far been more financially secure than my parents' at the same age, I hold a similar outlook. I tend to organize most of my life around challenges—athletic, professional, social, or personal—that I tend to accept before I feel ready, knowing that I will somehow find a way to rise to them. My assumptions about the value and responsibility of the individual striver are reinforced by my position as a professional academic, a career that I chose in fact largely because it is oriented around the idea of striving. I see pursuit of an education as part of a lifelong process of striving toward improvement.

SO HOW DOES THIS CULTURAL VALUE AFFECT MY CLASSROOM?

First, this value contributes to the fact that I love my job. In general, the student body at UNM is a community of strivers. As parents or caregivers, as full-time employees, or simply as first-generation college entrants, many UNM students are attempting to complete their degrees under difficult circumstances, knowing that their efforts will eventually empower them to excel in their communities, workplaces, and families. I have been frankly astonished by how hard some of my students work, and I appreciate and value the chance to work with these strivers every semester and to be part of their success.

Second, I impose this value on students by structuring classes in ways that require significant work and effort. I create syllabi that include numerous assignments in a variety of formats, and I repeatedly reinforce to students that hard work contributes to larger outcomes in their learning, degree progress, and lives.

I motivate, I provide opportunities, I even entertain, but the grading structures in my classes require individual work and a *demonstration* of effort. Probably the most notable example of this is that I expect students to attend class regularly. I do not record attendance itself, but a large portion of students' grades in every one of my courses comes from graded in-class activities or from participation that is recorded via a classroom-response system. Even if a student aces every take-home assignment and exam, she or he will not get a good grade in any of my classes without attending. I realize now that I've structured my classes this way because I believe effort is required for learning to occur. I see no value in a student taking a class if the student has already mastered its knowledge and skills. So I don't reward demonstrations of knowledge without accompanying demonstrations of effort. This approach surely stems from my belief that the value of education lies more in the striving than in the learning.

This cultural value makes me a good match for UNM at the same time that it probably produces a type of favoritism that I have not yet addressed. On the one hand, I am extremely flexible and accommodating with students because I believe they are strivers. For example, I often give students time in class to work on projects that I assume will be time-constrained outside of class, and I am responsive to requests for help or for deadline extensions. But on the other hand, I am much less likely to make a deadline exception for a student if the request is not supported by demonstrations of effort. Although I work to be even-handed with student requests surrounding special circumstances, I am almost always swayed to accommodate requests made by a student that I perceive as a hard worker, or a striver.

I judge "hard work" on the basis of consistency in attendance, apparent work rate, frequency of communications with me as instructor, and personal comportment in class. But this method of judgment is problematic and perception-based. There are perhaps less obvious ways of striving that I probably overlook, creating favoritism-based disadvantages for some who are working hard in less apparent ways. Some students may be committed to caregiving activities or personal improvement efforts, for example, that are necessarily private. These students may be true "strivers" in ways I will never know, leaving my perceptions of these students sorely incomplete, since they are based only on classroom observation. In addition, some hardworking students may even hold cultural values that lead them to *minimize* the appearance of effort, which problematizes my tendency to be most responsive to those students I perceive as strivers.

And then there is the issue of those students who *don't* work hard. I am fairly annoyed by students who skip all the classes but do well on tests, because their successes are not accompanied by any evidence of effort or striving. Accordingly, my syllabi and grading structures create a disadvantage for students who don't show up. A student who skips every class (and therefore misses all the graded in-class activities) yet demonstrates perfect mastery of course content (e.g., a perfect score on every test and take-home assignment) will get only a B-in my courses, by design. I suppose I should ask myself: Is this really fair? Hard work and learning are correlated, but they are not equal, so I wonder whether my cultural value is clouding my thinking about which one I am actually supposed to be grading.

Finally, I also now realize that it's somewhat problematic to categorize every student as either a "striver" or "non-striver." Some students are dealing with issues that extend well beyond their desire to work hard, including social distress, personal trauma, or mental illness, to name a few. Because I value striving so highly, I tend to focus mainly on the question of whether students are working hard, and I rarely account for issues other than motivation.

My focus on the value of striving for excellence and of engaging in hard work toward self-improvement confers some real benefit on my students. By setting high standards and offering multiple paths to achieve those standards, I feel that I provide students with a support structure that is biased toward their success. And just like the standards that were set for me by my parents, coaches, teachers, and professors, these standards convey a belief in students' ability to succeed. This belief is powerful and helpful for most students. But for some students, the motivation and direction and ability to invest oneself in a course is itself a difficulty or is simply not part of why the student is in college.

I VALUE TEAMWORK

In my classrooms, I regularly ask students to engage not only with course material but also with their peers. In introductory courses, I use pair-based or small-group activities to break down barriers to learning. In my World Regional Geography course, for example, I ask students to consult peers before answering graded conceptual questions, and I frequently assign in-class questions where small groups work together on challenging problems that require coordinated data analysis to understand complex geographical patterns. In upper-level classes, I use team-based activities to enable comprehensive learning experiences that are not possible in an individual format. In my class on the Geography of New Mexico and the Southwest, for example, students complete a multi-week field project in which groups work together to map different areas of Albuquerque and then analyze various geographic patterns in the urban landscape. In my graduate-level courses, I assign peer review and peer critique activities to help students develop professional skills related to scholarly communication and intellectual exchange.

I have thus made group- and team-based activities a requirement in every class, but there are a number of obstacles to implementing them. For many undergraduate students at the University of New Mexico, work schedules and family obligations often complicate the logistics surrounding group meetings outside of class. To overcome this obstacle, I design most group activities such that the bulk of student meeting time occurs within the normally scheduled class. But beyond this simple logistical challenge, group assignments can also induce profound student anxieties about social interaction, grading accountability, and the problem of uneven work rates among group members. In general, it has been my experience that students are resistant to group-based activities in class, especially when they are graded. So perhaps I should ask myself why I value them so highly.

My commitment to group activities in class does not stem from my own educational experience, since I can't remember *ever* working within a group in any of my own college classes. I've been exposed to recent pedagogical research that demonstrates the benefits of peer-based learning, but I have to be honest that I'm not engaging in this difficult undertaking simply for altruistic reasons associated with "best practices" in college teaching. It's more likely that I am committed to group work because many of my formative life experiences took place in team environments. I played competitive team sports for more than two decades, first on an elite team that won the Little League World Series and later on a university team that competed in two national championships. It was in the intense environments of team competition that I forged most of the confidence, self-discipline, and poise that still guide my personal and professional outlook today.

As much as I value individual striving, I also believe that most significant things in life can be accomplished only when a group of strivers is dedicated to a common cause. My experiences as an athlete have helped me achieve success in other group settings, in the workplace and at home. And although I don't play team sports anymore, I still view the world from a team-based perspective. I gravitate toward people who seem like "team players," and I can easily be convinced to "take one for the team" when I believe that my individual effort or sacrifice will provide a benefit to my group—whether family, friends, department, or classroom. In the classroom, in fact, I often think of myself as a "coach," charged with creating a "training" environment in which individual students will be motivated and enabled to maximize their own talents.

The manifestations of this value have some positive classroom impacts. In most of my classes, we develop a strong sense of camaraderie and community. I give students significant challenges, and they typically work together to rise to those challenges. I feel that my students, as a whole, are achieving high levels of subject-area mastery in a supportive environment where they see their peers and me as advocates and resources. I believe that my passion for teamwork inspires and enables students to engage with geography subjects more deeply than would be possible in a more individualized classroom setting.

But it nags at me that some students resist group work strenuously and seem so anxious or disengaged around peers that I fear they might actually be learning *less* in my class than in a more traditional classroom setting. In fact, I know that some students have dropped my classes because they are overwhelmed by requirements to engage with peers intensively and frequently. In general, I've taken these few students' discomfort as a challenge that I should meet by working harder and earlier to make students comfortable with team-based learning structures and to design collaborative learning activities in ways that provide flexibility for different types of engagement. But it is also possible that some students are extreme introverts or are in social distress, while others may see team-based learning as a challenge to their cultural values. Although I don't think this recognition should lessen my commitment to teamwork, I can probably be more mindful about how I engage these students in activities that challenge their preference for more solitary or reflective ways of learning.

I VALUE COSMOPOLITANISM

One of the reasons I am a professional academic geographer is because I believe that an educated worldview includes a sophisticated understanding of the forces and patterns that influence peoples, places, and landscapes around the world. Although I can appreciate that provincial attitudes function to maintain cultural coherence in specific places, I deeply detest narrow provincialism on an intellectual level. I believe that young Americans desperately need to explore the variability and complexity of the world beyond American borders and to develop open minds that are accepting of cultural and environmental norms outside the limits of their home culture areas. I believe this type of exploration leads to personal transformation and allows people to become more compassionate toward others, more tolerant of difference, and more committed to ideals that promote peace and social justice for all peoples.

I'm not sure exactly where this value came from, as I did not travel much as a child and did not talk much to my grandmother or mother about their experiences in Eastern Europe before immigrating to the United States. In addition, I grew up with a provincial attitude about the virtues of my coastal Florida home region. But I became interested in Latin America and the Caribbean during college and spent three months traveling through Central America one summer to see places I had read about in novels and course texts. This was a transformative experience for me, one that reinforced the positive experience of leaving my Florida hometown to attend college in the mid-Atlantic region, where I grappled with encountering others who had different accents and traditions than mine. I loved the way that travel forced me to confront and question my own assumptions on a minute-by-minute basis, simply by the fact that I had to face environments and attitudes and expectations that were different from home. Since then, I have become an active international traveler and am deeply committed to the belief that people of different cultures must find ways to respect, understand, and engage with one another. In my view, any college education that does *not* foster cosmopolitanism is incomplete.

This deep value manifests in my classroom both in the classes I choose to teach and also in the ways I teach. In my classes on world regions, I conceive my role as an intellectual tour guide who inspires and enables people to examine new places and new peoples with new eyes. Even when we don't leave the classroom, I am always working with students to gain perspectives on places they will encounter throughout their lives—as travelers, as participants in a global workforce, or as voters in one of the world's most geopolitically active nations. In terms of subject matter, my cosmopolitan values are a good match with the classes I teach.

In terms of pedagogical technique, I push hard in all of my courses for students to shed provincial ideologies and vocabularies. In my World Regional Geography course, I actually outlaw the use of personal pronouns in reference to ethnic or national groups. When students say "us" to refer to Americans and "them" to refer to non-Americans, I stop and request rephrasing that does not use personal pronouns. This is a deliberate attempt to help students develop habitually neutral perspectives on the world's culture groups, enabling them to better analyze phenomena such as geopolitical conflict without any provincial assumptions about the superiority of their own culture.

As another way of leading students to this type of intellectual discipline, all of my classes include exercises in which students must explore others' viewpoints or express others' perspectives. My lower-level world regional geography class, for example, requires students to analyze fiction from other world regions to more deeply explore non-American viewpoints. In my upper-level course on the Southwest, I assign writing projects in which students must assume the perspectives of different groups involved in environmental disputes or cultural conflicts. An underlying pedagogical goal of these assignments is to ensure that students are deep critical thinkers who can present and evaluate multiple points of view.

Writing this essay has helped me realize that the classroom manifestation of my cosmopolitan values influences almost everything about the subject matter I present, the assignments I create, the ways I motivate students, and the intellectual discipline that I enforce. I believe that this confers significant benefits: students leave my classes with improved abilities to inhabit others' perspectives, to seek out multiple points of view, and to systematically organize information about unfamiliar places and peoples. But for all of the benefits this cosmopolitan training confers in terms of promoting tolerance and developing an open mind, there are two potential problems with the way this value influences my classrooms.

First, I am asking (or forcing) students to adopt a mindset that represents a major leap for many of them. I have struggled, in fact, with the problem that students who are learning to cultivate tolerance for new viewpoints often lapse into relativistic thinking, rather than true cosmopolitanism. At an on-campus teaching workshop several years ago, I learned about recent neurological research showing that young adults have cognitive difficulty progressing from a black-white worldview to an ability to make reasoned judgments that account for the pros and cons in multiple perspectives. The workshop helped me realize that the development of a cosmopolitan worldview is a long and confusing process that cannot be accomplished in a single semester. An immersive experience, like my own early travel in Central America, can accelerate this cognitive transition, but a single semester in an Albuquerque classroom can never be more than a step along the way in a broader process of developing a true understanding of other perspectives or a deep tolerance for other cultures. In other words, I shouldn't expect students to walk out of my class wholly transformed, no matter how hard I try.

Second, and more problematically, my cosmopolitan values may be in direct conflict with some of my students' cultural worldviews. Especially for minority students, and especially in the Southwest where Native American communities have been forcibly assimilated via U.S. government policy, my explicit rejection of a provincial perspective that values one culture above others may be offensive and destructive to some students' cultural identity. As a modern mainstream American university, UNM is structured as a multicultural institution in which diversity and tolerance are cultivated in the service of education. But the struggles involved in protecting one's *own* culture while also trying to respect and accept *others'* cultural values are complex, and I should be mindful of the ways this struggle may play out in my classrooms at UNM. Although I am deeply committed to the ideal that all cultures should be respected and treated with equality, I could ask students to question this ideal itself, particularly in terms of arguments that the modern American educational system has caused and continues to cause disadvantage for indigenous people. Asking students to critique our cosmopolitan classroom may actually help them better understand cosmopolitanism.

CONCLUSIONS

This reflection has helped me to interrogate many values and behaviors that otherwise would have gone unexamined in relation to my work as an educator, but this short text seems like a meager starting point in a broader process of critically accounting for culture in the classroom. If my cultural values introduce numerous positive and negative influences in my classes, there are exponentially more cultural values introduced by my students as well. These myriad values interact at multiple scales—from the level of structural course design to the level of individual student interactions—in ways that seem too complex for anyone to control or even address in any meaningful way.

The lesson for me, then, is that I should work to cultivate a classroom environment in which both students and instructor are at least mindful of the values each person brings with them to campus. I already ask my students to write a first-week essay about their "personal geography," including a description of places they have traveled, places they would like to travel, and their own ethnic or ancestral identification with regions outside North America. Perhaps I will expand this assignment to include a discussion of the cultural values that each of us brings to the study of geography. Reading students' essays on culture and learning would certainly help me to be more thoughtful about the ways my own values interact with students' and could help me better identify ways of supporting students who are culturally both similar to and different from me. If I additionally share with students my own thoughts about how culture influences my teaching, I believe we might make collective progress toward harnessing our cultural strengths and minimizing our cultural limitations in the classroom.

CHAPTER TWENTY-ONE

Running From Religion

Finding My Reconstructionist Academic Culture

ROBERT NEUSTADT

Global Languages and Cultures
Northern Arizona University

I have spent most of my life running away from my religion. As a child, in Louisville, Kentucky, I felt annoyed when my father would pronounce with pride that some brilliant actor, author, or artist was Jewish, as if our religion had something to do with their accomplishments. The concept of a "chosen people" always struck me as arrogant and exclusionary. I never felt connected with Jewish religious services. As a boy, I would pass what felt like an eternity counting the big round lightbulbs that hung from the high ceiling in Temple Adath Israel. It was boring. I never felt comfortable praying to God. If God had the power to intercede on our behalf, the atrocities of the Conquest, the genocide of American Indians, the Holocaust, terrible accidents, diseases, and the famines that afflict people would not occur. If God were all-powerful, there would be no losers in football games. The nail in my coffin of religiosity came the day that Rabbi Waller repeated *ad nauseum* the importance of a new building, beseeching in his amplified tenor voice that congregation members dig deep and donate to raise the money to build "a new, a new, a new building" for a Temple in the suburbs. They sold the old downtown Temple—a neo-classical building with massive stone columns built in 1906, listed on the National Registry of Historic Places—to an Apostolic Church in 1977. I moved away for college and haven't lived in Louisville since. I have only visited the temple in the suburbs a couple of times.

As a child I attended Hebrew School. I don't know if I ever felt spiritually connected to Hebrew, but I have always liked learning languages. I enjoyed eating matzah balls and matzah on Passover. I even liked chopped chicken liver (times have definitely changed!). Reflecting back over my personal history, I enjoyed preparing for my Bar Mitzvah, the traditional coming-of-age ceremony that Jewish children perform when 13 years old. I was proud to read a long portion of the Torah, a significant challenge since the holy Jewish scrolls are written by hand in Hebrew without vowels. I liked manipulating the parchment scroll, following the Hebrew words with an antique silver pointer. I enjoyed sharing the accomplishment—in a new blue plaid suit!—with my large extended family that travelled to Louisville from all over the country. I prepared for the day, worked assiduously toward the goal, and then reveled in gifts and congratulatory energy showered on me. I appreciated my Bar Mitzvah, not as a religious ceremony per se, but perhaps in the manner that an actor takes pleasure from a successful performance.

Today, I am by no means a practicing Jew. Organized religion does not appeal to me now any more than it did as a child. I am moved by others' faith, especially when it translates to good deeds, but for me, personally, we may as well build sanctuaries to Flying Spaghetti Monster. That said, I sometimes think that it would be terrific if all 13-year-olds could have a Bar or Bat Mitzvah. Not for the content, but rather for the value of the experience. All too often I see students at my university who cannot give a coherent, well-organized presentation. Many of my students present while chewing gum, wiggling, and spinning around on one foot. I don't think I "became a man" on my Bar Mitzvah, but the rigorous, long-term preparation provided me with an experience that both deepened my appreciation for academic study and, of equal importance, helped me to develop skills in presenting to an audience. When I observe students' lack of public speaking skills, I acknowledge the usefulness of Jewish education as a valuable form of academic training. If all 13-year-olds prepared for and gave Bar Mitzvah–like presentations, they would be capable of better communicating information by the time they came to university.

My father's family, Reformed Jews from Evansville, Indiana, prayed to our "heavenly father, King of the Universe" twice a year on the high holidays. They didn't sing, chant, or wear funny ritualistic clothing (yarmulkes or taluses). Grandpa Mose was a quiet guy, bald as a bowling ball, who had stowed away on a ship from Russia as a boy because he didn't want to serve in the Czar's army. He forgot all of his Russian and never talked about the past. My mother's family, in contrast, were more observant Jews. New York Jews—"in your face" New Yorkers, who chanted in Hebrew. Their chanting and their use of traditional religious garments always seemed pretty weird to me as a kid.

As I mentioned above, I am no fan of organized religion. Too many have died in the name of God as a result of "holy wars" and religious conflicts. Too many continue to die in the name of this or that religion. To think that one religion can be better than another strikes me as ludicrous. When teaching the Conquest of the Americas to students at Northern Arizona University, I ask my students to contemplate the arrogance of the Spaniards who insisted that all of the "Indians" convert to Catholicism. Can you imagine, I ask them, that the Spaniards believed that their concept of religious "truth" was greater than the autochthonous spiritual cosmovisions of the natives? I wonder what students from evangelical churches are thinking; I know that some of my students go on missions to Latin American countries and attempt to convert people. Perhaps some are offended by my challenge to the concept of evangelism. My guess is that many do not catch my implication. Students are fairly skilled at tuning out their professors.

My academic research focuses on "cultural studies," and I have always been curious how my students' cultural identities shape their learning experiences in my classes. I strive to apply my understanding of different cultural traits and values as a vehicle to help my students succeed. This is particularly urgent at Northern Arizona University where first-generation Native American and Latino students pursue degrees in a state where a disproportionate percentage of students from their communities never make it through high school. Cultural sensitivity can help us to help our students. In this essay, however, I am exploring the inverse, my own cultural identity, in an effort to understand how *my* cultural background manifests itself in my teaching. I have always operated on a misconception, that culture is something that defines others, not me.

Who am I? The culture that formed me stems not only from my familiar background but also from those who I met, befriended, and studied with along the way. Attending college in the aftermath of the social, political, and cultural movements of the 1960s, I am, in some ways, a product of my generation. I identify myself as a long-haired Midwestern, New York–inflected, non-practicing Jew who became a political activist. My goal as a teacher is to encourage my students to have fun, to question authority, to think critically, to attain global awareness, to become politically conscious, and, ideally, to use their newly acquired knowledge to further social justice. My teaching behaviors and methodologies seek to instill these values. I clown around with and provoke my students. I employ vulgarity in the classroom to wake them up, to amuse them, and I hope to inspire them to take on an *active* role in their own education. I am convinced that if they want to learn, they can and will learn, so I try to stimulate their curiosity. Whether teaching literature, culture, or language, I focus on political and cultural issues—I try to present my students with material that really matters.

In academia today we are obliged to put an enormous amount of importance into our syllabi. We are told that syllabi are contracts, and consequentially, we stuff them with long tracts of boilerplate verbiage, rules, "learning outcomes," and disclaimers. I remember nostalgically that when I was in college my professors often didn't even hand out the syllabus until we were several weeks into the course. Were my professors less organized? I think not. My impression is that they were taking the pulse of the class before committing to a semester-long plan. Given that professors and students are human beings, each class will inevitably be a distinct interaction that will precipitate out of the unique chemistry between everyone present. The attempt to standardize education has, in my opinion, made it harder to tailor a class to its individual strengths, needs, and characteristics.

I attempt to make my classes "experiences," and often these experiences dismantle traditional power structures. For one class, I have my students form groups and perform one-act plays, without a director, in the non-hierarchical tradition of Latin American collective theater. In a writing class, I once departed from the syllabus halfway through the semester and had them write a collective novel, in Spanish, exploring how Chileans today confront the lasting effects of torture inflicted during the dictatorship.

I take students out of the classroom any chance I get. One time, I took a Spanish conversation class to Turf Paradise, the horse racetrack in Phoenix where they could practice their Spanish with some of the 2,000 Spanish-speaking employees at the track. A groom showed us the drugs with which they routinely, and illegally, medicate the horses. Being from Kentucky, I love horse racing. I grew up going to the horse races. Certainly my childhood culture as a Kentuckian influenced this trip. I still love to watch beautiful thoroughbreds gallop. I still feel uniquely alive at the races. That said, I do not condone or deny the problematic aspects that plague the "sport of kings," such as overmedicating horses and abusing jockeys. I took my students to the race track to practice their Spanish, and part of the experience was to discuss the problems associated with the racing industry.

Since 2010, I have taken students from seven classes on excursions to the Arizona/Mexico border. These field trips to the border are by far the most significant pedagogical experiences I have facilitated in my career. I do not tell my students what to think; rather, I put them face to face with recently deported migrants, have them talk with Border Patrol agents, have them see and touch the wall, and have them explore desert trails where people migrate and too often die. Seeing and feeling the border, through their own eyes, makes a huge impact on these students. Many have described it as a transformative, "life changing" experience. On the first trip they thanked me—one by one at a campfire—for making them aware. Some had never camped before. One student told me that the trip made him "realize that he had a soul." Another student told me that he felt like "the class had made him a better person."

Before my first field trip to the border, I had an academic understanding of undocumented immigration. It was on the trip, alongside of and with my students, that I became viscerally aware of the raw human suffering occurring on the border. It was on that first field trip to the border that I decided that I needed to reconstruct my *self*; I needed to find ways, in and outside of the classroom, to bring this crisis to people's awareness. Once I had seen this reality it was no longer acceptable to look the other way while thousands of people suffer and die, unseen, in our state. I became, for lack of another identity, a professor/activist who teaches border issues and who is willing, when necessary, to make noise to call attention to this humanitarian crisis.

Over the years, I have found myself struggling repeatedly with the administration of my public university in Arizona for the right to call attention to the humanitarian catastrophe that is occurring in Arizona. In fall 2011, when university administrators heard of my plans to take students to the border a second time, they denied permission. Due to a generalized travel warning in the area, they made a blanket decision to prohibit trips across the border into Mexico. I petitioned, explaining that I would take measures to ensure student safety during this very significant educational experience. Colleagues told me I would never obtain permission, but I continued to petition up through the chain of command. Surprisingly, I was given permission, though it required substantial perseverance (and the support of some key people at the university). That spring I again found myself in a tug-of-war with the university administration. My colleague, artist Shawn Skabelund, and I decided to put an art installation of 6,000 crosses on campus to honor and commemorate the people whose remains had been found on the border since 1994. Given the divisive political atmosphere in Arizona, we were denied permission twice. I convoked a group of supportive colleagues and asked for a meeting with the university president and provost. After several meetings and negotiations via an extensive series of emails and phone calls between 25 people, including the president, the provost, the vice president of capital assets, the head of campus security, various deans, chairs, directors, and others, we won permission to exhibit our installation. (I believe that I hold the record of the most crosses constructed by a Jewish cross-maker!) My role as professor who pushes the administration has continued. During spring 2015, I led the Northern Arizona effort, with a student group that I advise, to give DREAMers (young people who were brought to the country as children without documents) the right to pay in-state tuition. How did I end up in this position of faculty agitator? Did my culture or upbringing somehow prepare me for this role? Was there something in the pushiness of my mother's New York Jewish heritage that trained me to persevere?

Only as an adult did I realize that my mother was (and is) also a political activist. She was president of the Louisville section of the National Council of Jewish Women and she talked on the phone a lot. She worked on a variety of social issues, such as keeping the Juvenile Detention Center separate from a new jail. How did she come to take this path? While writing this essay I asked myself if someone or something further back in our family history connects with activism. It is here that I came to Colonel Sanders. Well, not really Colonel Sanders, but rather Rabbi Mordechai Kaplan, my mother's great uncle, who looked like Colonel Sanders and founded a new "American" branch of Judaism called "Reconstructionism." Seeking information for my cultural autobiography I discovered that this rabbi in my historical "closet" might have something to do with who I am today.

To my surprise and delight I discovered that Mordechai Kaplan, born in Lithuania in 1881, described by some as the "greatest American Jewish thinker," invoked a kind of Judaism that aligns ironically well with many of my own iconoclastic beliefs. On June 12, 1945, great-great-Uncle Mordechai was "excommunicated" by a group of orthodox rabbis who publically burned the prayer book that he authored, *Sabbath Prayer Book*. He was accused of "liturgical blasphemy." My kind of rabbi! Anyone accused of blasphemy deserves a second look, and any author whose book is burned has certainly succeeded in provoking a reaction, if not thought.

Mordechai Kaplan's major heresy lay in his rejection of right-wing fundamentalist orthodox Jewish traditions, including the notion that the Jews are the "chosen people." Kaplan rejected the notion of a God as a personal, supernatural Messiah and he rejected the idea that Jews must blindly reenact traditional rituals prescribed by authoritarian doctrine. For Kaplan, one does not pray to ask God to intercede; one prays, rather, to articulate a vision of what one wants to accomplish and/or change within himself or herself. For Kaplan, Judaism is "an evolving civilization," a community that needs to "reconstruct" itself in the new American reality within the context of modern scientific discoveries, rather than re-present a literal interpretation of the Bible. On March 18, 1922, Kaplan officiated at his daughter's Bat Mitzvah ceremony. This was the first Bat Mitzvah; in other words, this was the first time that a woman was allowed to take part in a religious ritual that had until this day been reserved for men. As historian Paula Hyman points out, Kaplan's gesture of allowing women to become Bat Mitzvah gave testimony both to his belief in gender equity and, at the same time, resulted from his belief in Jewish education: "Mordecai Kaplan intended *bat mitzvah* to give females equal standing with males and stimulate Jewish education for women so they would be better able to transmit Jewish knowledge to their children"(Hyman, as cited in *Jewish virtual library*, n.d., ¶4).

Uncle Mordecai's perspective rings urgently true today. In fact, we need to reconstruct all civilizations, not just Judaism, with the knowledge produced by science. We must, for example, respond to climate change. Furthermore, we must reconstruct our worldviews and practices with the cultural knowledge that we have gained from history. It is time, in other words, to start treating Others—no matter their country of origin, the color of their skin, their religion, their gender, their economic situation, or their sexual orientation—with dignity and respect.

Academia, like Judaism, and like culture at large, is always evolving. At times, nevertheless, members of the administration, and those who mandate from above, such as the Board of Regents and legislators, remind me of orthodox rabbis who reject the creativity and instead push faculty to stay between the lines—to repeat, over and over, empty ("prayer-like") institutional rituals. Rather than provoke thought, we are encouraged to isolate our teaching from politics. Rather than interpolating students' views and provoking them to think and take action—to reconstruct themselves and society—we are directed to craft "student learning outcomes" and to write assessment reports.

If there are fibers of my cultural heritage that manifest themselves in my identity as a professor, I believe these reveal themselves in my provocative teaching style and activism. Jews bicker. When we eat in restaurants we often have conflicts regarding where to sit, what to order, and whether everyone can find acceptable meals. Everyone in my family seems to ask for special accommodations—no onions, extra x, y on the side. Usually, someone's plate arrives not-quite-right and rectifying the problem turns into a group negotiation. It takes a village to order a meal in my family. That said, my professional persona is not only a legacy of my ethnic/religious culture. As I stated before, as a child of the post-1960s, I absorbed a strong antiestablishment mindset and a generalized distrust of authority and institutionalized hierarchy. Gender, as well, is cultural. Males in our society are encouraged to confront obstacles aggressively. This amalgam of cultural influences combines to form what I call my "academic reconstructionist culture." Rather than reenacting predigested knowledge by rote, as an apolitical academic ritual along the lines of Kaplan's view of orthodox prayers, my goal is to engage with an evolving civilization—a society we acknowledge, furthermore, is in need of perpetual reconstruction. The confluence of all of these cultural values, traits, and customs has shaped and continues to shape me as a professor—a reconstructionist academic, who seeks to inspire the construction, and perpetual reconstruction, of a better, more just, and more educated world.

REFERENCE

Jews in America: The first Bat Mitzvah in the United States. Retrieved from: http://www.jewishvirtuallibrary.org/jsource/Judaism/firstbat.html

CHAPTER TWENTY-TWO

Strengthening Our Teaching BY Honoring Our Culture

ROBIN MINTHORN

Educational Leadership & Native American Studies
University of New Mexico

My name is Robin Starr Williams, and I recently acquired Minthorn. My birth name was given to me by my grandma Toni, my father's mother. My Kiowa name is Zapetahholaw (sticks with bow), given to me by my grandma Roxie Kodaseet Tsotigh, who gave me her mother's Kiowa name, Bessie Catherine Kokoom. I am an enrolled member of the Kiowa tribe of Oklahoma but am also of Apache, Umatilla (and Cayuse), Nez Perce, and Assiniboine tribal descent. My father's side of the family is from Oregon, Idaho, and Montana. My father grew up on the Confederated Tribes of the Umatilla Indian Reservation (CTUIR) in Mission, Oregon. His name is David Williams and his parents were Donald Bruce Williams and Antoinette (Toni) (Conner) Williams. My mother's name is Rita Joyce Tsotigh (now Brewer); she is ¾ Kiowa and ½ Apache, from Oklahoma. She grew up in the southwest part of Oklahoma, where my grandfather Jacob Sherwood Tsotigh Sr. was a United Methodist pastor in the Oklahoma Indian Missionary Conference (OIMC), a predominantly Native American conference. He married my grandmother Roxie Kodaseet after his first wife Josephine passed away from tuberculosis. My grandmother grew up in the area by Carnegie, Oklahoma, called Zole-tone (stinking water in Kiowa). My mom, aunts, and uncles grew up in a household where they were constantly at church but also where they often had to take care of each other because my grandparents were busy serving the churches, congregations, and communities they were assigned to. Once my grandpa became a pastor, his connection to and participation in culture and tribal ceremonies was gone. But, my grandfather did continue to use and infuse his culture through the

Kiowa language into the songs and prayers. My grandpa was well-known in southwest and central Oklahoma.

I grew up mainly with the surroundings of my Kiowa family and always around my grandparents. Four of the values that were most important to my grandparents were having a relationship with God; family; education; and service. The relationship to God was evident in what they did on a daily basis. Family was also very important, and even though our family was very big, we always got together as often as possible. Education was very important to both my grandpa and grandma. My grandpa only received up to an eighth-grade education, and my grandma graduated from high school. My grandpa worked as a truancy officer in Elgin Public Schools going to get kids who didn't go to school (or helping to find them), and my grandma was a teacher's aide in an Elgin elementary school. So, although they didn't get advanced degrees, they valued education and always expressed the importance of getting one to better oneself and the communities. Service was also important to my grandparents, and my grandpa went above and beyond his call of duty as a pastor visiting people in their homes and the hospital, and going to help others when they needed it. It wasn't just a value that was expressed—it was a value that was acted out. On both sides of mom's and dad's family the value of family and service was important. My grandpa Don (my dad's dad) was in the military and served in World War II, and my grandma Toni (my dad's mom) worked with the Umatilla tribe. For our families it was important to be the best you can be and to give to others what you could—that is where the value of relationships, respect, and reciprocity emerged.

RELATIONSHIPS INTRICATELY BUILDING COMMUNITY

The value of relationships is very important for Native and tribal communities as they are how we function on a daily basis and how we find connections to each other. This is evident in how I grew up as my grandparents emphasized the value of relationships through their service to the communities they worked in. They also emphasized the value of relationships through strong family connections. This value has gone on to play an important role in my life through the many communities I am a part of. At each place that I have relocated to or professional environment I am a part of, good healthy relationships are important. This includes efforts in building strong relationships and networks on campus and within the communities I am a part of. This spirit of building relationships and community is evident throughout my academic and professional life. This value of honoring relationships and building community has trickled into how I do things in my prior profession in student affairs and now as an assistant professor.

The assumption and belief that underlie this value is that a community is important for an individual to be strong. Relationships and community are at the heart of who we are as Native and tribal people, and if we don't have that or are not connected with that we start to lose sight of the values and vision of our ancestors that have been embedded in us. I also think this is an attitude and motivation that guides me in building a strong community wherever I am, and being a part of that community. The Native communities that I find become a part of the community and relationships that I form.

This value of relationships manifests in my collegiate teaching and the way I interpret, judge, and interact with students and with my subject area. First, the layout in my syllabus I have not changed in its structure; rather, the assignments I give are more based on the students' understanding of their connection to the subject and how it manifests in their respective communities. My interaction with students within the classroom is about building a community within the classroom. I don't value myself as higher or better than the students, although unintentionally there may be some power dynamics that exist. In my courses we spend the first class period getting to know each other and sharing. It is important that each of us understand who we are and where we come from, including myself. I do share about myself, although not all of the time. I share when it is relevant and when it will help the students see me as a person who shares similar experiences, especially as an Indigenous person. The activities we participate in are interactive and hopefully speak to the diverse learning styles of each student. I often do talk about what we are going over for that day and sometimes include a PowerPoint presentation as a visual, but I also incorporate small-group discussions and activities. As well, one thing that I acknowledge is that not everyone is comfortable sharing in a large or small group, so I provide opportunities for students to do some self-reflection and write down their reaction to terms we are talking about for that day. This value is about valuing community, and as a part of that it is also about valuing the learning and sharing styles of each person in the community, including each student. It is important when I am going into a class to understand the students' experiences and connections to what we are going to learn. Once I get approval to highlight students' experiences they have shared with me, I incorporate those experiences into the discussions and assignments we are doing for class. Although I am acknowledged as the teacher, I also acknowledge I can learn from the students and that as a community valuing each person, each community member is essential.

This value of relationships is helpful as a teacher in that students can see from the beginning how important community is to me and how I am connected to my tribal and Indigenous culture. As well, this helps students to feel a part of the group and to be open to sharing their experiences and perspectives with respect to the learning and discussion. I think this is particularly helpful for the class I have recently taught, which is a community of teachers from two different pueblos who have unique experiences within their schools. So, building a community that is built on trust and confidence allows students who are also teachers to feel safe to share their experiences and how they apply them to their learning. This approach in value-based teaching could be limiting because there are non-Natives in some of my classes and so their values are not always based within the community. It is important for me to acknowledge the different experiences and cultural backgrounds of the students and to value those as an important part of the community.

RESPECT, AN EMBEDDED VALUE

Having respect for oneself and respect for others is another value that is highly regarded within our family and especially within our community. Respect means that you have respect for other people's views, perspectives, and what they represent. This value is carried into the interactions we have with others. This is especially true when it comes to Elders—when there are older people present you listen and don't speak as much. It is a value that our Elders have wisdom and with age we owe them the respect for their life experiences. This plays out in my life in how I interact with people and not just Native people. When I am around Elders or older adults, it is second nature to listen to them and make sure they are taken care of. I also do this with anyone who is an adult or child to show and give them the respect that was instilled in me to show others. Whether I am in a school, community, or professional atmosphere, it is important to show respect whether that means listening, giving time, or helping when others need it. The value and assumption that underlie this is that everyone is important to give and show respect to. Respect doesn't mean you agree with everything that someone does or says, but respect is listening and valuing their opinions, words, and actions. The only time that someone speaks up against others is when someone is disrespectful to others, especially Elders, either in word or action. I have incorporated respect as a value in how I live my life on a daily basis, both personally and professionally, with everyone I come in contact with. This also means taking notice when someone's voice is not being included or silenced and standing up for them so that they are respected. Respect is not something I strive to do; it is something that is a part of who I am for my family, for my tribe, and for our communities.

This value of respect is carried forward in my classroom, meaning that I value every person's experiences, opinions, and that this is a value that guides our classroom behavior. For example, at the beginning of the semester we introduce ourselves, talk about what would challenge us, and discuss our goals in life and for the class itself. It is important to listen to each person as they talk and to also make sure that every person's opinion is valued. This continues on into our class discussions and how we talk in the classroom. This is a part of the community building, to build a community with a foundation of respect for each other. I use respect when thinking of what activities to do, respecting that everyone has a different learning and sharing style. Therefore, it is respectful for me to incorporate diverse interactive learning approaches to help each student learn. I also acknowledge and respect that in my class everyone's purpose for learning and moving forward in their education is not the same. So, it is important for me to ask how they see the course helping them with their educational and professional goals and try to address and incorporate that when planning for activities. As a professor who values my students' opinions, one of the ways that I have shown this is to incorporate a self-reflection assignment where I get to see what the students have learned so far, how they find this applicable to them, and what they would improve for the second part of the semester. This demonstrates to the students understanding and respect in what they have learned, as well as asking for their opinions about what would help them learn better the second half of the semester. The true respect comes when I make adjustments to their suggestions in teaching and content so they can see their opinions being respected through my actions. The value of respect is carried out also in professional interactions. When we are respectful with our colleagues, students, and others on a daily basis, that leads to reciprocation by others—which leads to the next value.

RECIPROCITY: SHARING WITH OTHERS SELFLESSLY

The value of reciprocity is a part of my tribal and Native community and was definitely emphasized within my family as I was growing up. Reciprocity to me means that whatever we are given, we must also be willing to give that back. So, for instance, in my family, my grandpa as the United Methodist pastor in the Native communities in Oklahoma would receive gifts both monetary and in kind from church members and the community. There was never a hesitation from him to share that with his family and anyone who needed something. As my grandma got older she was giving away all of her possessions to family and friends to make sure what she had accumulated or had been given she shared with others. Another good example of this is traditionally when you walk into a Kiowa household as a guest you are immediately offered food, and when you leave you take something with you, whether that be fruit or a gift from the family or person you are visiting. The spirit of giving to others is a value that is embedded within our Kiowa community as we honor others who have done something to help us for a specific reason or on our life's journey. This value of reciprocity has always guided me in who I am and in how I serve others.

The value of reciprocity is carried out in how I teach and the community that is built within the classroom. My philosophy on learning is that we each have something to contribute to the learning experience. I will not ever let my students say, "I don't know what I have to contribute to that." Instead, I emphasize their lived experiences, whether professional or personal, and how those contribute to the respective subject matter. The focus is what their life experiences have been, how they relate to this subject, and what stories they can share. Relationships are built based on respect for students' learning and experiences and our willingness to share what we have learned through our life experiences with each other. Within our class discussions and activities, I try to use diverse learning opportunities where students can connect their learning to their experiences and where they currently are professionally and within their communities. Finally, when constructing my syllabus and assignments I strive to make them contextual and practical. I think the best way for students to learn is to find ways to practically use what they have learned through projects. This is embedding the value of reciprocity in the classroom; in what we learn, we find ways to give back that knowledge and use it to benefit our environment and communities.

THE EVIDENCE OF COMMUNITY, CULTURE, AND IDENTITY IN THE JOURNEY OF TEACHING—CONCLUDING THOUGHTS

I think my cultural identity, whether I acknowledge it or not, guides everything I do and who I am. When I acknowledge this I can draw on the strengths of my culture and values to help others, whether Native or not, to acknowledge who they are in their identity and to value their life experiences. Many undergraduate and graduate students are doubtful and hesitant in their higher education journey; when someone acknowledges and values who they are and builds a community of learners based on respect and reciprocity, I hope anyone could excel and connect their learning for future use throughout their life. I realize this process may seem idealistic and overly optimistic, but I would rather come in with an attitude like that and influence students with a hopeful attitude than one that is self-defeating and with deficit model thinking. I realize I have only been teaching for six years and have much growth ahead, but a strength I think I have is that I have found comfort in my identity and values and found ways to use them as a foundation for teaching.

This self-reflection and cultural autobiography have helped affirm what I already know and helped me articulate that. This is a wonderful way to have a constant reminder of what is important and true to me as a person in my culture and identity, connected to my family values and giving guidance to my teaching. It is also a way to be accountable to myself, and especially to the students to whom I have a great responsibility as a teacher. It is also a way to make sure if I find value in who I am, I should make sure I find value in each student's background and life experience, whether or not they are of my same cultural background. We each have a story to tell and a purpose in life to help positively influence our communities. It is my role to give those tools to my students to see them fulfill their potential and higher education goals.

CHAPTER TWENTY-THREE

The Power of Identity

LAURA SUJO-MONTES

Educational Specialties
Northern Arizona University

What is identity? I am tempted to answer, "it all depends." It depends on what the topic of the conversation is, if I am referring to social or personal identity, if I am engaged in a colloquial conversation or in an academic conversation, etc. Borrowing from Fearon (1999), I would say that identity is a social category that identifies membership and attributes; but it can also be said that identity is a set of specific *personal* characteristics that distinguish an individual and may produce feelings of pride and self-respect. In this document, I will refer to my identity as an immigrant to the United States, with the attributes that affords me, but I will also refer to my individual identity and the characteristics that generate a range of feelings: from being proud to feelings of inadequacy and everything in between.

I grew up in Mexico in a dusty town that was part of a conglomerate of three distinct and different towns that ran across state lines. When referring to the three towns, they are called "La Laguna"—The Lagoon—even though they are in the middle of the country, inland, and with no water bodies other than a river that ran through and was used for agricultural purposes. There were more than 300,000 inhabitants collectively in the three towns that seemed like one and were indistinguishable for nonlocals. Moving away from demographics, the point I want to make is that I never met anyone in my hometown with the same last name as mine. There were some people in one of the "sister" towns that shared the same last name, but we never approached each other to find out how and if we were related. So, even when I am a regular Mexican I feel that there is something distinct and individual about me. I had to learn how to spell my last name (Sujo) because it was usually misspelled, so I had to correct the person (when I was very young, it was hard for me to remember what sound the letter "j" made and would confuse it with the sound that the letter "g" makes). I have an uncommon last name because it is not a Mexican last name but a Japanese last name. I am the granddaughter of a man who was an immigrant to Mexico and died when my father was eight years old. My father would share with us vivid memories of the time he spent with him.

My father was born to Nepomuceno Sujo and Maria Ceniceros in a village about two hours from the town where I grew up. Nepomuceno was the child of a Chinese mother and a Japanese father. Maria was the youngest of five children born to a Mexican Indian (Apache) mother and a Spanish father. My paternal grandparents met when my grandfather immigrated to Mexico and ended up in that small mining village away from the three main towns. Because he settled away from the main towns, he did not stay close to any relatives of his, if any came with him. My father remembered that my grandfather was part owner of the only store in town. As is common in some Asian countries, the husband is in charge of making dinner, and my grandfather was not the exception. One of the stories that my father would share with us recounted how his father would tell him: Come with me, son; let's get dinner. Then, he would get his gun and he will aim at something like quails, kill several, and prepare them for dinner. He also remembered that my grandfather would like to grow his own vegetables, and he would go out to water the vegetable garden. My dad would tell us that many times he asked his dad what a ship looked like, and if it was big. He remembered that his father would answer and say that they were very big, more than the size of several street blocks. My grandfather died of an "empacho" (a digestive illness). My father would still remember the exact time that the house clock told when my grandfather died (he died at home, as was the norm back then). My middle sister has the clock, although it is broken and irreparable because of the lack of the parts needed to fix it.

My paternal grandmother, Maria, was an enigmatic person. She was the youngest of five siblings and the only female. Still, she would outride them on a horse, being able to shoot and hit an animal while riding. She would also outdrink them and would be the last one standing while her brothers were all drunk. Even though she was the youngest in the family, the older brothers would come to her for advice, something unheard of in those times (around 1918). I am saying all of this to make the point that she was a strong woman. I was always told that I inherited her character and that made me secretly proud. I say "secretly" because my grandma was the mother-in-law that never liked the daughter-in-law (my mother), and it would not have been proper, at least in my view, to publicly acknowledge that I was proud to be like my grandmother Maria.

My grandmother Maria was born to a family that had lots of land and was well-off. When she would drink from a cup, she would hold it with her pinky straight up, with all the "class" that she had. However, her family was not wealthy anymore by the time she married my grandfather; their land had already been taken away during the Mexican Revolution. My grandmother Maria believed in spirits and magic. She was superstitious and also very private with her feelings and possessions. My parents used to tell me that she shredded all of my grandfather's pictures, including their wedding picture, and all the pictures of the young family. I never had the opportunity to see a picture of my grandfather.

My mother came from a "lesser class" family, as I imagine my paternal grandmother would describe her. Her mother was a single mother who had children from different men. My mom remembered that she talked with her biological father a handful of times. I imagine he was married when my mother was conceived. Although my maternal grandmother had other children, only one other girl survived to be old. My mom dropped out of school when she was in third grade. I suppose my mother was retained several times before dropping out. She would tell me that she dropped school because she was too old to be shoeless and felt ashamed to go to school barefoot; my grandmother did not have money to buy her shoes. She always considered herself to be dumb, especially when compared to her only sister who was always smart and able to go to school and graduate with the equivalent of an associate degree to train as a secretary and, by age 15 (around 1950), was already holding her first job. Later in life, she earned two bachelor's degrees; she never married and my grandmother always lived with her. My mom used to say that maybe my grandmother loved her sister's father more than she loved my mom's because the little sister was always the preferred child.

My mom was far from dumb. She became a widow in 2004. At the beginning, after my dad passed away, she felt lost. She would tell me that since the day she was born, she always depended on somebody: first her mother, then her stepfather, and then her husband. Fortunately, she was able to adapt well. She would come to the United States and visit me every summer for about four months. In the times she stayed with me, she learned how to use the iPad to "attend" mass in Spanish every day, read her hometown newspaper, use Skype to talk with my sisters, and use Netflix to entertain herself. As I said, she was far from being dumb as she learned all of that at age 85; she passed away when she was 87 years old.

I was raised Catholic and I am still a Catholic. Life (or, should I say God?) has been good to me and I have not suffered major tragedies. I try to find comfort in God even in the worst of circumstances; I believe that life does not end at death because it is only a transition to get to the permanent home in heaven that God promised his children. I feel comfortable talking and thinking about death, maybe in part because the Mexican culture is that way and in part because of my faith. I am far from being a "good" Catholic; I find myself picking and choosing what church teachings I follow. For instance, I do not believe that the world was created or that women cannot use contraceptives. I mainly do not follow what priests or popes say because I believe that those are laws imposed by men and have nothing, or little, to do with what actually God wants for his creatures. The foundation of this value is the assumption that most people are intrinsically good and that they are somehow guided by God even if they refuse to be guided. In other words, God acts through every person regardless of the person and, as some may say, in mysterious ways. I am careful to have this guiding belief present in my mind when my students ask for an extension to turn in the assignment because "life happened." After all, who am I to judge if they are being truthful to me? According to my faith, they will be judged after they die.

While growing up in Mexico, public religious demonstrations and being religious were an integral part of society. My mother used to say, "You need to behave because God will punish you if you do such and such things." God is everywhere and can see all my actions—that is what I was taught, although I have come to the conclusion that God is not that interested in watching each one of us. After all, he has given us freedom to choose what to believe and how to behave.

I teach online graduate courses. I taught in-person, undergraduate courses for some time but I found it difficult to relate to the students' experiences at that young age. Being an immigrant to this country in my adulthood means that I did not have the American college experience. On the other hand, as an online teacher, I have students who may be immigrant themselves, have a family and a job, and are close to, or at, middle age; all of those are experiences to which I can relate. In a way, being a religious person makes it easier for me to try to step into my students' shoes. In my current position as a department chair, petitions of all types pass through my desk. As any administrator, I take into account the justification presented by the student for approval of a petition. I usually tend to believe what the students write. Sometimes their stories present such a hard life that I wish I could do something right away to help them. I have had students who are in the middle of a divorce, are male single parents, are battling cancer, just had a surgery or an accident, etc. When I read these petitions, I cannot help but thank God for the relatively easy life I carry. For instance, I remember a case that happened about 10 years ago. I had this female student online who was a Latina immigrant. She was a dedicated and intelligent student but she tended not to turn in assignments on time; I usually gave her opportunities to turn them in late. All of a sudden, she did not enroll in courses for probably two or three semesters. When she finally came back to finish the degree, she told me that she had cancer and had been under treatment, her father passed away, and she had a divorce. She was close to graduation and I did everything to help her. She graduated and I lost track of her until two years ago. She is now enrolled in a doctoral program and is teaching for the university where I work. I thank God because he has given her the strength to continue living her life. In hindsight, I am not sure if my actions made any impact on her graduation—probably not—and I wonder: Was I a benevolent teacher? Did I hold high expectations for her the same way I do for my students and for me? Did I show Christian charity toward her? How much of my actions were guided by my culture or by my religion? Can they even be separated?

Separation of state and church: that is the way I was educated in Mexico, and that is the way public schools work in the United States. I respect and follow this rule, and my religious beliefs must remain untold to my students. However, there have been times when my students have suffered a personal loss and I would like to try to console them and tell them that the person who passed away is now in a better place with God. I know I cannot say this because it may be offensive to some students who may not be religious or may think I am proselytizing; as a result, the consoling wishes stay only in my mind. My quest to honor my religious beliefs keeps me in a state of constant disequilibrium because I am always working toward improving myself and showing it through my actions; unfortunately, I have not been successful, and I usually regress to who I really am. Still, I try to constantly question myself: Am I being just and fair with my students? Should I believe the excuse they give me when they do not turn in work on time? What would it happen if I were in their situation? Would I want an instructor who is compassionate and understanding? My religious beliefs also make me question my ability to embrace everybody. Since "all of us are creatures of God," then I must love every one, which I do not do. Also, "love each other as I love you" guides me to try to be an accepting and caring person to everybody, but I still have a long way to go to be able to get there.

In the online classroom, my role is that of a facilitator. It is similar to the way Catholic religion tells us who God is. We are told that God provides the means to access all that we want: freedom of choice to behave or misbehave, freedom to select one path from another, etc. In a way, God is a facilitator. I do not believe I am God, but I believe I am a facilitator. Assignments in my courses are usually open ended to give students the opportunity to bring their own knowledge and experiences to complete the assignment. My role is to facilitate learning so students can discover knowledge and then share ideas and learn with and from each other. However, I expect students to know the material because part of my job is to teach them how to apply that knowledge to different situations in different circumstances in real life. I think that a student who does not want to excel and be the best he or she can be is a student who is just "surfing" in my class. In my present position as a chair, I feel disappointed and frustrated when faculty do not demonstrate that they are doing the best they can do for their programs. I dislike hearing what I believe to be excuses to justify a mediocre job in terms of student achievement or student enrollment; I think they do not put forward their best effort to increase the achievement and the enrollment, just as simple as that. As a chair, I expect faculty to be able to improve their academic programs and to attract and retain new students. I believe that the success of a program depends in great part on the faculty that teach in it and the care they put into the curriculum; all of those are influenced by faculty actions. At the end, I do not know how to connect this to my religious beliefs. At the least, I try to demonstrate and expect excellence, good behavior, and compassion.

The values of my heritage are that I need to take advantage of the opportunities that are presented to me because there may not be another opportunity. I was taught to value, believe, and act on the premise that children need to be better than their parents and they need to achieve more material value than what their parents achieved. But I also have the religious belief as part of my culture and heritage, and they seem sometimes to be in direct opposition to each other. How do I reconcile them? How do they affect my teaching? I am sure that they affect it in many ways—many more than the ones I am aware of—and, as a teacher, that is exciting and scary. However, that is my identity; there is no way it does not come shining through in my teaching.

REFERENCE

Fearon, J. D. (1999). *What is identity (as we now use the word)*. http://www.seminario2005.unal.edu.co/Trabajos/Fearon/What%20is%20identity%20(as%20we%20now%20see%20the%20world).pdf. Unpublished manuscript. Stanford, CA: Stanford University.

PART THREE

Moving Forward

CHAPTER TWENTY-FOUR

Developing a Culturally Introspective Practice

SUSAN DIANA LONGERBEAM & ALICIA FEDELINA CHÁVEZ

> I accept culture as a part of my teaching because it is the thing that I always wrestle with, and as a scholar, how can one effectively build a home around their ideas while inviting others to be a part of that home as well?
>
> —MJR Montoya

Teaching effectively across cultures requires a variety of developments in our practice. A critical one is developing a culturally introspective practice that will enable us to understand the role of our own cultural influences in our pedagogical choices, interactions with students, and judgments about values, priorities, and student behaviors. Another is going inward on a regular basis to observe our own interpretations of students and then going deeper to understand the meaning of our interpretations followed by considering the influence of our interpretations on our teaching takes courage, persistence, and a developing insight. As faculty develop a culturally introspective practice, this becomes both easier and more challenging. Easier because it becomes a habit of mind, more challenging because we begin to notice things about our own interpretations that can be uncomfortable, that can challenge our sense of self as we realize we are making judgments that may be unequal or unfair to specific populations of students.

> I accept culture as a part of my teaching because it is the thing that I always wrestle with, and as a scholar, how can one effectively build a home around their ideas while inviting others to be a part of that home as well? (MJR Montoya)

> I judge "hard work" on the basis of consistency in attendance, apparent work rate, frequency of communications with me as instructor, and personal comportment in class. But this

> method of judgment is problematic and perception-based. There are perhaps less obvious ways of striving that I probably overlook, creating favoritism-based disadvantages for some who are working hard in less apparent ways. Some students may be committed to care-giving activities or personal improvement efforts, for example, that are necessarily private. These students may be true "strivers" in ways I will never know, leaving my perceptions of these students sorely incomplete, since they are based only on classroom observation. In addition, some hardworking students may even hold cultural values that lead them to minimize the appearance of effort, which problematizes my tendency to be most responsive to those students I perceive as strivers. (K. Maria D. Lane)

> When I make quick judgments about my students, instead of being curious to know who they are and how they've come to know what they know, I limit our ability to create learning and I increase the power differential between me and my students. (Kersti Tyson)

> Thus, the contradictions inherent in culture serves as a pedagogical problem of the highest difficulty, and equally, of the noblest intent. We are asked to recognize cultural patterns in our students, provide access and greater sensitivity. Moreover, we are asked to help place those cultural patterns in the context of an ever-changing world, asking students to step inside and outside of themselves with sophistication and dedication. (MJR Montoya)

> [A]n exploration of aspects of my cultural legacy, sometimes spanning generations, bestows a stronger sense of identity on my work as a teacher in higher education, particularly in the context of a culture that is in many ways different from my own. It highlights some of the strengths and weaknesses inherent in my approach and provides additional room for reflection not only on my development as an educator but also in what I recognize and respond to in the learners I work with. I draw on my understanding that individuals are influenced by sometimes *tacit cultural legacies* and an appreciation of the many factors that students must balance in their decisions to pursue higher education and careers. (Melissa Birkett Greene)

Through purposeful cultural introspection, these faculty authors began to identify ways in which they interpreted students based in their cultural frameworks of assumptions, values, beliefs, and expected behaviors. They developed greater awareness of both the helpful and problematic aspects of these influences. In doing so the possibility of transforming their teaching to balance across cultural norms opened to them.

There are many ways to go inward and practice cultural introspection regularly in relation to our teaching. The following sections offer ideas and insights for some ways you might consider.

JOURNALING

Keeping a cultural introspection teaching journal can be a helpful practice for those who reflect naturally through writing as well as for many others who wish to more systematically record and process. Some find it helpful to free-write regularly, while others may choose to identify specific areas of reflection or teaching practices for concentration. It is helpful to set aside and even schedule time purposefully on a regular basis for this practice, because faculty carry so many responsibilities. It is often helpful to "make appointments with ourselves" so that cultural introspection becomes a regular habit of mind and practice. This is also helpful to a process of observing and going inward over the course of an academic term so that different periods receive reflection. Some of the faculty we worked with kept a paper-type journal with them, while others kept them electronically.

REGULAR DISCUSSIONS WITH A COLLEAGUE

Some faculty find it helpful to use a more shared or collective form of cultural introspection. A few of the faculty we worked with found it helpful to schedule time regularly with a colleague to discuss what they were noticing in their own teaching practices, judgments about students, interpretations, and assumptions. This can be an especially helpful technique for those who are more extroverted or external processors and for those who naturally learn through comparing and contrasting with others.

It can be especially helpful to find someone who leans toward the other side of the Cultural Frameworks continuum from you (see Chavez & Longerbeam, 2016) or who seems to have different values or ways of teaching than your own and regularly discuss "why you do that and do it that way" and "what are the assumptions underlying that practice" in relation to teaching. This can be done through conversation and also enhanced by observing and discussing each other's teaching. In our work with faculty we offered some of both to faculty ourselves, observing teaching and sharing what we noticed as well as meeting individually with faculty to process thoughts, ideas, observations, and suggestions toward more of a balance across cultural frameworks or epistemologies.

DISCUSSIONS WITH STUDENTS

It can be especially helpful to seek out and discuss teaching with students, especially with both students who we seem to connect with or relate to easily *and* with students we do not or who even might make us feel uncomfortable or irritated. One of the most powerful techniques toward understanding is to ask—and cultural introspection is no exception. Since one of the things humans do naturally is interpret things through our own cultural assumptions; it can be extremely helpful to seek out students and ask them the meaning of specific behaviors, how they learn most naturally, how they were taught by their families, cultures, communities, tribes, churches, etc., and how they are affected by our teaching practices and ways of interacting and evaluating. By doing so and then journaling or discussing this with colleagues, we are able to learn about other interpretations from our own and make choices to balance across the differences. This often opens our mind in more long-term ways to additional possibilities and interpretations of student behavior.

RESEARCHING OUR OWN CULTURES

Many of the faculty with whom we worked did some research on their own cultural origins and the values and meaning behind their teaching practices. Some started out knowing nothing more than their own surnames and feeling somewhat concerned that they "didn't have culture," to find indeed that they do have rich cultural values, traditions, and norms as well as underlying assumptions serving as foundations for their lives as well as for their teaching practices. This research, also a form of cultural introspection, often included discussions with family members, especially elders, as well as some Internet explorations and reading about specific cultural epistemologies within their own origins.

It can be helpful to identify specific values, beliefs, behaviors, and assumptions in our own teaching followed by reflection on where these originate—in something our parents always encouraged or stressed, something we were taught in church or in our tribe, something we were mentored in by early teachers. One faculty member who shared in our first retreat felt she didn't have any culture and through reading about the cultures of origin of her family names, began to understand that many cultural traits were strong in her family, and in her own life, and were manifesting in her teaching.

BLOGS

For those who wish to go inward by going outward through social networks, it can be helpful to start a blog or other interactive process online to reflect. A blog or other social network process could be developed within an academic discipline or more generally with others across professions who wish to explore the influence of culture in their professional practice. Blogs or other means could be developed on specific campuses among professionals or within a professional association.

PEN PAL

It can be meaningful and helpful to converse in writing over time with another individual. We, the editors, are scholars and friends, and we regularly interact through email—sharing our revelations, asking each other for meanings, and processing our struggles across cultural norms. We find this helpful not only to our developing understandings across our divergent cultures but also to our scholarship and writing in this area. We also interact regularly through phone discussions, writing retreats, and as conference roommates. Even after years of these pen pal-like written interactions and our shared work and friendship, we continue to gain new insights and surprising revelations. We continue to uncover the depth of our cultural distinctions, and how these distinctions show up on our teaching practices.

SYMBOLIC METAPHORIC PROCESSING

In our work with faculty, we often start by facilitating processes where individuals reflect for a moment, draw, chart, and discuss symbolic and metaphoric representations of cultural values and assumptions. Many individuals reflect and process most naturally through visual, kinesthetic, musical, storied, or rhythmic means. This process usually involves some form of introspection through symbol or metaphor as individuals use personal forms of expression to make meaning of specific values, assumptions, beliefs, and behaviors in their teaching. Newsprint and crayons or markers are important tools at our sessions, to allow faculty a variety of outlets, as are sharing of narratives and story. In our final retreat with faculty for this project, we asked faculty from both campuses to develop and facilitate activities to share and discuss what they learned and tried out to balance across cultural frameworks in their teaching. Two processes were especially powerful: a drawing and sharing exercise about cultural identity and a Pechakucha activity in which faculty shared stories about techniques they tried in their courses.

SELF-RECORDINGS

For those who process in auditory yet not shared ways, it may be helpful to conduct self-recordings to record and then listen back to reflections. This could be done regularly while driving, at home, or in the office. Alternatively, video recordings could be used. Both could also be used as forms of self-observation in classes to notice both our teaching and the responses of students to our teaching.

CULTURE AND TEACHING AUTOBIOGRAPHY

The faculty essays in this book were developed through the writing of a culture and teaching autobiography we required of participants in our yearlong culture and teaching faculty development project. For the complete set of instructions we gave to faculty for their essays in this book, see Chávez and Longerbeam (2016, pp. 209–214). The following are basic steps to writing a culture and teaching autobiography:

- Choose three to five values you hold in your teaching practices.
- Identify through written or visual processes some of the origins and personal experiences of these values, for example, family teaching, cultural norms, early teachers or religious edicts.
  o Write stories, narratives, or describe examples for each.
- Identify some of the ways these values play out or manifest in your teaching practices as well as in the ways you interpret students.
  o Write stories, narratives, or describe examples for each.
- Explore how each of these values might be construed by students who hold different values or who manifest the same values in ways different from your own norms.
  o Write stories, narratives, or describe examples for each.
- Finally, discuss ways you might over time develop a balance of teaching practices across your own and others' values.

COMBINING TECHNIQUES AND USING DIFFERENT TECHNIQUES OVER TIME

We believe that faculty benefit from the use of a variety of cultural introspection techniques and built many of these into our yearlong project. We encourage you to use techniques that feel natural and comfortable to you as well as some that are less so. This balance of resonance and dissonance will assist you to understand yourself more deeply in a cultural sense as well as to feel what it is like to be outside of your own comfortable processes. In doing so ourselves, we find that we are more able to understand the impact of our own teaching on those who do not originate in our natural processes and ways of being.

We wish you well on your journey of introspection toward improved teaching and more rewarding and enriching learning relationships with students.

CHAPTER TWENTY-FIVE

Reflecting Into THE Future

SUSAN DIANA LONGERBEAM & ALICIA FEDELINA CHÁVEZ

> I continue to learn from the lessons of my family and realized through cultural introspection that most of my teaching originates from the lessons of my family. … I am continually discovering underlying lessons and experiences of my cultures and family through introspection and through the catalyst of working with a diversity of students as people, learners, and professionals. This is a sacred responsibility and humbling reality of teaching. Through teaching, we ripple out through generations.
>
> —ALICIA FEDELINA CHÁVEZ

> As an educator, I seek to deepen cultural understanding. I want for students the truth I lacked, so they will know from whence they come. The process of understanding this historical context has been a long one and will continue throughout my life. Uncovering a dominant culture that was presumed the only relevant one is complex, but with help from mentors, with education, and with courage, I am getting to the heart of the artichoke, my cultures of origin. Now I want to offer students a pathway to wisdom, authenticity, and well-being.
>
> —SUSAN DIANA LONGERBEAM

When we reflect into the future, we share a vision and we have some dreams. We envision creating a higher education culture of belief in students and the strengths they bring with them to learning. We dream of a time when all students who choose higher education have opportunities to find their natural ways of learning, experience authentic connection with their professors, and graduate from college. Likewise, we wish for a time when all faculty have opportunities to form effective and even sometimes transformative learning partnerships with students. We wish for you, and for us, the deep joy of connecting with students in their own worlds, in sharing one another's cultures, in teaching to a balance of cultural strengths, and in learning about and appreciating all of our cultural ways of learning.

When we began our work together, we identified a shared sense of urgency about college graduation rates among Native, Latino, and African American peoples and cultures in the United States. Our dream going forward is that our work will contribute to a world where students of all cultures graduate from college at equitable rates and when college graduates of the United States reflect the cultures of the United States.

> We wish you deep contentment in your own going-inward journey, and in your going outward as you teach to and journey with students.

Editors

Susan Diana Longerbeam, Ph.D., is Associate Professor in Counseling and Human Development at the University of Louisville. She served as associate professor at Northern Arizona University, a university health services director and interim dean of students at Oregon State University, and she holds a Ph.D. in College Student Personnel from the University of Maryland, a master's degree in Health Services Administration from Antioch University, and a bachelor's degree in Community Studies from the University of California, Santa Cruz. She served on the ACPA Commission on Professional Preparation and the NASPA Faculty Fellows and Council.

Dr. Longerbeam's scholarship focuses on culture and college teaching, campus climate, and student success in higher education. Her publications include a coauthored book on culture and college teaching, *Teaching Across Cultural Strengths* (Stylus, 2016). Recent journal articles include "'We Cannot Reach Them'": Chinese Undergraduate Student Perceptions of the U.S. Campus Climate" (2013); "Putting Old Tensions to Rest: Integrating Multicultural Education and Global Learning to Advance Student Development" (2013); "Developing Openness to Diversity in Living-Learning Program Participants" (2010); and "Contemporary College Contexts: College Environments for Student Learning and Retention at a Southwestern U.S. University" (2010); and reflective work: "Encounters with Angels: A Struggle to Return Home from Study Abroad" (2015); "One Journey of

Compassion: My Search for Inspiriting Leadership' (2013); "'You Home? Meet Me on the Stairway': Lessons of Living Together" (2009).

Alicia Fedelina Chávez, Ph.D., is Associate Professor in Teacher Education, Educational Leadership and Policy at the University of New Mexico. She served as a collegiate leader, student affairs professional, and faculty member in universities around the country, including leading a campus in Northern New Mexico, serving as Dean of Students at the University of Wisconsin–Madison, and serving as the diversity development officer at Iowa State University. She holds a Ph.D. in Higher Education–Policy Studies from the University of Arizona, a master's degree in Student Affairs/Higher Education Administration from Iowa State University, and a bachelor's degree in psychology from New Mexico State University. She regularly works with faculty, student affairs professionals, and central administrators in the area of transforming colleges and universities to more effectively teach and serve diverse populations. Her current consulting, faculty development, leadership development, teaching, and scholarship are centered in facilitating understanding and balance between cultural epistemologies and ways of being in professional practice. She works from a belief that higher education institutions and societies benefit from garnering the strengths of many peoples, cultures, and nations.

Dr. Chávez's scholarship focuses in areas of culture and college teaching as well as identity and collegiate leadership. Her publications include two coauthored books on culture and college teaching, *Teaching Across Cultural Strengths* (Stylus, 2016) and *Web Based Teaching Across Culture and Age* (Springer, 2013), as well as two coedited books on identity and leadership in higher education, *Identity & Leadership: Informing Our Lives, Informing Our Practice* (NASPA, 2013) and *Indigenous Leadership in Higher Education* (Routledge, 2015). Her academic journal articles include "Clan, Sage, and Sky: Indigenous, Hispano and Mestizo Narratives of Learning in New Mexico Context"; "Leading in the Borderlands: Negotiating Ethnic Patriarchy for the Benefit of Students"; "Spirit of Place: Crafting a College in Northern New Mexico Rhythm"; "Spirit and Nature: Reflections of a Mestiza in Higher Education"; "Toward a Multicultural Ecology of Teaching and Learning"; and "Learning to Value the 'Other': A Model of Diversity Development."

Questions about the Purpose(s) of Colleges and Universities

Norm Denzin,
Shirley R. Steinberg
General Editors

What are the purposes of higher education? When undergraduates "declare their majors," they agree to enter into a world defined by the parameters of a particular academic discourse—a discipline. But who decides those parameters? How do they come about? What are the discussions and proposed outcomes of disciplined inquiry? What should an undergraduate know to be considered educated in a discipline? How does the disciplinary knowledge base inform its pedagogy? Why are there different disciplines? When has a discipline "run its course"? Where do new disciplines come from? Where do old ones go? How does a discipline produce its knowledge? What are the meanings and purposes of disciplinary research and teaching? What are the key questions of disciplined inquiry? What questions are taboo within a discipline? What can the disciplines learn from one another? What might they not want to learn and why?

Once we begin asking these kinds of questions, positionality becomes a key issue. One reason why there aren't many books on the meaning and purpose of higher education is that once such questions are opened for discussion, one's subjectivity becomes an issue with respect to the presumed objective stances of Western higher education. Academics don't have positions because positions are "biased," "subjective," "slanted," and therefore somehow invalid. So the first thing to do is to provide a sense—however broad and general—of what kinds of positionalities will inform the books and chapters on the above questions. Certainly the questions themselves, and any others we might ask, are already suggesting a particular "bent," but as the series takes shape, the authors we engage will no doubt have positions on these questions.

From the stance of interdisciplinary, multidisciplinary, or transdisciplinary practitioners, will the chapters and books we solicit solidify disciplinary discourses, or liquefy them? Depending on who is asked, interdisciplinary inquiry is either a polite collaboration among scholars firmly situated in their own particular discourses, or it is a blurring of the restrictive parameters that define the very notion of disciplinary discourse. So will the series have a stance on the meaning and purpose of interdisciplinary inquiry and teaching? This can possibly be finessed by attracting thinkers from disciplines that are already multidisciplinary, for example, the various kinds of "studies" programs (women's, Islamic, American, cultural, etc.), or the hybrid disciplines like ethnomusicology (musicology, folklore, anthropology). But by including people from these fields (areas? disciplines?) in our series, we are already taking a stand on disciplined inquiry. A question on the comprehensive exam for the Columbia University Ethnomusicology Program was to defend ethnomusicology as a "field" or a "discipline." One's answer determined one's future, at least to the extent that the gatekeepers had a say in such matters. So, in the end, what we are proposing will no doubt involve political struggles.

For additional information about this series or for the submission of manuscripts, please contact Shirley R. Steinberg, msgramsci@gmail.com. To order other books in this series, please contact our Customer Service Department at: (800) 770-LANG (within the U.S.), (212) 647-7706 (outside the U.S.), (212) 647-7707 FAX, or browse online by series at: www.peterlang.com.